Learning Chef

Mischa Taylor and Seth Vargo

Beijing · Cambridge · Farnham · Köln · Sebastopol · Tokyo

Learning Chef

by Mischa Taylor and Seth Vargo

Printed in the United States of America.

Published by O'Reilly Media, Inc., 1005 Gravenstein Highway North, Sebastopol, CA 95472.

O'Reilly books may be purchased for educational, business, or sales promotional use. Online editions are also available for most titles (*http://safaribooksonline.com*). For more information, contact our corporate/institutional sales department: 800-998-9938 or *corporate@oreilly.com*.

Editors: Courtney Nash and Brian Anderson	**Indexer:** WordCo Indexing Services, Inc.
Production Editor: Matthew Hacker	**Cover Designer:** Ellie Volckhausen
Copyeditor: Carla Thornton	**Interior Designer:** David Futato
Proofreader: Teresa Wilson	**Illustrator:** Rebecca Demarest

November 2014:   First Edition

Revision History for the First Edition:

2014-11-05:   First release

See *http://oreilly.com/catalog/errata.csp?isbn=9781491944936* for release details.

ISBN: 978-1-491-94493-6

[LSI]

Table of Contents

Preface

What Is This Book?

Learning Chef is an introductory book on the Chef infrastructure automation platform. This is a book for beginners who are new to Chef, configuration management, and automation coding.

Using Chef, you can model the setup, packaging, and delivery of applications in your infrastructure as code. We'll show you how using code makes actions easily repeatable, while running commands by hand is not. Once you have this code blueprint, you can then build or rebuild your whole infrastructure's application stack in minutes or hours, instead of the days or weeks it would typically take doing by hand. In this book, we'll cover the basics of Chef, assuming you have no prior experience with infrastructure automation or coding.

First, we'll get started by showing you how to set up a Chef development environment on your own local machine. This is where you will write Chef code and verify that it works. Learning how to code takes a lot of hands-on practice, so we try to get you to dive in and start writing code very early in the book. Then we progress slowly, introducing one new concept along with its accompanying Chef tool in each chapter. Hands-on examples are provided to help cement the concepts in your mind and to give you practice coding.

After you've read *Learning Chef*, you will understand all the basic concepts and be ready to pick up and benefit from two more advanced books on Chef, such as the O'Reilly books *Test-Driven Infrastructure with Chef, 2nd Edition*, by Stephen Nelson-Smith, and *Customizing Chef*, by Jon Cowie.

Who Should Read This Book?

We wrote this book for both system administrators and software developers new to Chef and the concept of infrastructure automation. It is assumed that you have some familiarity with using the command line and performing basic system administration tasks.

You may run Linux, Mac OS X, or Windows on your local machine and follow the hands-on exercises in this book. When necessary, we'll provide separate instructions for each platform. Because there is currently no easy-to-use graphical integrated development environment (IDE) for Chef, your primary interface to Chef will be through the command line. Thankfully, the command line interface has very few platform-specific differences, except with the initial installation, so the choice to cover three operating system platforms in this book shouldn't be too distracting while broadening your choice of environments in which to work with Chef.

We do not assume that you have any experience with automation coding, but we do assume that you've written scripts before, such as shell scripts, batch files, or PowerShell scripts. You should be familiar with scripting in some form before trying to learn Chef coding.

Why All the Culinary Terminology?

As you read this book, you might notice that the makers of Chef are fond of using culinary terms to describe infrastructure automation tools and concepts. The people at Chef Software discovered that words and phrases such as *cookbook* or *following a recipe* are good metaphors for abstract concepts such as *a collection of automation scripts* or *running code that consistently reproduces an infrastructure component*. The consistent use of cooking metaphors makes the topic of infrastructure automation more accessible to beginners and does not have the baggage of industry terms used in other contexts. Plus, it's a good way to market and brand Chef, as the cooking angle is unique and makes Chef memorable.

Conventions Used in This Book

The following typographical conventions are used in this book:

Italic
> Indicates new terms, URLs, email addresses, filenames, and file extensions.

`Constant width`
> Used for program listings, as well as within paragraphs to refer to program elements such as variable or function names, databases, data types, environment variables, statements, and keywords.

Constant width bold

Shows commands or other text that should be typed by the user.

Constant width italic

Shows text that should be replaced with user-supplied values or by values determined by context.

This element signifies a tip or suggestion.

This element signifies a general note.

This element indicates a warning or caution.

Using Code Examples

Supplemental material (code examples, exercises, etc.) is available for download at *http://learningchef.com*.

This book is here to help you get your job done. In general, if example code is offered with this book, you may use it in your programs and documentation. You do not need to contact us for permission unless you're reproducing a significant portion of the code. For example, writing a program that uses several chunks of code from this book does not require permission. Selling or distributing a CD-ROM of examples from O'Reilly books does require permission. Answering a question by citing this book and quoting example code does not require permission. Incorporating a significant amount of example code from this book into your product's documentation does require permission.

We appreciate, but do not require, attribution. An attribution usually includes the title, author, publisher, and ISBN. For example: "*Learning Chef* by Mischa Taylor and Seth Vargo (O'Reilly). Copyright 2015 Mischa Taylor and Seth Vargo, 978-1-491-94493-6."

If you believe your use of code examples falls outside fair use or the permission given, feel free to contact us at *permissions@oreilly.com*.

Safari® Books Online

 *Safari Books Online* is an on-demand digital library that delivers expert content in both book and video form from the world's leading authors in technology and business.

Technology professionals, software developers, web designers, and business and creative professionals use Safari Books Online as their primary resource for research, problem solving, learning, and certification training.

Safari Books Online offers a range of plans and pricing for enterprise, government, education, and individuals.

Members have access to thousands of books, training videos, and prepublication manuscripts in one fully searchable database from publishers like O'Reilly Media, Prentice Hall Professional, Addison-Wesley Professional, Microsoft Press, Sams, Que, Peachpit Press, Focal Press, Cisco Press, John Wiley & Sons, Syngress, Morgan Kaufmann, IBM Redbooks, Packt, Adobe Press, FT Press, Apress, Manning, New Riders, McGraw-Hill, Jones & Bartlett, Course Technology, and hundreds more. For more information about Safari Books Online, please visit us online.

How to Contact Us

Please address comments and questions concerning this book to the publisher:

O'Reilly Media, Inc.
1005 Gravenstein Highway North
Sebastopol, CA 95472
800-998-9938 (in the United States or Canada)
707-829-0515 (international or local)
707-829-0104 (fax)

We have a web page for this book, where we list errata, examples, and any additional information. You can access this page at *http://bit.ly/learning_chef*.

To comment or ask technical questions about this book, send email to *bookques tions@oreilly.com*.

For more information about our books, courses, conferences, and news, see our website at *http://www.oreilly.com*.

Find us on Facebook: *http://facebook.com/oreilly*

Follow us on Twitter: *http://twitter.com/oreillymedia*

Watch us on YouTube: *http://www.youtube.com/oreillymedia*

Acknowledgments

From Mischa: I would like to thank all the people who provided input and feedback on our book during the writing process. Thanks to my sister, Dr. Jane Maris Sinagub, who provided moral support and daily encouragement.

I want to give heartfelt thanks to all the people who helped contribute to this book, including but not limited to: Alex Vinyar, Alyssa Nabors, Anthony Stonebarger, Daniel DeLeo, Deluan Quintao, Eric Helgeson, Gene Harris, Glenna Gorlick, Jason Steele, Jennifer Davis, Jo Rhett, John Keiser, Jennifer Davis, John Fitzpatrick, Jon Cowie, Julian Dunn, Katherine Daniels, Kelly Setzer, Kimberly Lanning, Landon Medlock, Lejo Varughese, Mandi Walls, Michael Goetz, Michael Vitale, Nathen Harvey, Patricia Fernandes, Rhiannon Portwood, Sascha Bates, Sean Carolan, Serdar Sutay, Shane Robinson, Steve Taylor, and Thomas Petchel. Thanks to Chef Software for making Chef Fundamentals Training materials Creative Commons Attribution Share Alike licensed. Some of the diagrams and examples were reused in this book. Thanks as well to Courtney Nash, Brian Anderson, and all the marvelous people at O'Reilly. Your amazing Atlas authoring system made the writing process more delightful.

Special thanks go out to the following people: Mark Burgess for developing the theory to make Chef possible, John Keiser for providing the "written in stone" example, Jennifer Davis for providing valuable input on how to structure the initial chapters in the book, John Fitzpatrick for testing the installation examples and providing feedback, Nathen Harvey for helping with the introductory material, Sascha Bates for providing clear guidance on what beginners should first learn about Chef to be effective, Adam Jacob and Sean O'Meara for educating me on the theory behind the configuration management philosophy from which Chef was born, and Steve Taylor and Mark Andersen for providing training cohorts on which to try this book's material.

And finally I would like to thank my coauthor Seth Vargo, for being so gracious in allowing me to come on board to help finish the book.

From Seth: I would like to thank everyone who helped make this book possible. I would be remiss if I did not thank Nathen Harvey, Ramez Mourad, and Jake Vanderdray for introducing me to Chef and the Chef community. Without their knowledge and encouragement, I would not be here today.

In addition to everyone Mischa mentioned, I would like to extend my gratitude to my team, Seth Chisamore and Yvonne Lam, for their continued support throughout this endeavor; my roommate and best friend Joe Frick for supporting me as I quietly mumbled things at my laptop screen at all hours of the night; Prof. Larry Heimann and Prof. Jeria Quesenberry from Carnegie Mellon for giving me the experience and opportunity to be an educator; Stafford Brunk for forcing me to think outside of the box; and my parents Richard Stormer, Robbin Stormer, Robert Vargo, and Dara Vargo for being incredibly supportive while continually reminding me to finish this book.

Thanks as well to Courtney, Brian, Sonia, and the entire O'Reilly crew for making this an absolutely amazing experience. I would like to extend a special thank you to my coauthor Mischa Taylor for his amazing contributions and diligence in finishing this book. I could not have done it without you!

## CHAPTER 1

Configuration Management and Chef

Chef is a configuration management tool for information technology (IT) professionals, like you. Because there are a wide variety of definitions for the term *configuration management*, let's take a moment to explain what *configuration management* means in the context of this book and why you need a configuration management tool. We'll also cover what Chef is, and why you need it as well.

What Is Configuration Management?

With respect to IT, *configuration management* covers the set of engineering practices for managing the following entities involved in delivering software applications to consumers:

- Hardware
- Software
- Infrastructure
- People
- Process

Configuration management came about to address the fundamental challenges involved in doing group work. Managing change when you are a lone system administrator with a handful of servers to manage is relatively straightforward. Trying to coordinate the work of multiple system administrators and developers involving hundreds, or even thousands, of servers and applications to support a large customer base is complex and typically requires the support of a tool.

A modern IT configuration management tool usually involves an implementation inspired by the automation and policy-based theory originally developed by Mark

Burgess. He developed the following core ideas of this theory for automating IT when he was a professor at Oslo University College in the late 1990s and early 2000s:

- Changes must be handled in a systematic fashion to ensure that a system is configured in a correct and reliable manner.
- There must be some form of autonomy in the system so that it can automatically detect faults and repair them without being explicitly told to do so.

Examples of modern IT configuration management tools are CFEngine, Puppet, the Desired State Configuration engine in Microsoft Windows, Ansible, SaltStack, and of course, Chef.

Why You Need a Configuration Management Tool to Automate IT

There are a number of reasons why automated configuration management tools play a vital role in managing complex enterprise infrastructures. Here are four of the most popular reasons:

- **Consistency.** If your infrastructure is being configured manually, how do you know your servers are being set up in a consistent manner? Further, how do you know these changes are being performed in a way that meets your compliance and security requirements? (For instance, are administrators logging changes in the appropriate systems?)

  Make life easier for your system administrators by automating repeated tasks with a configuration management tool. When repeated tasks are tedious, humans are alarmingly bad at performing them consistently. Automate tedious administration tasks with a configuration management tool so your staff can focus on other important things that humans do best.

- **Efficient change management.** Whenever infrastructure is built manually without the aid of a configuration management tool, people tend to fear change. Over time, servers that are maintained by hand tend to become fragile environments that are hard to understand and modify.

  In these situations, organizations tend to develop a lot of processes for managing changes, usually with the sole intent on minimizing change or even delaying it as long as possible. This tends to delay introducing new features your customers need.

  When servers can be reproduced easily in a repeatable fashion, fewer processes are needed to manage change. Small change batches can be performed on a regular basis, such as daily, or even several times a day.

- **Simplicity in rebuild.** When servers are built manually, it's typically not easy to rebuild them from scratch. What would happen if you suddenly lost your servers in a catastrophic event? How quickly could you restore service if disaster struck?

  Automated deployments using a configuration management tool help quickly restore service. Rather than bothering to upgrade or patch applications, which can be inherently fragile operations, system administrators can build a new, upgraded system in an automated fashion and throw the old one away, returning it to the server pool. When rebuilds are easy, system administrators gain confidence to make changes to infrastructure more rapidly.

- **Visibility.** Configuration management tools include auditing and reporting capabilities. Monitoring the work performed by one system administrator doesn't require a sophisticated tool. But trying to understand what is going on with a team of, say, 10 system administrators and 10 software developers deploying software changes many times per day? You need a configuration tool.

  When infrastructure changes are handled by automated systems, changes can be automatically logged in all relevant tracking systems to raise visibility on the meaningful work your teams are doing.

What Is Chef?

Chef is an automation platform that configures and manages your infrastructure whether it is on-premises or in the cloud. You can deploy to the infrastructure type that makes the most sense for your business. You can use Chef to speed up application deployment, even creating a continual deployment pipeline. The key to Chef's power is that it turns infrastructure into code.

Infrastructure as code means that your computing environment has some of the same attributes as your application:

- Your infrastructure is versionable.
- Your infrastructure is repeatable.
- Your infrastructure is testable.

Figure 1-1 presents an overview of the major components of Chef.

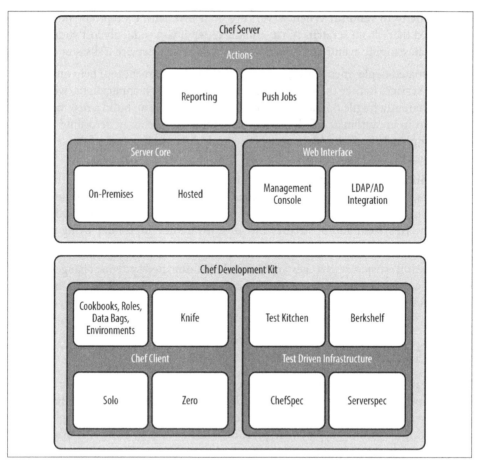

Figure 1-1. Chef architecture

The components of the Chef Development Kit help support you as you write Chef code on your development workstation. Chef Server provides additional components to help scale your configuration management capabilities to hundreds or thousands of servers, and beyond.

Why Chef Might Be a Good Tool for Your Enterprise

When Adam Jacob first created Chef in 2009, he had three key insights to address the shortcomings he saw in other configuration management tools:

1. A configuration management tool should easily enable web IT, providing first-class support for managing cloud infrastructure.

2. Everyone's infrastructure is unique. Complex, enterprise infrastructures benefit greatly from being able to model their IT infrastructure and application delivery process as code.

3. Great tools and ideas also come out of a vibrant and involved user community. You can't do it alone.

Over time with community support, Chef has evolved to have a powerful set of features that make it unique among configuration management tools:

Extreme scalability
Customers such as Facebook use Chef to manage tens of thousands of servers (*http://bit.ly/facebook_and_chef*) using only a handful of employees.

Power
Chef is built on top of the Ruby programming language. When you need it, you have full access to the power of Ruby to customize Chef.

Choice
You are not locked into one way of using Chef. Chef can operate in a distributed standalone mode or in a centralized mode requiring a server. There are also options to use pull or push models (or both) for deployment.

Open
Chef is open source and supported by a vibrant community of system administrators and developers. Chef open source has been used to power products from Dell (*http://bit.ly/dell_and_chef*), from Facebook (*http://bit.ly/fb_opscode_and_private_chef*), and from Amazon Web Services (*http://bit.ly/aws_opscode_chef*).

Visible
As a premium feature, the Chef Analytics Platform provides powerful enhancements to Chef integrated with the tool, so that you can be notified when important changes are made as a way to enforce compliance.

Chef's unique approach gives you tremendous flexibility. You don't need to struggle to conform to Chef. Chef adapts to you and your environment. You can deploy to the cloud or local infrastructure. You can describe any resource you have in code no matter how much it differs from a standard configuration.

With Chef there is no reason to start from scratch; many standard infrastructure configurations and tasks are already described in Chef cookbooks are available for free on the Chef Supermarket (*https://supermarket.getchef.com*) site.

Once you master Chef, you can use it to

- Fully automate deployments, including internal development and end-user systems

- Automate scaling of infrastructure
- Make your infrastructure self-healing

As an example, Tom Hallet used Chef to create a tool called SoloWizard, which he uses to automate deployments of his Mac OS X development machines. SoloWizard is based on the work Pivotal Labs has done to promote the use of automation for developer and end-user systems. As you can see from Figure 1-2, SoloWizard lets you create a new development environment with a single command. You can even personalize the output script to meet your needs by making choices on a simple website. This tool is publicly available at the SoloWizard site (*http://www.solowizard.com*).

Where Do We Go From Here?

In the first half of this book, we'll cover all the essential components of client-side Chef, showing you how to make your infrastructure versionable and repeatable with code. We'll cover:

- Test Kitchen
- Chef Solo/Chef Local
- Cookbooks

We'll also give you a firm foundation in the basics of infrastructure coding with Chef by providing lots of hands-on examples.

In the second half of this book, we'll introduce you to the essential topics related to Chef Server, showing you how to make your configuration management abilities scale as your infrastructure increases in complexity and scope:

- On-Premises Chef Server
- Chef Zero
- Roles, Data Bags, and Environments
- Knife

Tools covered in this book are freely available as open source downloads. Some paid tools will be mentioned, but are not required to learn or use Chef.

In the next chapter, we'll start your adventure with Chef by walking you through the Chef Development Kit installation process, so that you can get started right away writing Chef code.

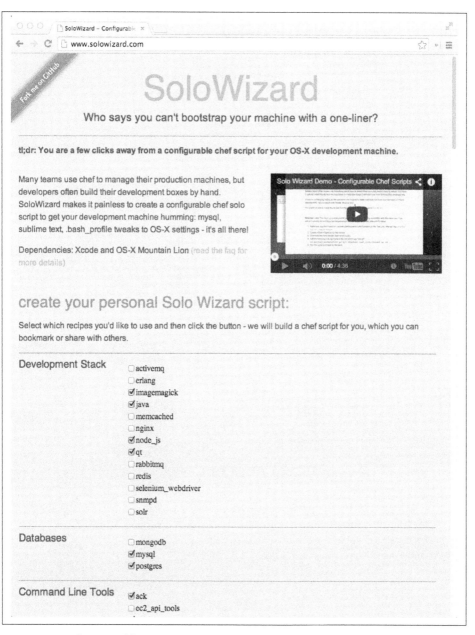

Figure 1-2. SoloWizard bootstraps Mac OS X development workstations

## CHAPTER 2

Configure Your Chef Development Environment

In this chapter, we'll walk you through the process of installing and configuring all the tools necessary to write Chef automation code. The setup covered is all you need for the hands-on exercises in this book. Linux, Mac OS X, and Windows are all first-class, supported development environments by Chef Software. We'll cover all these environments in this book, noting the platform-specific differences as necessary.

We Give You Options in This Book

There will be a little bit of a "Choose Your Own Adventure" aspect to this book, this chapter in particular. Chef supports a variety of environments: Linux, Mac OS X, and Windows. Also, in order to make Chef more accessible to new Chef developers, Chef Software now recommends the use of the Chef Development Kit. Unfortunately, as of this writing, the Chef Development Kit is not available on all the platforms supported by Chef.

You will find that you have to make two important choices as you start your adventures with Chef:

1. Choose a development platform: Linux, Mac OS X, or Windows.
2. Choose a Chef tool to install: Chef Development Kit or Chef Client.

The development platform is up to you. Chef supports development on Linux, Mac OS X, and Windows equally well.

We recommend that beginners use the Chef Development Kit, if you can, as that is now the recommended development platform for getting started with Chef. However, if the Chef Development Kit is not an option for you, we offer instructions on how to do Chef development simulating the Chef Development Kit with existing tools. We take care not to leave you out in the cold if you can't use the Chef Development Kit right now.

Once you have made a commitment to Chef in your production environment, you have also made a committment to learning Ruby. Many experienced Chef users prefer to manage their own Ruby development environment manually using Ruby virtual managers such as rvm, rbenv, or chruby, as any Ruby developer would. However, many beginners find this too daunting at first, so covering Ruby development environments in more detail is beyond the scope of this book. Since this book is aimed primarily at Chef beginners, we cover the installation options that provide prepackaged Ruby environments: the Chef Development Kit and Chef Client.

The section for each platform covers the choices you must make and the installation steps you must perform in more detail. Be prepared to skip around a bit in this chapter.

Install a Programmer's Text Editor

To write Chef code, you must use an editor designed to save files in raw text format. Do not use Microsoft Word, or a similar editor that saves text in a different file format, as Chef will have difficulty reading your files. Make sure that you have either a command line text editor or GUI text editor handy.

If you are comfortable using command line editors, vim, GNU Emacs, or nano are popular choices. Since it is difficult to perform system administration duties without a command line editor, we assume you have already configured one on your system.

If a text editor with a graphical user interface is more to your liking, we recommend Sublime Text (*http://www.sublimetext.com*). All the platforms covered in this book are supported by the Sublime Text editor—Linux, Mac OS X, and Windows. In addition to providing syntax highlighting and line numbers, Sublime Text also supports a project view for navigating through directory hierarchies as shown in Figure 2-1. You will find all these features handy as you write Chef code:

- Line number display
- Highlighted syntax
- Command autocomplete
- Ability to have multiple files open at once

Figure 2-1. Sublime text project view

Sublime Text offers some excellent plugins for writing Chef code as well. Sublime Text costs $70. We recommend giving Sublime Text a trial spin as you follow the coding examples in this book.

If Sublime Text isn't the right GUI editor for you, some other free alternatives to consider would be gedit (*http://bit.ly/gnome_gedit*) for Linux, TextMate 2 (*http://macro mates.com/*) for Mac OS X, and Notepad++ (*http://notepad-plus-plus.org/*) for Windows.

 Although there are currently no integrated development environments (IDEs) for Chef, Ruby IDEs work well with Chef—RubyMine (*http://www.jetbrains.com/ruby/*), IntelliJ IDEA (*http://www.jetbrains.com/idea/*), Eclipse (*http://www.eclipse.org/*) to name a few. A Ruby IDE will include a programmer's text editor as well.

Also, JetBrains supports Chef in its RubyMine and IntelliJ IDEs.

Chef Development Tools

The Chef Development Kit includes all the basic tools you need to get started writing Chef code. In the following sections we'll cover how to install the Chef Development Kit on Linux, Mac OS X, and Windows. Follow the applicable section that matches the operating system on your computer.

All Chef development tools are written in Ruby, a popular scripting language. The use of a scripting language eliminates the need to write and maintain native code individually for Linux, Mac OS X, and Windows. Instead, a single set of Ruby scripts implements the Chef development tools on these three supported platforms. For the scripts to function, you must install a native Ruby scripting engine to run the Chef development tools.

The Chef Development Kit installer for each platform comes bundled with the correct native Ruby scripting engine. The Chef development tools and the Ruby scripting engine are installed outside any commonly used system locations. This ensures that the Ruby bundled with Chef will not interfere with another copy of Ruby used elsewhere on your system.

As of this writing, the Chef Development Kit is relatively new and supports only recent versions of Linux, Mac OS X, and Windows. If you happen to be using an operating system version that isn't currently supported by the Chef Development Kit, you'll find additional instructions showing you how to manually install the extra development tools you'll need after installing Chef Client.

Chef Client versus Chef Development Kit

Chef Client (also known as the *Chef Omnibus Installer*) contains the core components of Chef needed to manage a server or workstation. The installer comprises the entire collection of things necessary to run Chef; thus, it is an *omnibus* installer. Chef Client bundles core application scripts along with the necessary Ruby scripting engine. In production environments, Chef Client is installed on every system intended to be managed by Chef.

The Chef Development Kit is a superset of Chef Client. If you install the Chef Development Kit, there is no need to install the Chef Client. Chef Development Kit includes all the components of Chef Client, plus the Chef Development Kit additional best-of-breed tools developed by the Chef community, in one package. Several community-developed tools have become part of the standard Chef development workflow for many, so now they are bundled together into an officially supported Chef product.

Skip ahead to the installation section for your operating system of choice:

- Linux: "Install the Chef Development Tools on Linux" on page 13
- Mac OS X: "Install the Chef Development Tools on Mac OS X" on page 20
- Windows: "Install the Chef Development Tools on Windows" on page 27

Install the Chef Development Tools on Linux

You will need an Internet connection and root access on your computer in order to install the Chef development tools on Linux.

Visit the Chef downloads page (*http://downloads.getchef.com/*) to download the installation package for your distribution of Linux.

Follow the Chef Development Kit link as shown in Figure 2-2 to see if there is an installation package available for your platform.

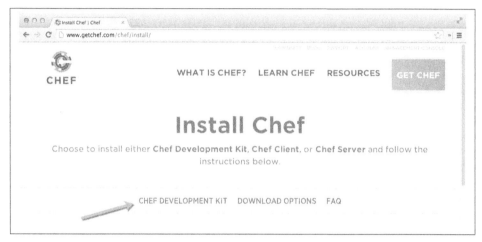

Figure 2-2. Choose to install the Chef Development Kit

Figure 2-3 shows the options available for Linux as of this writing. Choose your desired distribution and version of Linux. Once you've made your selection, a download link for an installation package will be displayed.

If there is no Chef Development Kit installer for your preferred version of Linux, you'll need to install the Chef Client for your platform instead and perform some additional steps manually. Using the Chef Development Kit installer is preferred because it makes installation more convenient, but it is not necessary. Go back to the main page (*http://downloads.getchef.com/*) and install the Chef Client instead.

On the Downloads page, under *Chef Client*, select the distribution and version of Linux installed on your computer as shown in Figure 2-4. Once you've made these selections, a download link for an installation package will be displayed.

The details for the installation process will vary by Linux distribution. Refer to the web page for more specific instructions. You will get a link to an installation package or a script.

Figure 2-3. Linux Chef Development Kit

The download page might not match the images in this book exactly. The download and installation procedure, however, should be the same.

For RedHat/CentOS and other Enterprise Linux variants, open your terminal and use `rpm` to install with a command prompt. As an example, if the installation package link was `chefdk-0.2.0-2.el6.x86_64.rpm`, you would enter in the following, replacing the last parameter with the package name from either the Chef Development Kit or Chef Client download link you just visited:

```
$ sudo rpm -Uvh chefdk-0.2.0-2.el6.x86_64.rpm
```

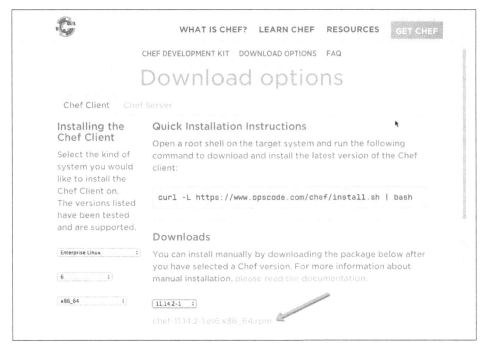

Figure 2-4. Downloading Linux Chef Client installer

For Ubuntu/Debian distributions, open your terminal and use dpkg to install with a command prompt. As an example, if the installation package link was chefdk_0.2.0-2_amd64.deb, you would enter the following, replacing the last parameter with the package name from the Chef Development Kit or Chef Client download link you visited:

```
$ sudo dpkg -i chefdk_0.2.0-2_amd64.deb
```

The Chef Development Kit installer will automatically install Chef and Ruby in the */opt/chefdk/embedded* directory on your local machine. Neither of these directories are commonly present in the default environment's PATH.

The Chef Development Kit includes a chef shell-init command to modify the current shell environment to use these paths. Assuming you are using the Linux default bash shell, run the following command to permanently enable this PATH setting:

Chef Development Kit installation:

```
$ echo 'eval "$(chef shell-init bash)"' >> ~/.bash_profile
```

If it was necessary to choose the Chef Client installation instead, the Chef and Ruby installation will be located under */opt/chef/embedded*.

We recommend you add this `bin` location to the following PATH. You should add this line to your `$HOME/.bash_profile` (or similar `*.profile` if you are using a different command line shell).

Chef Client installation:

```
export PATH="/opt/chef/embedded/bin:$PATH"
```

Once you change `$HOME/.bash_profile`, you will need to `source` the file to set up the correct $PATH. Alternatively, you can just close and open your terminal application to reload `$HOME/.bash_profile`.

```
$ source $HOME/.bash_profile
```

Verify the Chef Development Kit/Chef Client Install on Linux

Make sure the Ruby scripting engine in either */opt/chefdk/embedded/bin* or */opt/chef/embedded/bin* is being used with this $PATH change, depending on whether you installed the Chef Development Kit or the Chef Client, respectively. Enter `which ruby` in a terminal or command prompt. You should see the following:

Chef Development Kit installation:

```
$ which ruby
/opt/chefdk/embedded/bin/ruby
```

Chef Client installation:

```
$ which ruby
/opt/chef/embedded/bin/ruby
```

If you see no output at all, or if the output is not `/opt/chefdk/embedded/bin/ruby` or `/opt/chef/embedded/bin/ruby`, double-check that you have completed the preceding steps correctly.

If you do not want to change your $PATH, you could specify the full path to each embedded binary on the command line, such as

`/opt/chefdk/embedded/bin/ruby`

Going forward, so the command line entries fit better on our printed pages, this book will assume that you modified your PATH.

Verify that the basic Chef tools are present by checking */opt/chefdk/bin* or */opt/chef/bin* depending on whether you installed the Chef Development Kit or the Chef Client, respectively. You should see the following with the Chef Development Kit installation:

```
$ ls /opt/chefdk/bin
berks          chef-service-manager  fauxhai     nokogiri      ruby-rewrite
```

```
chef          chef-shell          foodcritic  ohai        shef
chef-apply    chef-solo           kitchen     rubocop     tt
chef-client   chef-vault          knife       ruby-parse
```

and with the Chef Client installation:

```
$ ls /opt/chef/bin
chef-apply  chef-service-manager  chef-solo  erubis  ohai    restclient
chef-client chef-shell            cher-zero  knife   rackup  shef
```

Run chef-client --version to ensure the chef-client command works properly. If your version differs, make sure that you have chef-client version 11.10.0 or higher to follow the hands-on exercises in this book:

```
$ chef-client --version
Chef: 11.14.6
```

If you installed the Chef Development Kit, you have now successfully installed the Chef development tools on Linux. Skip ahead to "Summary" on page 35. If you installed the Chef Client, you'll need to perform a few more installation steps, so keep reading.

Uninstalling the Chef Development Kit/Chef Client on Linux

You can use rpm to uninstall Chef Development Kit/Chef Client on RedHat Enterprise Linux-based systems.

Chef Development Kit uninstallation:

```
$ rpm -qa chefdk
$ sudo yum remove -y <package>
# If you installed custom gems, remove +/opt/chefdk+ manually
$ sudo rm -rf /opt/chefdk
# Remove PATH entry for Chef from $HOME/.bash_profile
```

Chef Client uninstallation:

```
$ rpm -qa chef
$ sudo yum remove -y <package>
# If you installed custom gems, remove +/opt/chef+ manually
$ sudo rm -rf /opt/chef
# Remove PATH entry for Chef from $HOME/.bash_profile
```

You can use dpkg to uninstall Chef Development Kit or Chef Client on Ubuntu-based systems.

Chef Development Kit uninstallation:

```
$ dpkg --list | grep chefdk # or dpkg --status chefdk

# Purge chefdk from the system.
# see man dkpg for details
$ sudo dpkg -P chefdk
# If you installed custom gems, remove +/opt/chefdk+ manually
```

```
$ sudo rm -rf /opt/chefdk
# Remove PATH entry for Chef from $HOME/.bash_profile
```

Chef Client uninstallation:

```
$ dpkg --list | grep chef # or dpkg --status chef

# Purge chef from the system.
# see man dkpg for details
$ sudo dpkg -P chef
# If you installed custom gems, remove +/opt/chef+ manually
$ sudo rm -rf /opt/chef
# Remove PATH entry for Chef from $HOME/.bash_profile
```

Install Test Kitchen on Linux (Chef Client Only)

We'll be using Test Kitchen to create virtualized sandbox environments in some of the
hands-on exercise. The Chef Client installer does not install Test Kitchen, so you'll need
to install it manually.

You need to install the test-kitchen gem. A *gem* is a supporting library or application
written in Ruby. You can think of a *gem* as the equivalent of an installer for Ruby.
Rubygems.org (*http://rubygems.org*) maintains a central registry of Ruby gems on the
Internet.

Run the gem install command as root to install the test-kitchen gem. The additional
--no-ri and --no-rdoc parameters save time by omitting the step that generates
documentation:

```
$ sudo gem install test-kitchen --no-ri --no-rdoc
Fetching: net-scp-1.2.1.gem (100%)
Fetching: safe_yaml-1.0.3.gem (100%)
Fetching: thor-0.19.1.gem (100%)
Fetching: test-kitchen-1.2.1.gem (100%)
Successfully installed net-scp-1.2.1
Successfully installed safe_yaml-1.0.3
Successfully installed thor-0.19.1
Successfully installed test-kitchen-1.2.1
4 gems installed
```

> If you see the error sudo: gem: command not found, your sudo is
> probably set up to use env_reset. As a workaround, use the following
> alternative command line to set the PATH for gem install:
>
> ```
> $ sudo env "PATH=$PATH" gem install test-kitchen --no-ri --no-rdoc
> ```

Where Do Ruby Gems Get Installed?

The `gem install` command installs gem files to the RubyGems *installation directory*. The Omnibus Install `gem` command stores gems in the directory containing Chef's private copy of Ruby: */opt/chef/embedded*.

You can verify this by using the `gem env` command to view the gem environment. It will list the `INSTALLATION_DIRECTORY` as */opt/chef/embedded/lib/ruby/gems/1.9.1*:

```
$ gem env
RubyGems Environment:
  - RUBYGEMS VERSION: 1.8.29
  - RUBY VERSION: 1.9.3 (2013-11-22 patchlevel 484) [x86_64-linux]
  - INSTALLATION DIRECTORY: /opt/chef/embedded/lib/ruby/gems/1.9.1
  - RUBY EXECUTABLE: /opt/chef/embedded/bin/ruby
  - EXECUTABLE DIRECTORY: /opt/chef/embedded/bin
  - RUBYGEMS PLATFORMS:
    - ruby
    - x86_64-linux
  - GEM PATHS:
    - /opt/chef/embedded/lib/ruby/gems/1.9.1
    - /home/misheska/.gem/ruby/1.9.1
...
```

 Why does the directory have 1.9.1 in it when the Ruby version is 1.9.3? The version of the installation directory refers to the *standard library version*, not the *core language version*. Every "batteries included" language like Ruby contains a large set of standard libraries to complement core language functionality. Historically, Ruby hasn't always changed the standard library at the same rate as the core language. Ruby 1.9.1, 1.9.2, and 1.9.3 all use the same standard library version: 1.9.1.

Verify the Test Kitchen Installation on Linux (Chef Client only)

You can verify that the `test-kitchen` gem is installed by using the `gem list` command. If Test Kitchen is already installed, the `gem list` command will display the output `true`:

```
$ gem list test-kitchen -i
true
```

You have now successfully installed the additional tools on Linux needed to follow the hands-on exercises in this book. Skip ahead to "Summary" on page 35.

Install the Chef Development Tools on Mac OS X

You will need an Internet connection and administrator privileges in order to install the Chef development tools on Mac OS X.

Visit the Chef downloads page (*http://downloads.getchef.com/*) to download the installer for your version of Mac OS X.

Follow the Chef Development Kit link as shown in Figure 2-5 to see if there is an installation package available for your version of Mac OS X.

Figure 2-5. Choose to install the Chef Development Kit

Figure 2-6 shows the options available for Mac OS X at the time of this writing. Currently, only the most recent version of Mac OS X, Mavericks (10.9), is supported, and not older versions like Mountain Lion (10.8) or Lion (10.8). When you click on the download link, an installation package will be displayed.

If there is no Chef Development Kit installation for your preferred version of Mac OS X, you'll need to install the Chef Client instead and perform some additional installation steps manually. Using the Chef Development Kit installation is preferred because it makes the installation more convenient, but it is not necessary. Go back to the main page (*http://downloads.getchef.com/*) and install the Chef Client instead.

WHAT IS CHEF?   LEARN CHEF   RESOURCES   GET CHEF

CHEF

Chef Development Kit

Accelerate Your Chef Workflow

The Chef Development Kit (ChefDK) brings the best-of-breed development tools built by the awesome Chef community to your workstation with just a few clicks. Download your package and start coding Chef in seconds.

Mac OS X   Ubuntu   Red Hat   Windows
              Linux   Enterprise
                           Linux

Version 0.2.0 ▾

Mac OS X 10.9

Download

MD5

Figure 2-6. Mac OS X Chef Development Kit

On the installation page, under *Chef Client*, choose the version of Mac OS X installed on your computer as shown in Figure 2-7. Once you've made your selection, a download link to a Mac OS X disk image *.dmg* file will be displayed.

> The download page might not match the images in this book exactly. The download and installation procedure, however, should be the same.

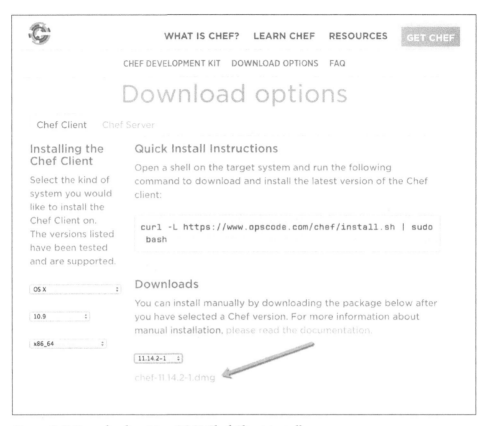

Figure 2-7. Downloading Mac OS X Chef Client installer

When you open the install *.dmg* file, you will see an icon with the Chef installation package as shown in Figure 2-8. Double-click on chef.pkg to run the installer.

Choose the default options and accept the license as you progress through the Chef Client installation. You might be prompted to enter your password. You'll need administrator privileges in order to make the necessary changes to run Chef on your machine.

 Don't forget to eject the Chef Client disk image once you have completed the installation.

Figure 2-8. Downloading Mac OS X Chef Client installer

The Chef Development Kit installer will automatically install Chef and Ruby in the */opt/ chefdk/embedded* directory on your local machine. Neither of these directories are commonly present in the default environment's PATH.

The Chef Development Kit includes a chef shell-init command to modify the current shell environment to use these paths. Assuming you are using the Mac OS X default bash shell, run the following command to permanently enable this PATH setting.

Chef Development Kit installation:

```
$ echo 'eval "$(chef shell-init bash)"' >> ~/.bash_profile
```

If it was necessary to choose the Chef Client installation instead, the Chef and Ruby install will be located under */opt/chef/embedded*.

We recommend that you add this bin location to the following PATH. You should add this line to your $HOME/.bash_profile (or similar profile file with your startup configuration and settings, if you are using a different command line shell).

Chef Client installation:

```
export PATH="/opt/chef/embedded/bin:$PATH"
```

Once you change $HOME/.bash_profile, you will need to source the file to set up the correct $PATH. Alternatively, you can just close and open your terminal application to reload $HOME/.bash_profile:

```
source $HOME/.bash_profile
```

Verify the Chef Development Kit/Chef Client Installation on Mac OS X

Make sure the Ruby scripting engine in either */opt/chefdk/embedded/bin* or */opt/chef/embedded/bin* is being used with this PATH change. Enter `which ruby` on a command line. You should see the following with the Chef Development Kit installation:

```
$ which ruby
/opt/chefdk/embedded/bin/ruby
```

or, with the Chef Client installation:

```
$ which ruby
/opt/chef/embedded/bin/ruby
```

If you see no output at all, or if the output is not `/opt/chefdk/embedded/bin/ruby` or `/opt/chef/embedded/bin/ruby`, double-check that you have completed the preceding steps correctly.

 If you do not want to change your $PATH, you could specify the full path to each embedded binary on the command line, such as

```
/opt/chefdk/embedded/bin/ruby
```

Going forward, so the command line entries fit better on our printed pages, this book will assume that you modified your $PATH.

Verify that the basic Chef Client tools are present by checking */opt/chefdk/bin* or */opt/chef/bin* depending on whether you installed the Chef Development Kit or the Chef Client. You should see the following with the Chef Development Kit installation:

```
$ ls /opt/chefdk/bin
berks           chef-service-manager  fauxhai   nokogiri     ruby-rewrite
chef            chef-shell            foodcritic  ohai         shef
chef-apply      chef-solo             kitchen    rubocop      tt
chef-client     chef-vault            knife      ruby-parse
```

and with the Chef Client installation:

```
$ ls /opt/chef/bin
chef-apply   chef-service-manager   chef-solo   erubis   ohai    restclient
chef-client  chef-shell             cher-zero   knife    rackup  shef
```

Run `chef-client --version` to ensure the `chef-client` command works properly. If your version differs, make sure that you have `chef-client` version 11.10.0, or higher to follow the hands-on exercises in this book:

```
$ chef-client --version
Chef: 11.14.6
```

If you installed the Chef Development Kit, you have now successfully installed the Chef development tools on Mac OS X. Skip ahead to "Summary" on page 35. If you installed the Chef Client, you'll need to perform a few more installation steps, so keep reading.

Uninstalling the Chef Development Kit/Chef Client on Mac OS X

You can uninstall the Chef Development Kit and Chef Client on Mac OS X using the appropriate commands.

Chef Development Kit uninstallation:

```
# Remove the installed files
sudo rm -rf /opt/chefdk

# Remove the system installation entry
sudo pkgutil --forget com.getchef.pkg.chefdk

# Remove the symlinks under /usr/bin for Chef Development Kit
ls -la /usr/bin | egrep '/opt/chefdk' | awk '{ print $9 }' | xargs rm -f

# Remove PATH entry for Chef from $HOME/.bash_profile
```

Chef Client uninstallation:

```
# Remove the installed files
sudo rm -rf /opt/chef

# Remove the system installation entry
sudo pkgutil --forget com.getchef.pkg.chef

# Remove the symlinks under /usr/bin for Chef Client
ls -la /usr/bin | egrep '/opt/chef' | awk '{ print $9 }' | xargs rm -f

# Remove PATH entry for Chef from $HOME/.bash_profile
```

Install Test Kitchen on Mac OS X (Chef Client Only)

for some of the hands-on exercises. The Chef Client installer does not install Test Kitchen, so you'll need to install it manually.

You need to install the test-kitchen gem. A *gem* is a supporting library or application written in Ruby. You can think of a *gem* as the equivalent of an installer for Ruby. Rubygems.org (*http://rubygems.org*) maintains a central registry of Ruby gems on the Internet.

Run the gem install command as root to install the test-kitchen gem. The additional --no-ri and --no-rdoc parameters save time by omitting the step that generates documentation:

```
$ sudo gem install test-kitchen --no-ri --no-rdoc
Fetching: net-scp-1.2.1.gem (100%)
Fetching: safe_yaml-1.0.3.gem (100%)
Fetching: thor-0.19.1.gem (100%)
Fetching: test-kitchen-1.2.1.gem (100%)
```

```
Successfully installed net-scp-1.2.1
Successfully installed safe_yaml-1.0.3
Successfully installed thor-0.19.1
Successfully installed test-kitchen-1.2.1
4 gems installed
```

Where Do Ruby Gems Get Installed?

The gem install command installs gem files to its *installation directory*. The Omnibus Install gem command stores gems in the directory containing Chef's private copy of Ruby: */opt/chef/embedded*.

You can verify this by using the gem env command to view the gem environment. It will list the INSTALLATION_DIRECTORY as */opt/chef/embedded/lib/ruby/gems/1.9.1*:

```
$ gem env
RubyGems Environment:
  - RUBYGEMS VERSION: 1.8.29
  - RUBY VERSION: 1.9.3 (2013-11-22 patchlevel 484) [x86_64-darwin11.2.0]
  - INSTALLATION DIRECTORY: /opt/chef/embedded/lib/ruby/gems/1.9.1
  - RUBY EXECUTABLE: /opt/chef/embedded/bin/ruby
  - EXECUTABLE DIRECTORY: /opt/chef/embedded/bin
  - RUBYGEMS PLATFORMS:
    - ruby
    - x86_64-darwin-11
  - GEM PATHS:
     - /opt/chef/embedded/lib/ruby/gems/1.9.1
     - /Users/vagrant/.gem/ruby/1.9.1
...
```

 Why does the directory have 1.9.1 in it when the Ruby version is 1.9.3? The version of the installation directory refers to the *standard library version*, not the *core language version*. Every "batteries included" language like Ruby contains a large set of standard libraries to complement core language functionality. Historically, Ruby hasn't always changed the standard library at the same rate as the core language. Ruby 1.9.1, 1.9.2, and 1.9.3 all use the same standard library version: 1.9.1.

Verify the Test Kitchen Installation on Mac OS X (Chef Client Only)

You can verify that the test-kitchen gem is installed by using the gem list command. If Test Kitchen is already installed, the gem list command will display the output true:

```
$ gem list test-kitchen -i
true
```

You have now successfully installed the additional tools on Mac OS X needed to follow the hands-on exercises in this book. Skip ahead to "Summary" on page 35.

Install the Chef Development Tools on Windows

You will need an Internet connection and administrator privileges on your computer in order to install the Chef development tools in Windows.

Visit the Chef downloads page (*http://downloads.getchef.com/*) to download the installer for your version of Windows. Follow the *Chef Development Kit* link as shown in Figure 2-9 to see if there is an installer available for your version of Windows.

Figure 2-9. Choose to install the Chef Development Kit

Choose your desired version of Windows. Once you've made your selection, a download link for an installation package will be displayed.

If there is no Chef Development Kit installation for your version of Windows, you'll need to install the Chef Client for your platform instead and perform some additional installation steps manually. Using the Chef Development Kit installation is preferred because it makes the installation more convenient, but it is not necessary. Go back to the main page (*http://downloads.getchef.com/*) and install the Chef Client instead.

On the installation page, under *Chef Client* choose the version of Windows installed on your computer as shown in Figure 2-10. Once you've made your selection, a download link to the corresponding Windows installer *.msi* file will be displayed.

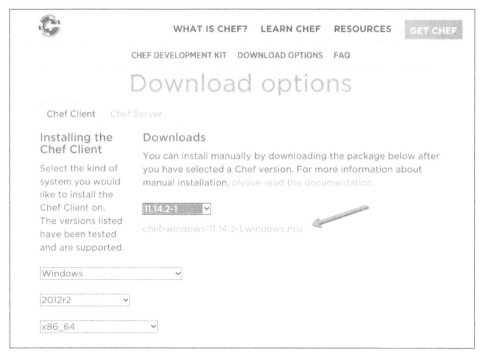

Figure 2-10. Downloading Chef Client Windows installer

 The download page might not match the images in this book exactly. The download and installation procedure, however, should be the same.

Run the installer for either the *Chef Development Kit* or the *Chef Client*, choosing the default options. The Chef Development Kit installer will install Chef and Ruby in the *C:\opscode\chefdk* directory on your local machine. If it was necessary to choose the Chef Client installer instead, the Chef and Ruby installer will be located under *C:\opscode\chef*. Either installer will automatically add all the correct directories for Chef and Ruby to the System PATH.

Verify the Chef Development Kit/Chef Client Installer in Windows

Make sure that the Ruby scripting engine in either *C:\opscode\chefdk\embedded\bin* or *C:\opscode\chef\embedded\bin* is being used with this PATH change, depending on whether you installed the Chef Development Kit or the Chef Client, respectively. Make sure you restart your command prompt after the installation and run the appropriate commands to verify.

Chef Development Kit installation—Windows Command Prompt:

```
> where ruby
C:\opscode\chefdk\embedded\bin\ruby.exe
```

Chef Development Kit installation—Windows PowerShell:

```
PS> (get-command ruby).path
C:\opscode\chefdk\embedded\bin\ruby.exe
```

Chef Client installation—Windows Command Prompt:

```
> where ruby
C:\opscode\chef\embedded\bin\ruby.exe
```

Chef Client installation—Windows PowerShell:

```
PS> (get-command ruby).path
C:\opscode\chef\embedded\bin\ruby.exe
```

If the output is not C:\opscode\chefdk\embedded\bin\ruby.exe or C:\opscode\chef\embedded\bin\ruby.exe, double-check that you completed the preceding steps correctly.

Verify that the basic Chef client tools are present by checking either *C:\opscode\chefdk\bin* as shown in Figure 2-11 or *C:\opscode\chef\bin* as shown in Figure 2-12.

Figure 2-11. C:\opscode\chefdk\bin

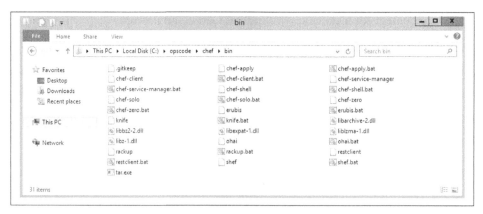

Figure 2-12. C:\opscode\chef\bin

Run `chef-client --version` to ensure the `chef-client` command works properly. If your version differs, make sure that you have `chef-client` version 11.10.0 or higher to follow the hands-on exercises in this book:

```
> chef-client --version
Chef: 11.14.6
```

If you installed the Chef Development Kit, you have now successfully installed the Chef development tools in Windows. Skip ahead to "Install Unix Tools for Windows" on page 32. If you installed the Chef Client, you'll need to perform a few more installation steps, so keep reading.

Uninstalling the Chef Development Kit/Chef Client in Windows

You can use Add/Remove Programs in Windows to remove the Chef Development Kit/Chef Client from your system.

Install Test Kitchen in Windows (Chef Client Only)

We'll be using Test Kitchen to create virtualized sandbox environments in some of the hands-on exercises. The Chef Client installer does not install Test Kitchen, so you'll need to install it manually.

You need to install the `test-kitchen` gem. A *gem* is a supporting library or application written in Ruby. You can think of a *gem* as the equivalent of an installer for Ruby. Rubygems.org (*http://rubygems.org*) maintains a central registry of Ruby gems on the Internet.

In Windows, you'll need to install the Test Kitchen gem as an administrator. Run `gem install test-kitchen` as *Run As Administrator* or *Command Prompt (Admin)*, depending on your version of Windows. The additional --no-ri and --no-rdoc parameters save time by omitting the step that generates documentation:

```
> gem install test-kitchen --no-ri --no-rdoc
Fetching: net-scp-1.2.1.gem (100%)
Fetching: safe_yaml-1.0.3.gem (100%)
Fetching: thor-0.19.1.gem (100%)
Fetching: test-kitchen-1.2.1.gem (100%)
Successfully installed net-scp-1.2.1
Successfully installed safe_yaml-1.0.3
Successfully installed thor-0.19.1
Successfully installed test-kitchen-1.2.1
4 gems installed
```

Where Do Ruby Gems Get Installed?

The gem install command installs gem files to the Rubygems *installation directory*. The Omnibus Install gem command stores gems in the directory containing Chef's private copy of Ruby: */opt/chef/embedded*.

You can verify this by using the gem env command to view the gem environment. It will list the INSTALLATION_DIRECTORY as */opt/chef/embedded/lib/ruby/gems/1.9.1*:

```
> gem env
RubyGems Environment:
  - RUBYGEMS VERSION: 1.8.28
  - RUBY VERSION: 1.9.3 (2013-11-22 patchlevel 484) [i386-mingw32]
  - INSTALLATION DIRECTORY: C:/opscode/chef/embedded/lib/ruby/gems/1.9.1
  - RUBY EXECUTABLE: C:/opscode/chef/embedded/bin/ruby.exe
  - EXECUTABLE DIRECTORY: C:/opscode/chef/chef/embedded/bin
  - RUBYGEMS PLATFORMS:
    - ruby
    - x86-mingw32
  - GEM PATHS:
     - C:/opscode/chef/embedded/lib/ruby/gems/1.9.1
     - C:/Users/misheska/.gem/ruby/1.9.1
  ...
```

 Why does the directory have 1.9.1 in it when the Ruby version is 1.9.3? The version of the installation directory refers to the *standard library version*, not the *core language version*. Every "batteries included" language like Ruby contains a large set of standard libraries to complement core language functionality. Historically, Ruby hasn't always changed the standard library at the same rate as the core language. Ruby 1.9.1, 1.9.2, and 1.9.3 all use the same standard library version: 1.9.1.

Verify the Test Kitchen Installer in Windows (Chef Client Only)

You can verify that the `test-kitchen` gem is installed by using the `gem list` command. If Test Kitchen is already installed, the `gem list` command will display the output `true`:

```
$ gem list test-kitchen -i
true
```

You have now successfully installed the additional tools in Windows needed to follow the hands-on exercises in this book.

Install Unix Tools for Windows

You'll need to install Unix-related tools in Windows for Test Kitchen. Test Kitchen requires the Secure Shell `ssh` to log in to your Enterprise Linux VM. The most painless way to install `ssh` is to install the Minimalist GNU for Windows (MinGW) tools that come bundled with Git for Windows. If you use Chef, you'll likely wind up using Git source control in some fashion as well.

Visit git-scm.com (*http://git-scm.com/downloads*) and refer to the git-scm.com site for more information on installing Git for Windows.

Make sure you choose *Run Git and included Unix tools from the Windows Command Prompt* when you see the *Adjusting your PATH environment* screen as shown in Figure 2-13. Except for this screen, feel free to choose the installation defaults if you like.

Figure 2-13. Add the accompanying Unix tools to your PATH

Verify that ssh is installed correctly by running ssh on the command line. You should see a usage screen resembling the following:

```
> ssh
usage: ssh [-1246AaCfgKkMNnqsTtVvXxYy] [-b bind_address] [-c cipher_spec]
           [-D [bind_address:lport] [-E log_file] [-e escape_char]
           [-F configfile] [-I pkcs11] [-i identity_file]
           [-L [bind_address:lport:host:hostport] [-Q protocol_feature]
           [-l login_name] [-m mac_spec] [-O ctl_cmd] [-o option] [-p port]
           [-R [bind_address:lport:host:hostport] [-S ctl_path]
           [-W host:port] [-w local_tun[:remote_tun]]
           [user@lhostname [command]
```

Install ConEmu (Optional)

Some of the tools included with Chef Client, such as Test Kitchen, use color in their output, as shown in Figure 2-14.

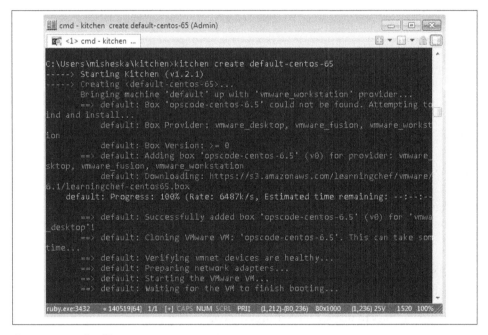

Figure 2-14. ConEmu

Neither the Command Prompt nor Windows PowerShell support the mechanism used by the Chef development tools to display text in color. We recommend you install a third-party terminal program for Windows that supports ANSI text color output.

We recommend ConEmu, as not only does it support colored text, but it also greatly improves the command prompt experience in Windows. ConEmu adds tabs, support for full screen, and a plethora of customization options. ConEmu also supports all the Windows command shells, so you can still use cmd.exe, PowerShell, bash, or another favorite. ConEmu does not replace existing Windows shells; it merely enhances their capabilities by providing user interface enhancements, such as adding support for color.

To install ConEmu, go to the primary download site for ConEmu (*http:// www.fosshub.com/ConEmu.html*) and download a ConEmu Installer, as shown in Figure 2-15.

Figure 2-15. Installing ConEmu, a third-party program that supports colored text

By default, ConEmu will use the cmd.exe shell, but you are not limited to this choice. Click on the *New console dialog* dropdown to choose from other shells, such as PowerShell, as shown in Figure 2-16.

To change the default shell, change the ConEmu settings (see Figure 2-17):

1. Click on the icon in the upper-left corner to display the application menu.

2. Choose *Settings* to display the Settings dialog.

3. In the settings dialog, choose *Startup* from the tree.

4. Choose your desired default shell from the pulldown under *Specified named task*.

5. Click on the *Save settings* button to make the setting your default.

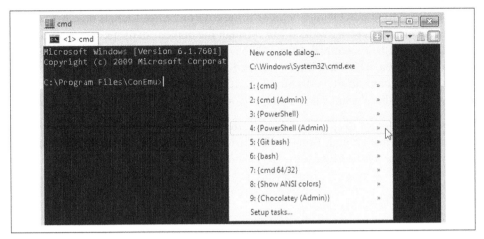

Figure 2-16. ConEmu lets you choose from among multiple shells

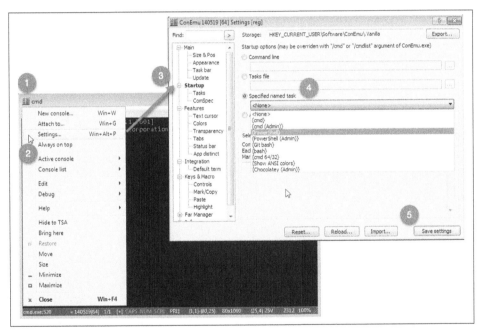

Figure 2-17. Setting your preferred default shell in ConEmu

Summary

Now that you have installed the Chef development tools on your computer using either the Chef Development Kit installer or the Chef Client installer, you have all the basic tools you need to interact with Chef. For some environments, there is no Chef Development Kit available, so we walked you through the manual steps necessary to make a Chef Client installation equivalent to a Chef Development Kit installation, for the purposes of this book. The Chef Development Kit is a superset of the Chef Client, with some additional community tools bundled with the installer. You can install these extra tools by hand if there is not yet a Chef Development Kit available for your platform.

Before we delve more deeply into Chef, in the next chapter we'll take a brief, related detour covering just enough Ruby to get started with Chef. Chef is based on Ruby, so you have to know a little bit of Ruby to get started with Chef.

## CHAPTER 3

Ruby and Chef Syntax

As briefly discussed in Chapter 2, both the Chef Development Kit and Chef Client are written and implemented in Ruby. However, prior experience with Ruby is not a requirement for writing Chef code. Most people who use Chef have no prior experience with the Ruby programming language. So let's spend some time going over the basics of Ruby and how it relates to Chef syntax.

Overview of Ruby

Ruby is an object-oriented programming language that was originally designed in 1993 as a replacement for Perl. Yukihiro Matsumoto (or "Matz" for short) designed and created Ruby in Japan. Ruby became very popular in the United States after two things occurred: 1) Dave Thomas wrote the book "Programming Ruby" in English in 2000, as until then most of the documentation on Ruby was in Japanese, and 2) David Heinemeier Hansson created the Ruby on Rails framework in 2003, which came to be viewed as an incredibly productive way to build web applications. The rapid adoption of Ruby on Rails, along with great documentation written in English, led people outside Japan to appreciate the Ruby language for other purposes besides web development. As illustrated in the next section, Ruby boasts a very English-like syntax.

Although Ruby is object oriented, it also supports functional and imperative programming paradigms. Unlike C or Java, which implement static typing, Ruby is a dynamically typed language. In this way, Ruby is similar to Python and Lisp. Ruby is designed for programmer productivity and fun. Usability and interface design are often given preference over speed or concurrency:

> Often people, especially computer engineers, focus on the machines. They think, "By doing this, the machine will run faster. By doing this, the machine will run more effectively. By doing this, the machine will something something something." They are focusing on machines. But in fact we need to focus on humans, on how humans care about

doing programming or operating the application of the machines. We are the masters. They are the slaves.

— Yukihiro Matsumoto

Similarly, Ruby follows the Principle of Least Surprise (also called the Principle of Least Astonishment), which aims to minimize confusion for both new and experienced users. The principle encourages consistency, common design patterns, and reusable code. The Ruby principles of simplicity and ease of use are echoed throughout Chef as well.

There is much more to the Ruby programming language, but that knowledge is not required to use Chef. For a more detailed explanation of Ruby and the Ruby programming language, check out *Programming Ruby 1.9 & 2.0 (4th edition): The Pragmatic Programmers' Guide* by Dave Thomas with Chard Fowler and Andy Hunt, or *Learning Ruby* by Michael Fitzgerald (O'Reilly).

Ruby Syntax and Examples

Let's cover the basics of Ruby syntax through the use of real-world examples.

Checking Syntax

Ruby provides a built-in mechanism to verify that a file contains valid Ruby syntax. You can check a file's syntax by passing the `-c` flag and the path to the file to the Ruby interpreter.

```
$ ruby -c /path/to/ruby/file
```

This will return `Syntax OK` if the syntax is correct. Otherwise, it will print a stack trace pointing to the line where the error occurred.

Comments

In Ruby, the hash character (#) is used to represent a comment. Comments contain documentation for your code. Everything after the \# on the same line is treated as a comment intended to be read by humans and ignored by the Ruby interpreter:

```
variable = 2 # This is a comment

# This is a multiple line comment because each
# line starts with a hash symbol
```

It is important to document *why* you are writing code. Use comments to explain why you chose to implement your code in the way you did and describe the alternative approaches you considered. Jeff Atwood, of Stack Exchange and Discourse fame, brilliantly explains the purpose of comments this way: *"Code tells you how, comments tell you why."*

For example, consider the following Ruby code snippet, which buys bacon if there are currently fewer than five strips. By reading the code you can understand *what* the code does, but it is not clear *why* the code was written in the first place:

```
if bacon.strips < 5
  buy_bacon
end
```

The following code adds a simple comment explaining why we should buy more bacon when there are fewer than five strips. It is helpful to understand the context around this bacon purchase: Jake likes to eat five pieces of bacon in the morning, so we want to have enough bacon on hand at all times:

```
# Jake eats 5 pieces of bacon each morning
if bacon.strips < 5
  buy_bacon
end
```

Variables

As we just saw in the preceding example, variables in Ruby are assigned from left to right:

```
variable = 2 # This assigns the value 2 to variable.
```

Because Ruby is not a statically typed language, you do not need to declare the type of variable when assigning it. The following examples assign very different kinds of values to variables: a number, the string *hello*, and even an object. There is no need to tell Ruby the kind of content that will be stored in a variable before assigning values:

```
a = 1
b = 'hello'
c = Object.new
```

In Ruby, a variable is accessible within the outermost scope of its declaration. Consider the following example that better demonstrates variable scope. First, a top-level variable named bacon_type is declared and assigned the value *crispy*. Next, the bacon is cooked twice and an additional variable named temperature is assigned the value 300. Finally, the script attempts to access the temperature variable, which is now out of scope:

```
bacon_type = 'crispy' ❶

2.times do
  puts bacon_type ❷
  temperature = 300 ❸
end

puts temperature ❹
```

❶   The bacon_type variable is declared at the top-level scope, so it will be accessible everywhere within this context.

❷   We can access the bacon_type variable inside a more specific scope, such as a loop.

❸   A variable declared inside a scope is accessible only from inside that scope.

❹   Outside of the scope of declaration, attempting to access a variable will result in an exception (undefined local variable or method 'temperature').

Wait... what are you saying?
It's worth noting that if you're feeling a bit lost at this point, this book presumes a basic level of experience with object-oriented programming concepts. If you're not clear about variables, scope, and loops, you'll probably want to brush up on some of the basics of object-oriented programming and then head back here to get up to speed on Ruby and Chef. A great book on object-oriented programming with Ruby is *Practical Object-Oriented Design in Ruby*, by Sandi Metz.

Mathematical Operations

Ruby exposes basic arithmetic operations such as addition, multiplication, and division as a core feature of the language:

```
1 + 2       #=> 3
3 * 4       #=> 12
5 / 6.0     #=> 0.8333...
```

Let's say that to ensure a productive and collaborative work environment, your company policy requires that your team take a bacon break every three hours, on the hour. Even though the policy is strict, the team often becomes engrossed in its work and forgets to check the clock. You could write a short Ruby script that alerts the team when it should stop and enjoy some freshly-cooked bacon:

```
# Bacon time is every third hour
if hour % 3 == 0
  puts "It's BACON time!"
end
```

More complex operations, such as rounding or polynomial distributions, are exposed in Ruby's Math module. You can use the Math.hypot method in a Ruby script to calculate the length of a diagonal for a right triangle by returning the sum of the squares of its two sides:

```
Math.hypot(43, 57) #=> 71.40028011149536
```

Additional functions and constants such as log, sin, sqrt, e, and π are also contained in the *Math* module.

Strings

There are two common ways to create strings in Ruby: with single quotes and with double quotes. Single-quoted strings have the advantage of one fewer keystroke and do not apply *interpolation*.

Double-quoted strings are useful when variables need to be evaluated as part of the string content—this evaluation process is known as *string interpolation*. A hash symbol is used as a placeholder within a double-quoted string to indicate to Ruby that the placeholder should be replaced with the evaluated content of a variable. In the following example, #{x} is used to insert the value of x within a string.

Both double and single-quoted strings use the backslash (\) character to escape special characters.

```
"double quoted string" #=> "double quoted string"
'single quoted string' #=> "single quoted string"

x = "hello"
"#{x} world" #=> "hello world" ❶
'#{x} world' #=> '#{x} world' ❷

"quotes in \"quotes\"" #=> "quotes in \"quotes\""
'quotes in \'quotes\'' #=> "quotes in \"quotes\""
```

❶ Double-quoted strings interpolate

❷ Single-quoted strings use the literal

You might need to escape special characters. For example, when storing the player name *Jim O'Rourke* as a string, you need to escape the single quote in his last name:

```
player = 'Jim O\'Rourke'
```

Alternatively, you can use double quotes and avoided escaping the character altogether:

```
player = "Jim O'Rourke"
```

Heredoc Notation

In Chef, you might see the "heredoc" notation for strings. Heredoc is especially useful when having a multiline string. Heredoc notation starts with two "less than" symbols (<<) and then some identifier. The identifier can be any string, but should not be a string that is likely to appear in the body of text. In the following example, we chose METHOD_DESCRIPTION as the heredoc identifier:

```
<<METHOD_DESCRIPTION
This is a multiline string.

All the whitespace is preserved, and I can even apply #{interpolation} inside
```

```
this block.
METHOD_DESCRIPTION
```

True and False

In addition to the literal *true* and *false*, Ruby supports "truthy" and "falsey" values. Expressions evaluate as true or false in a situation where a boolean result is expected (such as when they are used in conditionals like the if statement). Table 3-1 demonstrates the common truthy and falsey values and their actual evaluations.

Table 3-1. Truthy and falsey values

value	evaluates as
true	*true*
false	*false*
Bacon	*true*
Object	*true*
0	*true*
1	*true*
-1	*true*
nil	*false*
" "	*true*
[]	*true*
{}	*true*

The results of those expressions can also be negated using the not keyword or the bang (*!*) operand:

```
!true      #=> false
not true   #=> false
not false  #=> true
!!true     #=> true
not nil    #=> true
```

Arrays

Ruby's native array support allows you to create lists of items. Ruby's arrays use the bracket notation as shown in the following example. Arrays are *zero-indexed* and the Ruby interpreter automatically allocates memory as new items are added; there is no need to worry about dynamically resizing arrays:

```
types = ['crispy', 'raw', 'crunchy', 'grilled']
types.length        #=> 4 ❶
types.size          #=> 4 ❷
types.push 'smoked' #=> ["crispy", "raw", "crunchy", "grilled", "smoked"] ❸
```

```
types << 'deep fried' #=> ["crispy", "raw", "crunchy", "grilled",
                           "smoked", "deep fried"] ❹
types[0]      #=> "crispy" ❺
types.first   #=> "crispy" ❻
types.last    #=> "deep fried" ❼
types[0..1]   #=> ["crispy", "raw"] ❽
```

❶ The length method tells us how many items are in the array.

❷ You'll sometimes see size used as a synonym for length; Ruby offers the choice
    to use either.

❸ Add one or more items to the end of the array with push.

❹ << is a helpful alias for push when you want to add just one item to the end.

❺ Arrays are zero-indexed, so we can access the first element using 0 as the index.

❻ The first element is also accessible via the convenient first method.

❼ To complement the first method, Ruby also exposes a last method.

❽ Specifying a range inside the brackets will slice the array from the first index up
    to and including the second index.

For example, you could use Ruby arrays to store an ordered list of all employees in the
order in which they were hired. Each time a new employee joins the team, he is added
to the list. The first employee is at index 0, the second employee is at index 1, and so on:

```
employees[0] #=> Chase
employees[1] #=> Jake
```

When a new employee joins the team, his name is pushed onto the end of the array:

```
employees << 'Bob'
employees.last #=> Bob
```

Hashes

Ruby also supports *hashes* (sometimes called *dictionaries* or *maps* in other languages).
Hashes are key-value pairs that behave similarly to arrays. Hashes are created using
literal curly braces (*{}*):

```
prices = { oscar: 4.55, boars: 5.23, wright: 4.65, beelers: 6.99 }
prices[:oscar] #=> 4.55 ❶
prices[:boars] #=> 5.23

prices[:oscar] = 1.00 ❷
prices.values #=> [4.55, 5.23, 4.65, 6.99] ❸
```

❶ Individual elements are accessed using the bracket notation, much like arrays.

❷ The same bracket notation can be used to set elements at a particular key.

❸   Hashes respond to helpful methods like `keys` and `values`.

Strings, Symbols, and Mashes

So far, we have been using the symbol syntax for hashes. The syntax is:

```
key: value
```

This is Ruby syntactic sugar for the following:

```
:key => value ❶
```

❶   The `=>` is called a *hash rocket*.

Symbols are immutable strings in Ruby. Other languages would call them constants. We are using symbols in the preceding example, but the next code snippet demonstrates using strings as hash keys:

```
hash = { 'key' => value }
hash['key'] #=> value ❶
```

❶   Notice that the way in which the key is accessed also changes.

In Chef, you'll most commonly see string keys for consistency. However, Chef actually uses a custom data structure known as a *mash*. Mashes do not care about the data type you use to access a given element in a hash. In a mash, the following are all equivalent:

```
mash = Hashie::Mash.new({key: value}) ❶

mash[:key]   #=> value
mash['key']  #=> value
mash.key     #=> value
```

❶   `Hashie::Mash` is not part of the core Ruby library.

Mashes are great because they do not enforce a specific key construct. You can use the form that makes the most sense to you.

For example, you can use Ruby hashes to store information about popular baseball players and their current statistics. The `key` in this hash was the name of the baseball player. The `value` was another hash whose key is the name of the statistic and whose value is the number of that statistic. This is better illustrated by the following sample data:

```
players = {
  'McCutchen, Andrew' => {
    'AVG' => 0.311,
    'OBP' => 0.385,
```

```
      'SLG' => 0.507
    },
    'Alvarez, Pedro' => {
      'AVG' => 0.236,
      'OBP' => 0.297,
      'SLG' => 0.477
    }
  }
```

An individual player is accessed using his name as the key in the `players` hash. Because `players` is a hash of hashes, the returned value is also a hash:

```
players['McCutchen, Andrew'] #=> { 'AVG' => 0.311, 'OBP' => 0.385, 'SLG' => 0.507 }
```

A particular statistic is accessible by nested bracket notation where the first key is the name of the player and the second key is the name of the statistic:

```
players['McCutchen, Andrew']['AVG'] #=> 0.311
```

Regular Expressions

Ruby supports Perl-style regular expressions using the `=~` operator:

```
"Bacon is good" =~ /lie/    #=> nil
"Bacon is good" =~ /bacon/  #=> 0
"Bacon is good" !~ /lie/    #=> true
```

Remembering the order

It's easy to forget the order of the equal-tilde matcher. Is it `=~` or `~=`? The easiest way to always get the order correct is to think in alphabetical order. "Equals" comes before "tilde" in the dictionary, so the equal sign comes before the tilde in the expression.

For example, you could try using regular expressions to find names in a list of players on a baseball team beginning with a certain letter of the alphabet. Regular expressions can be anchored using the caret (^), which starts a match at the beginning of the string. The following snippet searches for all players that have a last name beginning with the letter F:

```
players.select do |name, statistics|
  name =~ /^F/
end
```

Conditionals and Flow

Like most programming languages, Ruby supports conditionals to manage the flow and control of application logic. The most common control gate is the `if` keyword. The `if` keyword is complemented by the `unless` keyword, which is the equivalent of `if not`:

```
# Using if
if some_condition
  puts "happened"
else
  puts "didn't happen"
end

# Using unless
unless some_condition
  puts "didn't happen"
else
  puts "happened"
end
```

It is also possible to have multiple levels of conditionals using the `elsif` keyword:

```
if false ❶
  puts "this can't possibly happen"
elsif nil ❷
  puts "this won't happen either"
elsif true
  puts "this will definitely happen"
else ❸
  puts "this won't happen, because the method is short-circuited
end
```

❶ If the result of an expression is falsey, the body of that block will not be executed.

❷ `nil` is considered a falsey value, so this block will not be evaluated.

❸ Because the former `elsif` block will always execute, this else block is unnecessary.

Less common in Ruby (but common in Chef) is the `case` statement. Very similar to the `if` statement, the `case` statement applies more syntactic sugar and logic for the developer:

```
case some_condition
when "literal string" ❶
  # ...
when /regular expression/ ❷
  # ...
when list, of, items ❸
  # ...
else ❹
  # ...
end
```

❶ If a literal object is supplied, the `case` statement will perform a pure equality match.

❷ If a regular expression is supplied, Ruby will attempt to call `match` on the receiving object.

❸ If multiple items are given, they are interpreted as "or" (if the item matches "list", "of", or "items").

❹ `case` statements also support a default case, in the event that nothing else matches.

For example, you could use Ruby's `case` statement to classify players on a baseball team based on their age. Players younger than 12 are considered to be in the minor league. Players between 13 and 18 are developing. Players between 19 and 30 are in their prime. Players still in the league between 31 and 40 are on their decline, and anyone over 40 is in retirement. This logic is captured by the following Ruby `case` statement:

```ruby
case player.age
when 0..12
  'Minor League'
when 13..18
  'Developing'
when 19..30
  'Prime'
when 31..40
  'Decline'
else
  'Retirement'
end
```

Methods, Classes, and Modules

Although not necessary until more advanced interactions with Chef, Ruby also supports methods, classes, modules, and an object-oriented hierarchy. Ruby methods are defined using the `def` keyword. Ruby classes are defined using the `class` keyword. Ruby modules are defined using the `module` keyword:

```ruby
class Bacon ❶
  def cook(temperature) ❷
    # ...
  end
end

module Edible ❸
  # ...
end
```

❶ Classes are created using the `class` keyword.

❷ Methods are created using the `def` keyword and can accept arguments (or parameters).

❸   Modules are created using the `module` keyword.

Methods may be invoked by name. Although optional, parentheses are highly recommended for readability and code portability:

```
my_method(5)        ❶
my_method 5         ❷
```

❶   This will execute the method named `my_method` with the parameter 5.

❷   `my_method` call without parentheses does the same thing.

Methods are also *chainable* in Ruby, so you can continue to call a method on a chain, provided the return value responds to the method:

```
"String".upcase.downcase.reverse  #=> "gnirts"
```

Chef Syntax and Examples

The *Domain Specific Language* (DSL) used by Chef is actually just a subset of Ruby. The full power of the Ruby programming language is accessible in Chef code. This allows developers to conditionally perform actions, perform mathematical operations, and communicate with other services easily from within Chef code. Before diving into the more advanced features of Chef's DSL, we will explore the basic syntax first.

Here is an example of the Chef DSL in action, demonstrating how a user account can be created with a Chef resource. In Chef, resources are the building blocks used to define specific parts of your infrastructure. For example, the following statement manages a user account named `alice` with a user identifier (UID) of 503:

```
user 'alice' do
  uid '503'
end
```

The following code sample demonstrates the more abstract syntax for invoking a DSL method in Chef code, on which the previous example is based:

```
resource 'NAME' do
  parameter1    value1
  parameter2    value2
end
```

The first part is the name of the resource (such as `template`, `package`, or `service`). The next part is the `name_attribute` for that resource. The interpretation of this value changes from resource to resource. For example, in the `package` resource, the `name_at tribute` is the name of the package you wish to install. In the `template` resource, the `name_attribute` is the path on the target node where the compiled file should reside. Next comes the Ruby keyword do. In Ruby, the do must always be accompanied by a closing end. Everything that resides between the do and end is called the block. Inside the block, resource parameters and their values are declared. This varies from resource to resource. A valid parameter for the package provider is version, whereas a valid parameter for the template provider is source.

It might help to think about the code in a more object-oriented approach as follows. The Chef DSL creates a new resource object for you, sets the correct attributes and parameters, and then executes that resource when Chef evaluates the code:

```
resource = Resource.new('NAME')
resource.parameter1 = value1
resource.parameter2 = value2
resource.run!
```

 Please note that the preceding code is not valid syntax and is only used for instructional purposes.

template, package, and service are just three of the many types of resources built into the Chef DSL. The following code demonstrates using the template, package, and service resources in Chef code:

```
template '/etc/resolv.conf' do ❶
  source 'my_resolv.conf.erb'
  owner  'root'
  group  'root'
  mode   '0644'
end

package 'ntp' do ❷
  action :upgrade
end

service 'apache2' do ❸
  restart_command '/etc/init.d/apache2 restart'
end
```

❶ This declares a template resource in Chef's DSL. The template will be compiled from the local file *my_resolv.conf.erb*, be owned by root:root, have 0644 permissions, and be placed at */etc/resolv.conf* on the target machine (where Chef evaluates the code).

❷ This declares a package resource in Chef's DSL. The "ntp" package will be upgraded.

❸ This declares a service resource in Chef's DSL. The "apache2" service will be accessible and manageable by Chef.

If you specify an invalid parameter (either one that does not exist or is misspelled), Chef will raise an exception:

```
NoMethodError
-------------


undefined method `not_a_real_parameter' for Chef::Resource
```

Chef uses a *multiphase* execution model, which lets you include logic switches or loops inside Chef code. For example, if you wanted to execute a resource on an array of objects, you could do so using the following code. The `file` resource is used to manage a file. `content` is a Chef DSL expression used to specify a string that is written to the file:

```
['bacon', 'eggs', 'sausage'].each do |type|
  file "/tmp/#{type}" do
    content "#{type} is delicious!"
  end
end
```

In the first phase of evaluation, Chef will dynamically expand that Ruby loop. After the first phase, internally the code becomes equivalent to:

```
file '/tmp/bacon' do
  content 'bacon is delicious!'
end

file '/tmp/eggs' do
  content 'eggs is delicious!'
end

file '/tmp/sausage' do
  content 'sausage is delicious!'
end
```

Even though the resources were dynamically created using Ruby interpolation and looping, they are still available as individual items in the resource list, because of Chef's multiphase execution.

Similarly, top-level Ruby code is computed during the first phase of execution. When dynamically calculating a value (such as the total free memory on a target node), those values are cached and stored during the first phase of execution:

```
free_memory = node['memory']['total']

file '/tmp/free' do
  contents "#{free_memory} bytes free on #{Time.now}"
end
```

In the second phase of evaluation, the resource contained in the resource list will be:

```
file '/tmp/free' do
  contents "12904899202 bytes free on 2013-07-24 17:47:01 -0400"
end
```

So far, you have seen the `file` resource, `template` resource, `service` resource, and `package` resource. These are all resources packaged into the core of Chef. You can find a complete listing of all resources on the resources page (*http://docs.getchef.com/chef/resources.html*). Here are some of the most commonly used Chef resources, followed by examples of their basic usage:

bash

Execute multi-line scripts written in the Bourne-again shell (bash) scripting language using the bash shell interpreter:

```
# Output 'hello' to the console
bash 'echo "hello"'
```

chef_gem

Install a gem inside of Chef, for use inside Chef; useful when a Chef code requires a gem to perform a function:

```
# Install the HTTParty gem to make RESTful requests
chef_gem 'httparty'
```

cron

Create or manage a cron entry that schedules commands to run periodically at specified intervals:

```
# Restart the computer every week
cron 'weekly_restart' do
  weekday '1'
  minute  '0'
  hour    '0'
  command 'sudo reboot'
end
```

deploy_revision

Control and manage a deployment of code from source control (such as a Rails application):

```
# Clone and sync an application from revision control
deploy_revision '/opt/my_app' do
  repo 'git://github.com/username/app.git'
end
```

directory

Manage a directory or directory tree, handling permissions and ownership:

```
# Recursively ensure a directory exists
directory '/opt/my/deep/directory' do
  owner     'root'
  group     'root'
  mode      '0644'
  recursive true
end
```

execute

> Execute an arbitrary one-line command (as if it were entered on the command line):
>
> ```
> # Write contents to a file
> execute 'write status' do
>   command 'echo "delicious" > /tmp/bacon'
> end
> ```

file

> Manage a file already present (but not already managed by Chef):
>
> ```
> # Delete the /tmp/bacon file
> file '/tmp/bacon' do
>   action :delete
> end
> ```

gem_package

> Install a gem for use outside of Chef, such as an application or utility:
>
> ```
> # Install bundler to manage dependencies
> gem_package 'bundler'
> ```

group

> Create or manage a local group definition with local user accounts as members:
>
> ```
> # Create the bacon group
> group 'bacon'
> ```

link

> Create and manage symlinks and hard links:
>
> ```
> # Link /tmp/bacon to /tmp/delicious
> link '/tmp/bacon' do
>   to '/tmp/delicious'
> end
> ```

mount

> Mount or unmount a file system:
>
> ```
> # Mount /dev/sda8
> mount '/dev/sda8'
> ```

package

> Install a package using the operating system's underlying package manager:
>
> ```
> # Install the apache2 package (on Debian-based systems)
> package 'apache2'
> ```

remote_file

> Transfer a file from a remote location (such as a website):
>
> ```
> # Download a remote file to /tmp/bacon
> remote_file '/tmp/bacon' do
> ```

```
      source 'http://bacon.org/bits.tar.gz'
    end
```

service
> Start, stop, or restart a service:

```
    # Restart the apache2 service
    service 'apache2' do
      action :restart
    end
```

template
> Manage plain-text file contents parsed as an Embedded Ruby template:

```
    # Write the /tmp/bacon template using the bits.erb source
    template '/tmp/bacon' do
      source 'bits.erb'
    end
```

user
> Create or manage a local user account:

```
    # Create the bacon user
    user 'bacon'
```

These examples illustrate Chef's DSL, as well as showcase some of the common resources used when working with Chef. Although our list is not comprehensive, it does include some of the most common Chef resources you will encounter. The full list of Chef's built-in resources can be found in the online resource documentation (*http://docs.opscode.com/resource.html*).

The material presented in this chapter is all you need to know about Ruby to write Chef code. Only when you need to extend Chef beyond what is provided out of the box will you have to worry about delving more deeply into Ruby coding. When you need to level up your Ruby knowledge for this task, we highly recommend Customizing Chef by Jon Cowie (O'Reilly).

Now that we have covered all the necessary fundamentals of Ruby, let's get back to more Chef coding! In the next chapter, we will put your new Ruby knowledge to use by writing some Chef code.

## CHAPTER 4

Write Your First Chef Recipe

Create a Directory Structure for Your Code

Since we will be writing a lot of code over the remainder of this book, let's create a simple directory structure—organizing the code by chapter—like the one below (There is no need to use this exact directory structure to organize your files. It is only a suggestion. Use a system that makes sense to you):

```
learningchef
|_ chap04
|_ chap05
...
|_ chap16
```

In your home directory, create a subdirectory named *learningchef*, making it the current directory:

```
$ cd
$ mkdir learningchef
$ cd learningchef
```

Then create a *chap04* subdirectory for the code examples you will be writing in this chapter. Make *chap04* the current directory:

```
$ mkdir chap04
$ cd chap04
```

Follow a similar pattern for each new chapter, creating a new subdirectory underneath *learningchef* to contain each chapter's examples. The code examples for this book (*http://learningchef.com*) follow this convention. When a specific directory structure is required for an example, we'll let you know; otherwise, assume you can put the files anywhere you find convenient.

Write Your First Chef Recipe

To show you the basics, let's write the simplest form of Chef code to make a "Hello World" *recipe*. A *recipe* is a file that contains Chef code.

Using your favorite text editor, create the recipe file *hello.rb* to match Example 4-1. This file can be anywhere—no specific directory structure is required. By convention, files that contain Chef code have the extension *.rb* to show they are written in Ruby.

The Chef coding language is a Ruby Domain Specific Language (DSL). It contains additional Ruby-like statements specialized for expressing Chef system administration concepts.

Example 4-1. hello.rb

```
file 'hello.txt' do
  content 'Welcome to Chef'
end
```

 It's not necessary to place *hello.rb* or any of the other **.rb* example files in this chapter in a special directory. To find the *hello.rb* file containing the code from the preceding example, look among the source code examples for the book (*http://learningchef.com*) in the *chap04/* directory. Other examples in this and subsequent chapters can be found in similarly titled chapter directories.

We'll go over what all the statements in this file mean in more detail in "Examine hello.rb" on page 58. Enter the code using a text editor, making sure you match the capitalization, spacing, and syntax exactly.

The `file` statement code you entered in *hello.rb*. is a *resource*. Resources are the building blocks for assembling Chef code. A *resource* is a statement within a recipe that helps define actions for Chef to perform. This particular `file` resource in *hello.rb* tells Chef to:

- Create the file *hello.txt*.
- Write the content `Welcome to Chef` to *hello.txt*.

Use the `chef-apply` command to get Chef to perform the actions indicated in your newly created *hello.rb* file.

---

chef-apply

The `chef-apply` tool is a wrapper built on top of Chef Solo (which will be discussed in more detail in Chapter 9). Chef Solo allows you to run Chef code locally without needing

---

a Chef Server. As you'll see in Chapter 9, it is not convenient to execute Chef code in a *.rb* file using Chef Solo. The chef-apply tool was designed to provide an easy-to-use wrapper on top of Chef Solo.

 Chef requires administrator privileges to run. If you are running User Account Control (UAC) on Windows, make sure you *Run As Administrator*. On Linux/Mac OS X, run chef-apply with sudo privileges if you are not running as root.

When you run chef-apply hello.rb, the output should resemble, for Linux/Mac OS X:

```
$ sudo chef-apply hello.rb
Recipe: (chef-apply cookbook)::(chef-apply recipe)
  * file[hello.txt] action create
    - create new file hello.txt
    - update content in file hello.txt from none to 40a30c
    --- hello.txt    2014-08-10 22:27:44.000000000 -0700
    +++ /tmp/.hello.txt20140810-14225-6e7qc7    2014-08-10 22:27:44.000000000
    -0700 @@ -1 +1,2 @@
    +Welcome to Chef
```

For Windows (Run As Administrator):

```
> chef-apply hello.rb
Recipe: (chef-apply cookbook)::(chef-apply recipe)
  * file[hello.txt] action create
    - create new file hello.txt
    - update content in file hello.txt from none to 40a30c
        --- hello.txt    2014-07-11 12:38:30.000000000 -0700
        +++ C:/Users/misheska/AppData/Local/Temp/hello.txt20140711-2344-mf17rh
        @@ -1 +1,2 @@
        +Welcome to Chef
```

Verify Your First Chef Recipe

Congratulations, you just automated the creation of the *hello.txt* file using Chef!

Verify that your *hello.rb* recipe performed the correct action. Look to see if a *hello.txt* file exists in the current directory alongside your *hello.rb* file and that it has the correct content:

```
$ more hello.txt
Welcome to Chef
```

Examine hello.rb

Let's go over each line in *hello.rb* from Example 4-1 in more detail, exploring the purpose of each component. As mentioned earlier, Chef code uses a *domain-specific language* (DSL) built on top of the Ruby programming language. Having expressions tailored for system administration makes Chef code more accessible to beginners. The DSL is also designed to make you focus more on describing *what* the desired configuration of a machine should be, rather than *how* it should be accomplished. *Desired configuration* is a concept we'll cover in more detail in "Recipes Specify Desired Configuration" on page 59.

 Because Chef recipes are code, we recommend that you use some form of source control to manage your Chef source. It is beyond the scope of this book to show you how to use version control to manage source. However, use version control for everything you do with Chef. Any version control system will do: Git, Subversion, Mercurial, Team Foundation Server, and so on.

The first line of *hello.rb* contains a `file` resource referring to the file *hello.txt*:

```
file 'hello.txt' do
```

Remember that *resources* are building blocks that Chef uses to configure things on a system. The `file` resource is used to manage a file on a computer. The `file` resource takes a string parameter specifying the path to the file. In a Chef recipe, this is denoted by enclosing the string in double quotes ("") or single quotes ("). For example, use the following `file` resource syntax, to specify the filename */usr/local/hello.txt*:

```
file "/usr/local/hello.txt"
```

It doesn't matter whether you use double or single quotes for string literals; either choice is valid:

```
file '/usr/local/hello.txt'
```

Now, what is that do clause at the end of the first line? The do statement at the end of the first line denotes the start of a *block*. To specify extra parameters in a resource statement, it must span multiple lines. When resource statements span multiple lines, everything but the first line must be enclosed by a `do..end` pair. The do...end pair containing the extra lines is referred to as a *block*.

Line two contains a reference to a `content` *attribute*, specifying a string that should be written to the file:

```
content 'Welcome to Chef'
```

For now, just think of an *attribute* as yet another variable maintained by Chef that can be used as a parameter to a resource. We'll delve more deeply into attributes in Chapter 8. By convention, statements in Chef recipes are indented with spaces when they are inside a block. Thus, the `content` attribute is indented two spaces, following Ruby convention.

The string `Welcome to Chef` is passed as a `content` attribute to the `file` resource. The `file` resource writes out the specified `content` string attribute to the *hello.txt* file.

Finally, line three completes the block for the `file` resource with an `end` statement, finishing off the `do..end` pair:

```
end
```

This example should give you an idea of what Chef code looks like, building on the introduction to Ruby, the core of Chef, which we covered in Chapter 3.

Recipes Specify Desired Configuration

Let's explore the concept that you only need to tell Chef *what* the desired configuration should be, not *how* to achieve it, that we touched on earlier. Figure 4-1 illustrates this concept. Before Chef performs actions, it refers to the resources and attributes in a recipe to answer the question "*What* do I care about?" Then Chef decides *how* to put the system in the desired configuration by reasoning about the current state of the system. As a result, Chef code tends to be more succinct than equivalent bash or PowerShell scripting code as you only need to specify the desired configuration in your code, not how this configuration must be achieved. Chef determines *how* automatically and autonomously.

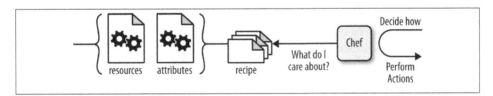

Figure 4-1. Recipes specify desired configuration

Let's make this concept more concrete by writing some Chef code. Create a new recipe alongside *hello.rb* called *stone.rb* following Example 4-2. Similar to *hello.rb*, *stone.rb* does not need to be in any specially named directory structure.

Example 4-2. stone.rb

```
file "#{ENV['HOME']}/stone.txt" do
  content 'Written in stone'
end
```

stone.rb is just a slight modification of the earlier *hello.rb* recipe in Example 4-1. The string *Written in stone* will be written to *stone.txt*. However, in this example, the *stone.txt* file will be written to your home directory instead of the directory where you run `chef-apply`.

Why did we make this change? It is not safe to use implied relative paths like *stone.txt* with Chef resources. On some platforms, behind the scenes, Chef could be running in a different place than you expect. We constrained the things you did in the first *hello.rb* example, so it was safe, but in general you must use absolute paths when specifying a filename to a resource. Plus, keep in mind that Chef recipes are intended to be run on different machines and even different operating systems producing the same configuration. Chef steers you toward using absolute paths in recipes because it would be difficult to specify consistent file locations using relative paths.

 On Windows, Chef will convert absolute paths with forward slashes (/) to use the Windows-style backslash character (\). You can use the backslash character, but Chef code uses the backslash (\) as an escape character in strings. So, you have to specify a double backslash (\\) to insert a literal single backslash in a string. In this book, we'll stick with using forward slashes (/) on Windows.

Let's explain the `#{ENV['HOME']}` construct and why we changed the file string to use double quotes ("") instead of single quotes ('\'). In Chef code, it doesn't matter if you use double quotes or single quotes for *string literals*. However, it does matter when you want to evaluate the value of a variable in a string (also known as *string interpolation*).

`#{ENV['HOME']}` is a variable referring to the current user's home directory. Variable references within strings are denoted by `#{<variable>}` (a hash character followed by the variable enclosed by a set of curly braces). A string must be enclosed in double quotes ("") when it contains a variable reference. Otherwise, Chef will not replace the variable reference with its value when the string is evaluated.

The `ENV['HOME']` variable is a reference to a collection of name-value pairs. Chef calls a collection of name-value pairs a *Hash*. Other languages refer to this construct as dictionary, associative array, or a map—it's all the same thing. In a Chef recipe, you can retrieve the value for a system environment variable by referring to the variable `ENV['<name>']`. *name* refers to a string with an environment value name. This is the code equivalent of:

- echo $HOME on Linux/Mac OS X/Windows PowerShell

- echo %USERPROFILE% on Windows Command Prompt

For example, my home directory is *Users/misheska*. Chef evaluates the string "#{ENV['HOME']}/stone.txt" as "/Users/misheska/welcome.txt".

 Sharp-eyed readers might wonder how we could get away with using the $HOME reference if you are using the Windows Command Prompt. If you try to echo %HOME% using the Windows Command Prompt, you'll discover the environment variable doesn't exist. By default on Windows, internally Chef uses PowerShell to evaluate command-line references, even when you run Chef on the Windows Command Prompt. PowerShell is more Unix-like than the Windows Command Prompt, so Chef uses PowerShell by default.

Now that we've explained the changes to the source, run your Chef code using chef-apply on a command line. The output should resemble, for Linux/Mac OS X:

```
$ sudo chef-apply stone.rb
Recipe: (chef-apply cookbook)::(chef-apply recipe)
  * file[/Users/misheska/stone.txt] action create
    - create new file /Users/misheska/stone.txt
    - update content in file /Users/misheska/stone.txt from none to ba4fda
    --- /Users/misheska/stone.txt    2014-08-10 22:33:40.000000000 -0700
    +++ /tmp/.stone.txt20140810-14302-1nfmi0r    2014-08-10 22:33:40.000000000
    -0700 @@ -1 +1,2 @@
    +Written in stone
```

For Windows (Run As Administrator):

```
> chef-apply stone.rb
Recipe: (chef-apply cookbook)::(chef-apply recipe)
  * file[C:/Users/misheska/stone.txt] action create
    - create new file C:/Users/misheska/stone.txt
    - update content in file C:/Users/misheska/stone.txt from none to ba4fda
        --- C:/Users/misheska/stone.txt 2014-07-11 15:48:46.000000000 -0700
        +++ C:/Users/misheska/AppData/Local/Temp/stone.txt20140711-2232-1wpswfb
        @@ -1 +1,2 @@
        +Written in stone
```

Now the file *stone.txt* should be created in your home directory with the content *Written in stone*. Verify with the following command for Linux/Mac OS X/Windows PowerShell:

```
$ more $HOME/stone.txt
Written in stone
```

or, for Windows Command Prompt:

```
> more %USERPROFILE%\stone.txt
Written in stone
```

Try running chef-apply using the same *stone.rb* recipe one more time. You should notice that the output is a little different executing the same recipe for the second time.

Linux/Mac OS X:

```
$ sudo chef-apply stone.rb
Recipe: (chef-apply cookbook)::(chef-apply recipe)
  * file[/Users/misheska/stone.txt] action create (up to date)
```

Windows (Run As Administrator):

```
> chef-apply stone.rb
Recipe: (chef-apply cookbook)::(chef-apply recipe)
  * file[C:/Users/misheska/stone.txt] action create (up to date)
```

chef-apply reports that file[...stone.txt] action create is *up to date* and that no action was performed. This is a good example of how chef-apply behaves differently depending on the machine's state. Chef performs actions autonomously without being explicitly told to do so:

- If *stone.txt* does not exist, chef-apply creates the file with the appropriate content.
- If *stone.txt* already exists, chef-apply will do nothing.

Do you think that chef-apply is smart enough to detect someone tampering with file content outside of Chef? Let's try an experiment. Change the contents of *stone.txt* with the following command for Linux/Mac OS X:

```
$ sudo sh -c 'echo "Modifying this file written in stone" > $HOME/stone.txt'
```

For Windows Command Prompt:

```
> echo Modifying this file written in stone > %USERPRFOILE%\stone.txt
```

For Windows PowerShell:

```
$ echo "Modifying this file written in stone" > $HOME\stone.txt
```

Verify that the file contents were changed by running one of the following for the Linux/Mac OS X/Windows PowerShell platform:

```
$ more $HOME/stone.txt
Modifying this file written in stone
```

For Windows Command Prompt:

```
$ more %USERPROFILE%\stone.txt
Modifying this file written in stone
```

Run chef-apply again for Linux/Mac OS X:

```
$ sudo chef-apply stone.rb
Recipe: (chef-apply cookbook)::(chef-apply recipe)
  * file[/Users/misheska/stone.txt] action create
    - update content in file /Users/misheska/stone.txt from 283cb7 to ba4fda
    --- /Users/misheska/stone.txt    2014-08-10 22:35:22.000000000 -0700
    +++ /tmp/.stone.txt20140810-14428-1uxzrvv    2014-08-10 22:35:46.000000000
    -0700 @@ -1,2 +1,2 @@
```

```
    -Modifying this file written in stone
    +Written in stone
```

or, for Windows (Run As Administrator):

```
> chef-apply stone.rb
Recipe: (chef-apply cookbook)::(chef-apply recipe)
  * file[C:/Users/misheska/stone.txt] action create
    - update content in file C:/Users/misheska/stone.txt from 7400c9 to ba4fda
        (current file is binary, diff output suppressed)
```

Notice that `chef-apply` reports that it performed an action. What action was performed? Check the content of *stone.txt* again on Linux/Mac OS X/Windows PowerShell:

```
$ more $HOME/stone.txt
Written in stone
```

or, for Windows Command Prompt:

```
> more %USERPROFILE%\stone.txt
Written in stone
```

Notice that `chef-apply` reverted the content back to `Written in stone`.

This is how Chef prevents *configuration drift*. Chef not only decides whether or not files are created, but it also checks file content. When a file is inadvertently modified, Chef makes sure the file reverts back to the content specified in the recipe.

The only way you can change the contents of *stone.txt* is by specifying different content in the *stone.rb* recipe. Otherwise, `chef-apply` reverts the content of *stone.txt* back to what the recipe specifies.

Chef decides the actions to perform to make the system configuration match what the recipe specifies. As a Chef developer, you only need to tell Chef the *desired configuration*. Chef takes care of all the rest automatically.

To Uninstall, Specify What Not to Do

You might wonder if it is possible to get Chef to automatically uninstall everything it installs. Not quite, but you can perform the equivalent of an uninstallation by telling Chef explicitly what *not* to do.

This might seem like Chef falls short in the uninstallation department, but that's not the case. Remember, Chef tries to be smart. You don't need to tell Chef *how* to do something. Instead you define the desired configuration you want in a recipe, and Chef determines *what* to do. Your recipe tells Chef when to stop reasoning about the configuration of the machine by defining what the desired configuration looks like.

There is no reasonable way for Chef to automatically reverse changes or uninstall and ensure that a system will consistently be in a known good configuration. You probably already know this is an impossible problem to solve in general. Every system administrator has come to the point in troubleshooting an issue caused by unknown changes to a computer where he gives up, wipes the box, and starts over again from scratch.

You might have thought that if you merely had enough time or were more persistent in your troubleshooting, you could solve an issue. Mark Burgess, the computer scientist introduced in Chapter 1 who made significant contributions to the automation theory upon which Chef is based, did the math and proved otherwise (*http://markburgess.org/papers/totalfield.pdf*), because *order matters*. Based on the theory supported by this math, Chef restricts itself in trying to reason about the state of the system only to the extent of what is explicitly defined in a recipe. This ensures that your system will always be consistently what the recipe defines as a "good" configuration. Then Chef can be smart and repair the system, as in the example from the previous section when you skirted around Chef and modified the content of *stone.txt* manually. Chef was able to assess that there was a change in the configuration and reverted *stone.txt* back to the configuration defined in the recipe.

Thus, if you want Chef to perform an uninstall, you must explicitly define what *not* to do. All resources support this kind of definition in some fashion. In the case of a *file* resource, you can tell Chef that a file is no longer supposed to be present on the system. Then Chef will perform the inverse of the reasoning it performed to create the file:

- If the file exists, `chef-apply` deletes the file.
- If the file is verifiably not present, `chef-apply` will do nothing.

To close out this chapter, let's write a recipe to clean up the *stone.txt* file we just created. Create *cleanup.rb* following Example 4-3.

Example 4-3. cleanup.rb

```
file "#{ENV['HOME']}/stone.txt" do
  action :delete
end
```

Let's review this code before running `chef-apply`.

The `file` resource performs the `:create` action by default, but you can override this default with the `:delete` action instead. `action` is an attribute that can be specified in a `file` resource, to override the default setting. In *cleanup.rb* we've specified that our recipe perform the `:delete` action.

In Chef code, a string prefaced by a single colon (:) is called a *symbol*. In other languages this is equivalent to a string constant.

Now let's perform a Chef run using the *cleanup.rb* recipe on Linux/Mac OS X:

```
$ sudo chef-apply cleanup.rb
Recipe: (chef-apply cookbook)::(chef-apply recipe)
  * file[/Users/misheska/stone.txt] action delete
    - delete file /Users/misheska/stone.txt
```

or, in Windows (Run As Administrator):

```
> chef-apply cleanup.rb
Recipe: (chef-apply cookbook)::(chef-apply recipe)
  * file[C:/Users/misheska/stone.txt] action delete
    - delete file C:/Users/misheska/stone.txt
```

 In Chef, using relative paths with :delete is problematic on some platforms, so just delete the *hello.txt* file by hand that you created in the first exercise.

We've cleaned up the *stone.txt* we created in this final hands-on exercise in the chapter. chef-apply deleted *stone.txt*.

Summary

In this chapter we introduced the chef-apply command, showing you how to run *.rb* files containing Chef code.

We introduced the following Chef concepts and terminology:

recipe
> A set of instructions written in a Ruby DSL that indicate the *desired configuration* to Chef.

resource
> A cross-platform abstraction for something managed by Chef (such as a file). Resources are the building blocks from which you compose Chef code.

attribute
> Parameters passed to a resource.

You created recipe files with Chef code, and ran chef-apply to perform the actions specified in the recipe. You learned that in Chef code, you need only tell Chef the *desired configuration* using *resources* as building blocks. We showed you how to use the file resource to create a file, and how to use the action :delete attribute to delete a file.

In the next chapter, we will show you how to create a sandbox environment using Test Kitchen, so that you have a safe place to experiment and learn more about Chef.

## CHAPTER 5

Manage Sandbox Environments with Test Kitchen

For the rest of this book, we're going to want to deploy to sandbox environments that closely simulate a production environment. Running Chef on your local development workstation, like we did in Chapter 4, is not the best approach. Your development workstation probably doesn't match your production operating environment. Even if your development workstation does match your production environment, you probably don't want to take the risk of running untested Chef code locally. Untested Chef code might make unintended configuration changes to your local development environment. Neither is it a good idea to run your experimental Chef code in your production environment before it is validated, for similar reasons.

We'll use Test Kitchen to create a *sandbox environment* that simulates a production environment. Test Kitchen works in concert with two other tools, Vagrant and Virtual-Box, to produce a sandbox locally in a virtual machine. This sandbox environment is a safe, isolated place in which to experiment with Chef.

The CentOS 6 operating system will be used in our sandbox environment. CentOS is a free operating system compatible with RedHat Enterprise Linux. RedHat Enterprise Linux is a popular choice for a production environment. CentOS is a compatible variant of RedHat intended for open source projects. CentOS does not require the purchase of a commercial license for use. The skills you will learn in this book aren't specific to RedHat Enterprise Linux, however. You should be able to translate what you learn to your operating system of choice.

If you would like to easily follow along with the examples in this book, use the Vagrant and VirtualBox setup as outlined in this chapter. If you would prefer to use an alternative method, you can still follow the exercises in the book—all you really need is a separate machine, cloud instance, or virtual machine that is not your main development workstation. Refer to the website for this book (*http://learningchef.com*) for more information on alternative setups in which you can create sandbox environments with Test Kitchen.

More choices

You are not required to use the Vagrant/VirtualBox-based setup highlighted in these exercises in order to use Chef. We had to pick one way, as the whole book can't all be choices. It also helps to provide a prescriptive approach for beginners who might not have a lot of sysadmin experience. Running the sandbox environment in a virtual machine is a great way to learn Chef for many, as it does not require a production setup of Chef.

There is an article on *http://learningchef.com* that gives you more setup options, should the local desktop virtualization approach not be a good fit for you. Experienced sysadmins should be able to translate the examples in this book to different production setups.

Before we can get started using Test Kitchen with the setup we use as default for the exercises in this book, first you need to install the necessary virtualization software: Vagrant and VirtualBox.

As shown in Figure 5-1, Test Kitchen uses Vagrant to create sandbox environments as virtual machines. Vagrant provides a single abstraction layer for Test Kitchen so it can work with many different kinds of virtualization software on a host OS. Vagrant currently supports VirtualBox, VMware Workstation, VMware Fusion, and Hyper-V virtualization software. We chose to use VirtualBox for the examples in this book because it is a free, open source virtualization solution that works on all the supported Chef platforms—Linux, Mac OS X, and Windows.

Installing Vagrant and VirtualBox

In order to use the most straightforward Test Kitchen setup based on open source software, you'll need to install Vagrant and VirtualBox. The machine requirements for this setup are:

- At least 6 GB of memory total
- At least 2 GB of free memory before running the sandbox environments
- Roughly 10 GB of free disk space to hold the extracted sandbox environments

If your machine does not meet these requirements, take a look at *http://learning chef.com* for alternatives where you can configure your sandbox environments on another machine besides your development workstation.

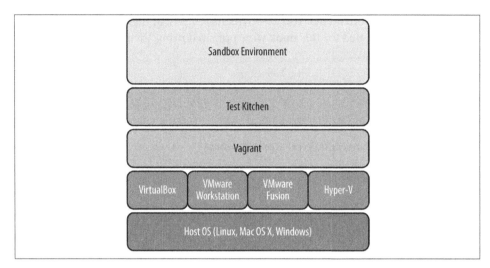

Figure 5-1. Vagrant provides an API for virtualization software

Both Vagrant and VirtualBox are available as free downloads on the Internet. Visit the following web pages to download the Vagrant and VirtualBox installers, running each in turn:

- Vagrant—http://www.vagrantup.com/downloads.html
- VirtualBox—https://www.virtualbox.org/wiki/Downloads

 You might need to restart your computer after installing Virtual-Box. Make sure you run VirtualBox at least once to make sure it is working properly.

To verify that Vagrant is installed properly, run `vagrant --version` on a command line. As we will be using images distributed via VagrantCloud, you must be using Vagrant 1.5.0 or higher. VagrantCloud is a directory of Vagrant images on the Internet. Further, we recommend that you use Vagrant 1.6.3 or higher, especially if you are using Windows. The Vagrant 1.6.x series is the first to officially add support for Windows guests:

```
$ vagrant --version
Vagrant 1.6.3
```

To verify that VirtualBox is installed properly, check the version with `VBoxManage`. Vagrant is compatible with VirtualBox versions 4.0.x, 4.1.x, 4.2.x, and 4.3.x, as you can read about in the documentation (*http://docs.vagrantup.com/v2/virtualbox/*

index.html). We recommend that you use VirtualBox 4.3.12 or higher because the sandbox environments created for this book were prepared using VirtualBox 4.3.12.

Linux/Mac OS X:

```
$ VBoxManage --version
4.3.12r93733
```

Windows Command Prompt:

```
> "C:\Program Files\Oracle\VirtualBox\VBoxManage" --version
4.3.12r93733
```

Windows PowerShell:

```
PS> & "C:\Program Files\Oracle\VirtualBox\VBoxManage" --version
4.3.8r92456
```

Host versus Guest

When talking about virtual machines and sandbox environments, it helps to explain two terms: *host* and *guest*. Figure 5-2 presents an overview of the logical architecture for a virtualization system like VirtualBox.

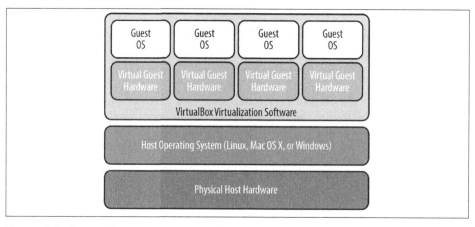

Figure 5-2. Guest OS overview

Virtualization software such as VirtualBox allows you to run practically any kind of operating system (OS) on your physical hardware. Virtualization software accomplishes this feat by running a target operating system in an isolated environment. Within this isolated environment, the virtualization system simulates the operating system running on separate, dedicated hardware, even though it is sharing resources with the main host. This isolated environment only consumes resources when needed and is easily replaced if something goes wrong. It's the perfect place for experimenting with Chef.

VirtualBox allows your single workstation to behave as if it were multiple machines. You have your physical machine, running Linux, Mac OS X, or Windows (and the VirtualBox virtualization software). This is commonly referred to as the *host* environment. Each isolated environment that runs a separate copy of an operating system, behaving as if it were a separate machine, is referred to as a *guest*. On a single machine, there is only one host environment, but there can be many guest environments. There can be as many guest environments as the physical resources on the host allow.

For this book, you have installed the Chef Development Kit on your host environment. In Chapter 4, you wrote Chef code on the host, and deployed Chef code on the host. Going forward, you will continue to write Chef code on the host environment. But from now on, you will deploy your code to a guest running CentOS 6. The guest environment will simulate a production environment running CentOS 6.

It is a good idea to develop your Chef code in a separate environment from your production machines. To make it more convenient to do work on just one machine, you can use virtualization software to simulate having multiple machines. To follow the exercises in this book, you will need to enter commands on one machine or the other. The terms *host* and *guest* are a convenient way to be more specific about precisely which environment we expect you to be using.

Introducing Test Kitchen

You installed Test Kitchen in Chapter 2, either as part of the Chef Development Kit, or manually, if you chose the Chef Client option. Test Kitchen will create a number of supporting files in the current working directory while it is being used. You should create a project directory for each sandbox environment to organize these files. For your first sandbox environment, create a directory called *kitchen* and make it the current directory:

```
$ mkdir kitchen
$ cd kitchen
```

Run the `kitchen init --create-gemfile` command in your newly created *kitchen* directory. The `kitchen init` command generates all the config files needed to add Test Kitchen support to a project. We need to use the `--create-gemfile` option, because if we don't, Test Kitchen will immediately try to run `gem install` as a user instead of as an admin. This fails on some platforms because the Chef Development Kit installation doesn't always make its gem directory user-writeable:

```
$ kitchen init --create-gemfile
      create  .kitchen.yml
      create  test/integration/default
      create  Gemfile
      append  Gemfile
```

```
     append  Gemfile
  You must run `bundle install' to fetch any new gems.
```

The bundle install command referenced in the preceding command line output refers to the *Bundler* tool. Bundler is a tool that downloads and manages Ruby gems. Test Kitchen needs you to run bundle install to download and install the kitchen-vagrant driver and some supporting gems.

 You might be prompted for your administrator/root password when running bundle install.

kitchen-vagrant is a *driver* for Test Kitchen that adds support for managing VirtualBox and VMware virtual machines using Vagrant. Nearly all Test Kitchen functionality is implemented via these drivers, as Test Kitchen is itself is nothing more than a generic framework for managing environments and running tests. Add-on drivers actually implement functionality. Run bundle install, like kitchen init, suggests installing those extra dependencies:

```
$ bundle install
Fetching gem metadata from https://rubygems.org/.........
Resolving dependencies...
Using mixlib-shellout (1.4.0)
Using net-ssh (2.9.1)
Using net-scp (1.2.1)
Using safe_yaml (1.0.3)
Using thor (0.19.1)
Using test-kitchen (1.2.1)
Using kitchen-vagrant (0.15.0)
Using bundler (1.5.2)
Your bundle is complete!
Use `bundle show [gemname]` to see where a bundled gem is installed.
```

Let's go over the directory structure and files kitchen init just created:

```
.
├── .kitchen
│   └── logs
│       └── kitchen.log
├── .kitchen.yml
├── Gemfile
├── Gemfile.lock
└── test
    └── integration
        └── default
```

.kitchen.yml

Used to configure virtual environments for Test Kitchen.

Gemfile

Bundler uses this file to configure the gem repository and the list of gems to download. Bundler will automatically determine a gem's dependencies by its references to other gems, so you need only list the top level gems you require.

Gemfile.lock

Records all the versions of the gems Bundler downloaded for the current project, plus the versions of all dependencies. This file can be used by another Chef developer to reproduce your current gem environment using `bundle install`.

.kitchen/

Hidden directory that Test Kitchen uses to store persistent data it needs to function properly.

.kitchen/logs/kitchen.log

Text file that contains the output from the last run of Test Kitchen.

test/

Directory structure that contains tests (initially just a skeleton structure with the subdirectory tree *test/integration/default/*).

Spinning Up Your First Virtual Machine

Before spinning up the virtual machine, you'll need to modify the *kitchen.yml* configuration file created by `kitchen init`. You'll need to change the *.kitchen.yml* configuration file so it loads the environment prepared exclusively for this book. Open *.kitchen.yml* with your programmer's editor and edit the `platforms:` section to make sure *.kitchen.yml* resembles what you see in Example 5-1.

Example 5-1. kitchen/.kitchen.yml

```
---
driver:
  name: vagrant

provisioner:
  name: chef_solo

platforms:
  - name: centos65
    driver:
      box: learningchef/centos65
      box_url: learningchef/centos65

suites:
  - name: default
    run_list:
    attributes:
```

Spacing matters in the *.kitchen.yml* file. Make sure you use the space character and not the tab character for white space. The *.kitchen.yml* should be tab free! Vertical alignment of the statements in this file also matters, so make sure the spacing lines up exactly as shown in Example 5-1.

This change will tell Test Kitchen to download the CentOS 6.5 image from VagrantCloud prepared for this book. The `box:` field must match the VagrantCloud box name listed on *https://vagrantcloud.com/learningchef/centos65*. The box name is `learningchef/centos65`. Because we will be typing in the `name:` field in Test Kitchen command prompts as an alias string for this box, we shorten it to `centos65`.

In Test Kitchen lingo, an *instance* is an environment that includes a way to create a virtual machine with an operating system and a way to deploy automation code. Run the `kitchen list` command to print out the available instance names:

```
$ kitchen list
Instance          Driver   Provisioner  Last Action
default-centos65  Vagrant  ChefSolo     <Not Created>
```

Notice that the `default-centos65` instance is set up to use the *Vagrant* driver (kitchen-vagrant) and to use the *ChefSolo* provisioner. We'll cover the `ChefSolo` provisioner more in Chapter 9.

If you are using a Windows PC, make sure you have hardware virtualization support enabled in your BIOS. For more information, see the VirtualBox User Manual (*https://www.virtualbox.org/manual/ch10.html*).

To create a virtual environment on your Chef Development Workstation running CentOS, use the `kitchen create` command, passing it a Test Kitchen instance name. Depending on the speed of your Internet connection, this download might take anywhere from 5 to 15 minutes the first time:

```
$ kitchen create default-centos65
-----> Starting Kitchen (v1.2.2.dev)
-----> Creating <default-centos65>...
       Bringing machine 'default' up with 'virtualbox' provider...
       ==> default: Box 'learningchef/centos65' could not be found.
           default: Box Provider: virtualbox
           default: Box Version: >= 0
       ==> default: Loading metadata for box 'learningchef/centos65'
           default: URL: https://vagrantcloud.com/learningchef/centos65
       ==> default: Adding box 'learningchef/centos65' (v0.2.0) for provider:
           virtualbox
           default: Downloading: https://vagrantcloud.com/learningchef/centos65
```

```
==> default: Successfully added box 'learningchef/centos65' (v0.2.0) for
    'virtualbox'!
==> default: Importing base box 'learningchef/centos65'...
==> default: Matching MAC address for NAT networking...
==> default: Checking if box 'learningchef/centos65' is up to date...
==> default: Setting the name of the VM: default-centos65_default_
    1407741726274_31370
==> default: Clearing any previously set network interfaces...
==> default: Preparing network interfaces based on configuration...
    default: Adapter 1: nat
==> default: Forwarding ports...
    default: 22 => 2222 (adapter 1)
==> default: Booting VM...
==> default: Waiting for machine to boot. This may take a few minutes...
    default: SSH address: 127.0.0.1:2222
    default: SSH username: vagrant
    default: SSH auth method: private key
        default: Warning: Connection timeout. Retrying...
    ==> default: Machine booted and ready!
    ==> default: Checking for guest additions in VM...
    ==> default: Setting hostname...
    ==> default: Machine not provisioning because `--no-provision`
    is specified.
    Vagrant instance <default-centos65> created.
    Finished creating <default-centos65> (1m43.54s).
-----> Kitchen is finished. (1m43.79s)
```

 When there is only one instance name in a *.kitchen.yml* file, there is
no need to specify an instance name. The command line kitchen
create would have been sufficient in the previous example. We'll
continue to specify the instance name on all kitchen command lines
in this book for clarity. But feel free to omit them if you want to save
typing a few extra characters.

The flowchart in Figure 5-3 presents an overview of the logic kitchen create uses to
create a virtual environment.

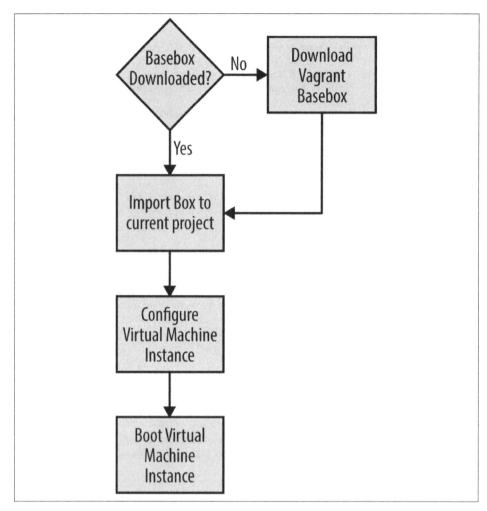

Figure 5-3. kitchen create logic

The kitchen-vagrant driver uses prepackaged basebox templates to accelerate the virtual machine creation process. A *basebox* contains a bare-bones OS installation, just enough to enable Chef to run. Test Kitchen comes preconfigured to use baseboxes that Chef Software makes available on the Internet via VagrantCloud. The baseboxes vary in size, depending on the operating system, and are roughly the size of a CD—a 400-MB to 600-MB download. Test Kitchen downloads a basebox only once, if it is not already present on your system. Vagrant maintains the catalog of baseboxes, which you can view with the command vagrant box list.

Do you want to create your own custom baseboxes? Packer can be used to create baseboxes from small configuration scripts. The Packer tool (*http://packer.io*) is available for download. Chef Software makes the configuration scripts for the Test Kitchen baseboxes freely available on the Internet; you can use these as a starting point.

Chef sponsors two projects: Bento and Box-Cutter. The Bento project (*https://github.com/opscode/bento*) contains Packer definitions that Chef uses internally to build software. Box-Cutter (*https://github.com/box-cutter*) offers configuration management tool-agnostic Packer templates that go beyond the platforms Chef uses for its internal builds, offering more cutting-edge, experimental features.

Once a basebox has been downloaded, the box is imported to your virtualization software. Test Kitchen then works with the virtualization provider to configure a virtual machine instance according to the parameters set in the *.kitchen.yml* file. Finally, it boots up the virtual machine so that it is ready to use, creating an instance.

You can verify that Test Kitchen performed all these steps by running the `kitchen list` command, noting that its *Last Action* changed to *Created*:

```
$ kitchen list
Instance          Driver   Provisioner  Last Action
default-centos65  Vagrant  ChefSolo     Created
```

You can also verify that a virtual machine got created in the VirtualBox Manager as shown in Figure 5-4 and that `VBoxManage list runningvms` shows that a VM is running.

On Linux/Mac OS X:

```
$ VBoxManage list runningvms
"default-centos65_default_1407741726274_31370"
{70b5e95a-d5f5-4956-b8b6-86dbf00e7218}
```

On Windows Command Prompt:

```
> "C:\Program Files\Oracle\VirtualBox\VBoxManage" list runningvms
"default-centos65_default_1404514741641_54313"
{2db0fb6c-ab8e-4c65-99aa-2d4d4a4d27ff}
```

On Windows PowerShell:

```
PS> & "C:\Program Files\Oracle\VirtualBox\VBoxManage" list runningvms
"default-centos65_default_1404514741641_54313"
{2db0fb6c-ab8e-4c65-99aa-2d4d4a4d27ff}
```

Figure 5-4. CentOS 6.5 virtual machine running in VirtualBox

You might be tempted to manage these virtual machines directly in the VirtualBox Manager GUI. Be careful, because you might confuse Test Kitchen. It is intended that you use the Test Kitchen command line interface to manage the lifecycle of these virtual environments.

Now that the virtual machine has been created and started, you can log in to the instance via the kitchen login command, using the same instance name we used for kitchen create:

```
$ kitchen login default-centos65
Last login: Fri Jul  4 14:48:27 2014 from 10.0.2.2
Welcome to your Packer-built virtual machine.
```

You should notice that you are now logged into the CentOS 6.5 guest virtual machine running on your Chef Development Workstation host via Oracle VM VirtualBox. To verify that the operating system is indeed CentOS Enterprise Linux, run cat /etc/redhat-release to print out the operating system release information:

```
[vagrant@default-centos65 ~]$ cat /etc/redhat-release
CentOS release 6.5 (Final)
```

If you get an error message that includes "No such file or directory - ssh," make sure that you have the ssh program in your $PATH. On Windows, make sure you install the Unix tools for Windows, which includes the required ssh command (see "Install Unix Tools for Windows" on page 32).

In this book, you will see that all the virtual machine command lines will have the Test Kitchen instance name in them before the $ prompt. For example, note that the command lines you just ran in the virtual machine were all prefaced by [*vagrant@default-centos65* ~]. This should make it less confusing as to whether commands should be run in the Chef Workstation *host* environment or the virtual machine *guest* environment.

To exit back out to your host command prompt, run the `exit` command. You should notice that the command prompt changes from [*vagrant@default-centos65* ~] to the default prompt for your host platform:

```
[vagrant@default-centos65 ~]$ exit
logout
Connection to 127.0.0.1 closed.
Atwood:kitchen misheska$
```

We're done with this sandbox environment. Run the `kitchen destroy` command to shut down the virtual machine and release all the associated system resources:

```
$ kitchen destroy default-centos65
-----> Starting Kitchen (v1.2.2.dev)
-----> Destroying <default-centos65>...
       ==> default: Forcing shutdown of VM...
       ==> default: Destroying VM and associated drives...
       Vagrant instance <default-centos65> destroyed.
       Finished destroying <default-centos65> (0m2.83s).
-----> Kitchen is finished. (0m3.07s)
```

YAML Overview

The *.kitchen.yml* configuration file used to configure Test Kitchen is in the YAML file format. YAML is a recursive acronym that stands for *YAML Ain't Markup Language*. A sequence of three hyphens (---) denote the beginning of a YAML document, so you'll see this at the beginning of every *.kitchen.yml* file. Comments are indicated by the hash symbol (#), just like in Ruby. Space and indentation matter in a YAML file. Tab characters should never be used in a YAML file, only spaces.

YAML files work with two fundamental kinds of a data:

- Key-value pair
- List

A key-value pair has the form *<key>*: *<value>* like:

```
name: vagrant
```

The space after the colon is required. The value for `name` is `vagrant`. The value `vagrant` can be looked up by the `name` key.

Key-value pairs can be nested, so that the value for a key is another key-value pair. When a key-value pair is nested, the value portion for the parent is written on separate lines, indented by at least one space. For example:

```
driver:
  name: vagrant
  aws_access_key_id: 12345
```

Having more spaces is perfectly fine, as long as the values belonging to the same nested key-value pair are all aligned vertically, with the same number of spaces:

```
driver:
          name: vagrant
          aws_access_key_id: 12345
```

You can also include as many spaces as you like before the colon, like so:

```
driver:
  name             : vagrant
  aws_access_key_id : 12345
```

If there were no spaces before each line, the nested values would not be interpreted correctly, however:

```
driver:
name: vagrant
aws_access_key_id: 12345
```

There is an alternate format for nested key-value pairs. They can also be in the form of `{<key>: <value>, <key>: <value>, …}`, also known as JavaScript Object Notation format, or JSON. For example:

```
mysql: {server_root_password: "rootpass", server_debian_password: "debpass"}
```

It is interpreted the same as:

```
mysql:
  server_root_password: "rootpass"
  server_debian_password: "debpass"
```

Lists are the other kind of data that can be stored in a YAML file. Lists contain ordered data. Each value is not associated with a key, like in a key-value pair. Lists are used when having a key for each value does not make sense. The items in a list are on separate lines, similar to nested key-value pairs. The items start with a dash followed by a space. Here's an example from a *.kitchen.yml* for a list of supported platforms, as key-value pairs with the name key, `name`:

```
platforms:
- name: ubuntu-10.04
- name: ubuntu-12.04
- name: ubuntu-12.10
- name: ubuntu-13.04
- name: centos-5.9
- name: centos-6.4
- name: debian-7.1.0
```

The previous example also shows how you can put key-value pairs inside of a list. (You can also put lists inside of a key-value pair as well.) Similar to key-value pairs, the items in a list can have any number of spaces before, as long as all the items have the same number of spaces. The following would be equivalent to the last example:

```
platforms:
    - name: ubuntu-10.04
    - name: ubuntu-12.04
    - name: ubuntu-12.10
    - name: ubuntu-13.04
    - name: centos-5.9
    - name: centos-6.4
    - name: debian-7.1.0
```

Values can also have a type. *kitchen.yml* files mostly deal with integers, strings, or arrays. Values that start with a digit are interpreted as integers. Values that start with an alphabetical character, enclosed by single quotes (") or double quotes (""), are interpreted as strings. Arrays are enclosed by square brackets ([ ]), with values separated by commas. Here's an example that puts all these concepts together:

```
network:
- ["forwarded_port", {guest: 80, host: 8080}]
- ["private_network", {ip: "192.168.33.33"}]
```

Test Kitchen Configuration with .kitchen.yml

Now that you understand the basics of YAML, let's go over the *.kitchen.yml* file that Test Kitchen generated:

```
---
driver:
  name: vagrant

provisioner:
  name: chef_solo

platforms:
  - name: ubuntu-12.04
  - name: centos-6.4

suites:
  - name: default
```

```
    run_list:
    attributes:
```

The three hyphens at the beginning denote that *kitchen.yml* is a YAML file.

The *.kitchen.yml* contains four main sections:

`driver:`
Specifies the driver plugin to use, plus configuration parameters to manage Test Kitchen environments. You can get a list of drivers running the command `kitchen driver discover`. We're using the default driver `kitchen-vagrant`. By convention, the `kitchen-` part of the driver name is dropped when specified in *kitchen.yml*.

`provisioner:`
Determines which configuration management tool will be used to provision the driver's environment(s). We're using the `chef_solo` provisioner. When you run `kitchen setup` it will install Chef Client on the node, if it is not already installed.

`platforms:`
A list of operating systems for which Test Kitchen will create instances.

`suites:`
In the case of the Chef configuration management tool, specifies a configuration to be run on each instance. Among other things, a suite contains a list of recipes to run on each instance.

The platform names in your *.kitchen.yml* file are aliases that point to baseboxes managed by Chef Software. When you see values such as:

```
---
platforms:
  - name: ubuntu-12.04
  - name: centos-6.4
```

Test Kitchen expands the values to the following internally:

```
platforms:
- name: ubuntu-12.04
  driver:
    box: opscode-ubuntu-12.04
    box_url: https://opscode-vm-bento.s3.amazonaws.com/vagrant/\
            opscode_ubuntu-12.04_provisionerless.box
- name: centos-6.4
  driver:
    box: opscode-centos-6.4
    box_url: https://opscode-vm-bento.s3.amazonaws.com/vagrant/\
            opscode_centos-6.4_provisionerless.box
```

Each platform item can have a `driver` key-value pair that specifies a `box` and a `box_url`, denoting the name of the box in the `vagrant box list` catalog and the URL from which the basebox file can be downloaded, respectively. When they are not specified, the `kitchen-vagrant` driver assumes you want to download baseboxes from the standard Chef Software site on the Internet.

Summary

In this chapter, we introduced the following commands that Test Kitchen uses to manage sandbox environments:

`kitchen init`
 Add Test Kitchen support to a project

`kitchen list`
 Display information about Test Kitchen instances

`kitchen create`
 Start a Test Kitchen instance, if it is not already running

`kitchen login`
 Log into a Test Kitchen instance

`kitchen destroy`
 Shut down an instance and destroy the virtual machine

We introduced the following configuration files that control the behavior of Test Kitchen:

.kitchen.yml
 Configures Test Kitchen environment settings

Gemfile
 List of gems needed and the repository from which Bundler should download gems via `bundle install`

Gemfile.lock
 List of gem dependencies determined by Bundler when `bundle install` runs. Used to reproduce an identical setup on another developer's machine

We explained the YAML file format used by *.kitchen.yml* files in great detail, including how to configure synced folders to synchronize source between your host and guest environments.

Also, we pointed you at *http://learningchef.com* should you wish to use an alternative to the Vagrant + VirtualBox setup around which we've tailored the hands-on exercises in this book. You can find some great *.kitchen.yml* file examples there as well.

In the next chapter, we'll learn more about *nodes*. *Node* is the generic term Chef uses to refer to any system managed by Chef.

CHAPTER 6

Manage Nodes with Chef Client

Now that you have a sandbox environment in which to experiment with Chef, let's set up your guest system to be managed by Chef. In this chapter, you will use Test Kitchen to install Chef Client on your guest virtual machine so it can run Chef recipes. As a reminder, in Chapter 4 you learned that a Chef recipe is a file that contains Chef code.

What Is a Node?

Before we show you how to install Chef Client on the guest with Test Kitchen, let's first introduce some Chef-specific terminology to describe the different types of machines that we are now using.

The machine on which you author Chef code is referred to as the *Chef Developer's Workstation* or *Chef Administrator's Workstation*. Your host machine is your Chef Developer Workstation. In Chapter 2 you installed the Chef Development Kit on your host so that you have all the tools necessary to write Chef recipes using a programmer's editor and to manage changes to your Chef code with a source control system.

A machine that is managed by Chef is called a *node*. A machine is managed by Chef when it runs Chef recipes to ensure the machine is in a desired configuration, as shown in Chapter 4. A *node* can be a physical machine, a virtual machine, a cloud instance, or a container instance—it makes no difference to Chef. As long as the node has Chef Client installed, it can be managed by Chef and it can run Chef recipes.

Because the Chef Development Kit is a superset of Chef Client, you could install the Chef Development Kit on a node. This is what we did in Chapter 4, making your host act as both a Chef Developer Workstation and as a node managed by Chef. However, the Chef Development Kit is about double the footprint of Chef Client. All of the extra tools included with the Chef Development Kit are for writing Chef code, not running Chef code. In Chapter 5 we made the case that in real-world production environments, these roles are split between two different machines because you do not write Chef code on every machine in your infrastructure. We are using Test Kitchen to manage a sandbox environment running CentOS 6 as a guest virtual machine. Now we need to make the guest virtual machine a Chef node.

 Chef uses the generic term *node* because Chef is not limited to managing servers or compute nodes. Chef can manage other components in your infrastructure as well, such as switches, routers, and storage.

Going forward, we will refer to your guest virtual machine sandbox environment simply as a *node*. In fact, you might not even be using a guest virtual machine if you decided to opt for the alternative setups covered on *http://learningchef.com*. So it makes sense to just refer to the "other machine" being managed by Chef generically as a *node*.

Create a New Sandbox Environment for a Node

Within the directory structure you have created for this book's code, as outlined in "Create a Directory Structure for Your Code" on page 55, create a project directory to contain the sandbox environment for your node. Create a new directory called *node* and make it the current directory, just like you did in Chapter 5. For example:

```
$ mkdir node
$ cd node
```

Then perform the same steps you performed in Chapter 5, running `kitchen init` to generate all the required Test Kitchen configuration, and `bundle install` to install the supporting gems:

```
$ kitchen init --create-gemfile
$ bundle install
```

In this case, running `bundle install` is really not necessary, because you are setting up a sandbox environment identical to the one you created in Chapter 5. However, it is a good idea to acquire the habit of running `bundle install` after `kitchen init`.

Edit the *.kitchen.yml* file as shown in Example 6-1, and make it resemble the state of the final *.kitchen.yml* when you finished Chapter 5.

Example 6-1. node/.kitchen.yml

```
---
driver:
  name: vagrant

provisioner:
  name: chef_solo
```

```
platforms:
  - name: centos65
    driver:
      box: learningchef/centos65
      box_url: learningchef/centos65

suites:
  - name: default
    run_list:
    attributes:
```

Then run `kitchen create` to spin up a new sandbox environment to serve as your node. As before, it will use the cached version of the `learningchef/centos65` box, and Test Kitchen will not try to download the box again if it sees the box in the cache. So the sandbox environment should start fairly quickly, in less than a minute:

```
$ kitchen create default-centos65
```

Installing Chef Client with Test Kitchen

Use the `kitchen login` command to connect to your node (a.k.a. the sandbox environment), and access the command prompt of the node running CentOS 6. Then, check to see if the Chef Client is installed on the node by running `chef-client --version`:

```
$ kitchen login default-centos65
Last login: Fri Jul  4 14:48:27 2014 from 10.0.2.2
Welcome to your Packer-built virtual machine.
[vagrant@default-centos65 ~]$ chef-client --version
-bash: chef-client: command not found
```

Nope, doesn't seem to be installed. How do we install `chef-client` on the node? Although we could follow the instructions again for *Installing Chef Client on Linux* from Chapter 2 by running the following, don't do this:

```
curl -Lk https://www.getchef.com/chef/install.sh | sudo bash
```

There is an easier way. Type in the `exit` command on your node to get back to your host prompt:

```
[vagrant@default-centos65 ~]$ exit
logout
Connection to 127.0.0.1 closed.
```

Double-check to make sure that the prompt being displayed is actually your host prompt (no `vagrant@default-centos65`). Run the command `kitchen setup default-centos65` to install `chef-client`:

```
$ kitchen setup default-centos65
-----> Starting Kitchen (v1.2.2.dev)
-----> Converging <default-centos65>...
       Preparing files for transfer
```

```
        Berksfile, Cheffile, cookbooks/, or metadata.rb not found so Chef will
        run with effectively no cookbooks. Is this intended?
        Removing non-cookbook files before transfer
-----> Installing Chef Omnibus (true)
        downloading https://www.getchef.com/chef/install.sh
          to file /tmp/install.sh
        trying wget...
        trying curl...
...
-----> Setting up <default-centos65>...
        Finished setting up <default-centos65%gt; (0m0.00s).
-----> Kitchen is finished. (0m19.93s)
```

If you inspect the output, the `kitchen setup` command installed the `chef-client` for you. The `kitchen setup` command is used to run a *provisioner*. Provisioner is a generic term for any kind of configuration management software, as Test Kitchen can be used with other configuration management tools besides Chef. By default, Test Kitchen is configured to use the ChefSolo provisioner, which installs Chef Client without configuring the tools to use a Chef Server. `kitchen setup` will automatically install `chef-client` for you using the commands you entered in Chapter 2 if `chef-client` is not present.

SSL Warning

During the Chef run, you might have noticed the following SSL warning:

```
* * * * * * * * * * * * * * * * * * * * * * * * * * * * * * * * * * * * *
SSL validation of HTTPS requests is disabled. HTTPS connections are still
encrypted, but chef is not able to detect forged replies or man in the middle
attacks.

To fix this issue add an entry like this to your configuration file:

  ```

    # Verify all HTTPS connections (recommended)
    ssl_verify_mode :verify_peer

    # OR, Verify only connections to chef-server
    verify_api_cert true
  ```


  To check your SSL configuration, or troubleshoot errors, you can use the
  `knife ssl check` command like so:

  ```

    knife ssl check -c /tmp/kitchen/solo.rb
  ```


* * * * * * * * * * * * * * * * * * * * * * * * * * * * * * * * * * * * *
```

When you are developing Chef code, it is perfectly fine to run without validating HTTPS requests with Chef Server. At the moment, you don't even have a Chef Server anyway, so if verification was turned on, you'd just get an error.

In order to support ease of development, Chef by default does not verify certificates when it makes HTTPS connections, and chef-client is informing you of this fact. When you are developing Chef code, oftentimes you will run your code without using a Chef Server, or even if you are using a Chef Server, it will be an in-memory version of Chef Server such as Chef Zero, where you don't want the bother of setting up a valid SSL configuration.

In production, you'll want to override this setting in the */etc/chef/client.rb* configuration file on nodes. We'll show you how to enable SSL verification in an automated fashion with Chef in Chapter 10. For the moment, just ignore the warning.

If you run kitchen list now, you'll notice that the Last Action column changed from *Created* to *Set Up*:

```
$ kitchen list
Instance        Driver   Provisioner  Last Action
default-centos65  Vagrant  ChefSolo     Set Up
```

Now, if you log into the guest node, you should see that chef-client is present:

```
$ kitchen login default-centos65
Last login: Sat Jul  5 09:15:07 2014 from 10.0.2.2
Welcome to your Packer-built virtual machine.
[vagrant@default-centos65 ~]$ chef-client --version
Chef: 11.14.6
```

Your First Chef-Client Run

Although you could use chef-apply to execute code in a Chef recipe file like you did in Chapter 4, the chef-client tool is more commonly used in production environments. chef-client provides the ability to execute Chef code across multiple recipe files, which we'll see more of in Chapter 7. In order to manage real-world production environments, you'll be running a lot of Chef code. In order to make maintenance easier, one normally spreads production code across multiple recipe files. Although chef-apply will do in a pinch for simple management tasks, you'll end up using chef-client most of the time to manage a node with Chef.

To show you the basics of using chef-client, let's create a new Chef recipe file that prints out some of the information Chef maintains about each node.

The log resource can be used to print out strings from a recipe. For example, the statement log "Hello" in a recipe would write out the string Hello. Let's give this a try. We assume you're still logged in to the node environment. Create the file *hello.rb* on the node with the following command:

```
[vagrant@default-centos65 ~]$ echo 'log "Hello, this is an important message."' \
> hello.rb
```

 In Chapter 7 we will show you how to edit files in your host environment and automatically transfer them to the node. Until then, we're showing you commands that you can use to create *hello.rb* in lieu of using editors such as vi or nano directly on the node. Some readers might not feel comfortable with editing files in a Linux-based operating environment. Feel free to use a text editor instead.

This command will produce the following source file.

Example 6-2. node/hello.rb

```
log "Hello, this is an important message."
```

When you use chef-client to perform actions in a recipe, this is referred to as a *Chef run*. Execute your first *Chef run* by entering chef-client --local-mode hello.rb --log_level info on a command line. The --local-mode option will prevent chef-client from trying to time out looking for a nonexistent Chef Server. We will introduce Chef Server later in this book. The --log_level info option is also necessary because by default, chef-client will only print errors, not informative messages. This option will tell chef-client to print out the strings from any Chef::Log.info commands.

 Chef requires administrator changes to run. If you are running User Account Control (UAC) on Windows, make sure you *Run As Administrator*.

When you run chef-client --local-mode hello.rb on the node, the output should resemble the following:

```
[vagrant@default-centos65 node]$ chef-client --local-mode hello.rb
[2014-08-14T12:28:43-07:00] WARN: No config file found or specified on command
line, using command line options.
[2014-08-14T12:28:43-07:00] WARN: No cookbooks directory found at or above
current directory.  Assuming /learningchef.
Starting Chef Client, version 11.14.6
resolving cookbooks for run list: []
Synchronizing Cookbooks:
Compiling Cookbooks...
[2014-08-14T12:28:46-07:00] WARN: Node default-centos65.vagrantup.com has an
empty run list.
```

```
Converging 1 resources
Recipe: @recipe_files::/learningchef/hello.rb
  * log[Hello, this is an important message.] action write


Running handlers:
Running handlers complete
Chef Client finished, 1/1 resources updated in 2.308460088 seconds
```

During your `chef-client` run, the following output indicates that "Hello, this is an important message." was written to the log for the Chef run:

```
log[Hello, this is an important message.] action write
```

To actually see the log message, you need to change the `chef-client` log level. Every message written to the log has severity level. The levels, in order of priority from lowest to highest, are `debug`, `info`, `warn`, `error`, and `fatal`. The `log` resource uses the `info` level as a default, which is appropriate for your "Hello" message. However, `chef-client` only prints out messages of severity `warn` or greater unless you change the `chef-client` log level.

To change the log level, use the `--log_level` option. The `--log_level` option takes a parameter (`--log_level <level>`), changing the lowest level severity messages `chef-client` will write to its log. If you add the option `--log_level info` to your `chef-client` command line, it will display the log message you just added. Try that now:

```
[vagrant@default-centos65 learningchef]$ chef-client --local-mode hello.rb \
  --log_level info
[2014-08-14T12:30:43-07:00] WARN: No config file found or specified on command
line, using command line options.
[2014-08-14T12:30:43-07:00] WARN: No cookbooks directory found at or above
current directory.  Assuming /learningchef.
[2014-08-14T12:30:43-07:00] INFO: Starting chef-zero on host localhost, port
8889 with repository at repository at /learningchef
  One version per cookbook
...
Converging 1 resources
Recipe: @recipe_files::/learningchef/hello.rb
  * log[Hello, this is an important message!] action write[2014-08-14T12:30:45
  -07:00] INFO: Processing log[Hello, this is an important message.] action
  write (@recipe_files::/learningchef/hello.rb line 1)
[2014-08-14T12:30:45-07:00] INFO: Hello, this is an important message.


[2014-08-14T12:30:45-07:00] INFO: Chef Run complete in 0.040486944 seconds


Running handlers:
[2014-08-14T12:30:45-07:00] INFO: Running report handlers
Running handlers complete
[2014-08-14T12:30:45-07:00] INFO: Report handlers complete
Chef Client finished, 1/1 resources updated in 2.275689636 seconds
```

By default, `chef-client` prints out log messages to the screen. Now that you have reset the log level, you see your important message in the log output (along with some other messages that are also at the `info` level of severity).

 If you would prefer to write the `chef-client` log to a file, use the `--logfile <LOGLOCATION>` option (or the short form `-l`).

Chef Client Modes

Chef Client can operate in one of three modes:

- Local mode
- Client mode
- Solo mode

When `chef-client` is running in *local mode*, it simulates a full Chef Server instance in memory. Any data that would have been saved to a server is written to the local directory. The process of writing server data locally is called *writeback*. This is why `client-client` created the *nodes/* directory. Local mode was designed to support rapid Chef recipe development by using Chef Zero, the in-memory, fast-start Chef server.

On the other hand, when `chef-client` is running in *client mode*, it assumes you have a Chef Server running on some other system on your network. In production, this is how most people use Chef. In client mode, `chef-client` is an agent (or service/daemon) that runs locally on a machine managed by Chef. Chef Server is a centralized store for the information needed to manage infrastructure with Chef. It is recommended that you set up Chef Server when you need to manage more than one machine at a time.

Before `chef-client` local mode was implemented in version 11.8, the only way to run Chef recipes without a Chef Server was to use `chef-solo`. `chef-solo` offers an additional client mode called *solo mode*. Solo mode provides a limited subset of Chef functionality intended to be able to run Chef locally. `chef-solo` does not support *writeback*. In most cases, *local mode* is far more convenient to use than *solo mode*. Eventually, Chef software plans to retire solo mode once local mode has feature parity with solo and when the majority of customers have migrated to `chef-client` 11.8 or higher. Solo mode is most popular in places still using older versions of Chef.

Ohai

When Chef Client performs a Chef run, a separate command-line tool called ohai is used to collect system information. Ohai exposes this collection of node information to Chef as a set of *automatic attributes*.

Try running ohai yourself, so you can see what information is being collected about your node. On our system, ohai generates 1058 lines of output, so make sure you pipe the command's output through the more command to present the information a screen at a time. You don't have to look through the whole output. When you're done, hit the *q* key to exit back to the command line:

```
$ ohai | more
{
  "network": {
    "interfaces": {
      "lo": {
        "mtu": "16436",
        "flags": [
          "LOOPBACK",
          "UP",
          "LOWER_UP"
        ],
        "encapsulation": "Loopback",
        "addresses": {
          "127.0.0.1": {
            "family": "inet",
            "prefixlen": "8",
            "netmask": "255.0.0.0",
            "scope": "Node"
          },
...
--More--
```

As you can see, ohai collects a lot of information about the current state of the computer: networking configuration, CPU state, operating system type and version, memory consumption, and much, much more.

As an example, let's take a look at this subset of the information generated by ohai. As you can see in the following, ohai collects the node's IP address, MAC address, OS information, hostname, and even that we are running in a virtualized guest:

```
{
...
  "ipaddress": "10.0.2.15",
  "macaddress": "08:00:27:1C:AD:B6",
...
  "os": "linux",
  "os_version": "2.6.32-431.el6.x86_64",
  "platform": "centos",
```

```
    "platform_version": "6.5",
    "platform_family": "rhel",
...
  "virtualization": {
    "system": "vbox",
    "role": "guest"
  }
...
  "hostname": "default-centos65"
...
}
```

In the next section, we'll access the information collected by ohai in our Chef code. Let's learn more about how the information gets into Chef and how we can refer to this information in our code.

ohai output is in JavaScript Simple Object Notation (JSON) form. JSON is a commonly used format for machine-readable output, as it can be easily parsed into the object-representation used for programming languages like Ruby. Although you can run ohai as a standalone application, this is not very common. Instead, the output of ohai is intended to be read by machines, specifically by chef-client and associated tools, so JSON is the perfect format. chef-client reads the JSON output from ohai and converts it into a node object, which is accessible by your Chef code.

You can refer to the node's IP address in your code with the following *attribute*. An attribute is a variable maintained by Chef. In your code, you specify a quoted string in a pair of brackets with the name used as an index in the collection, then Chef will return the value. In this case, we want to know the IP address. By referring to the prior ohai output, Chef knows the index name is *ipaddress*:

```
node['ipaddress']
```

We used an attribute variable in our Chef code back in "Recipes Specify Desired Configuration" on page 59. node is another attribute Chef makes available to your code. It contains all the information generated by running ohai on the node. Similar to the ENV attribute we used in "Recipes Specify Desired Configuration" on page 59, the node attribute is a collection of name/value pairs.

Name/value pair collections can be nested. This is what is indicated in the multiple levels of indentation in the ohai output. So to access the kind of virtualization software we are using (the "virtualization system"), use the following nested set of name/value pair references, because system is a name/value pair within the virtualization collection:

```
node['virtualization']['system']
```

The string variant node['virtualization']['system'] tends to be the most commonly used node attribute form. However, because attribute expressions are evaluated as a Mash, you'll encounter Chef code that uses the other possible Mash variants:

- node[:virtualization][:system]
- node['virtualization']['system']
- node.virtualization.system

Use a form that makes the most sense to you.

Let's make these examples more concrete by using them in a Chef recipe.

Accessing Node Information

As we discussed in the last section, chef-client collects a lot of information about the state of a node using ohai. Collecting this information is necessary so that Chef can intelligently reason how to put the node into the desired configuration specified in a recipe. Chef does not keep this information to itself. It makes this information available to your Chef code as a node attribute. An attribute is a variable maintained by Chef.

Let's use the log resource that you just used in "Your First Chef-Client Run" on page 89 to print out some node information. Create a new file called *info.rb* on the node with the following sequence of commands:

```
[vagrant@default-centos65 ~]$ cat << EOF > info.rb
> log "IP Address: #{node['ipaddress']}"
> log "MAC Address: #{node['macaddress']}"
> log "OS Platform: #{node['platform']} #{node['platform_version']}"
> log "Running on a #{node['virtualization']['system']} \
> #{node['virtualization']['role']}"
> log "Hostname: #{node['hostname']}"
> EOF
```

This command will produce the source file seen in Example 6-3.

Example 6-3. node/info.rb

```
log "IP Address: #{node['ipaddress']}"
log "MAC Address: #{node['macaddress']}"
log "OS Platform: #{node['platform']} #{node['platform_version']}"
log "Running on a #{node['virtualization']['system']} \
#{node['virtualization']['role']}"
log "Hostname: #{node['hostname']}"
```

The syntax using #{<variable>} to print out information contained in variables should be familiar to you. This is similar to what we did in Chapter 4 to access #{ENV['HOME']}. In this case, the variable is node instead of ENV.

The log statements in Example 6-3 will produce the following output during your Chef run. The use of log statements to show the content of attributes is a recommended Chef recipe debugging technique:

```
INFO: IP Address: 10.0.2.15
INFO: MAC Address: 08:00:27:1C:AD:B6
INFO: OS Platform: centos 6.5
INFO: Running on a vbox guest
INFO: Hostname: default-centos65
```

You should still be logged into the node. Perform a Chef run using chef-client in local mode. This time we will use the short options for --local-mode and --log_level. The output should resemble the following:

```
[vagrant@default-centos65 learningchef]$ chef-client --local-mode info.rb \
--log_level info
...
Starting Chef Client, version 11.14.6
...
Converging 5 resources
Recipe: @recipe_files::/learningchef/info.rb
  * log[IP Address: 10.0.2.15] action write[2014-08-14T12:36:05-07:00] INFO:
    Processing log[IP Address: 10.0.2.15] action write (@recipe_files::/learning
    chef/info.rb line 1)
[2014-08-14T12:36:05-07:00] INFO: IP Address: 10.0.2.15


  * log[MAC Address: 08:00:27:1C:AD:B6] action write[2014-08-14T12:36:05-07:00]
    INFO: Processing log[MAC Address: 08:00:27:1C:AD:B6] action write
    (@recipe_files::/learningchef/info.rb line 2)
[2014-08-14T12:36:05-07:00] INFO: MAC Address: 08:00:27:1C:AD:B6


  * log[OS Platform: centos 6.5] action write[2014-08-14T12:36:05-07:00] INFO:
    Processing log[OS Platform: centos 6.5] action write (@recipe_files::/learning
    chef/info.rb line 3)
[2014-08-14T12:36:05-07:00] INFO: OS Platform: centos 6.5


  * log[Running on a vbox guest] action write[2014-08-14T12:36:05-07:00] INFO:
    Processing log[Running on a vbox guest] action write (@recipe_files::/learning
    chef/info.rb line 5)
[2014-08-14T12:36:05-07:00] INFO: Running on a vbox guest


  * log[Hostname: default-centos65] action write[2014-08-14T12:36:05-07:00]
    INFO: Processing log[Hostname: default-centos65] action write (@recipe_files
```

```
  ::/learningchef/info.rb line 6)
[2014-08-14T12:36:05-07:00] INFO: Hostname: default-centos65


[2014-08-14T12:36:05-07:00] INFO: Chef Run complete in 0.039998861 seconds

Running handlers:
[2014-08-14T12:36:05-07:00] INFO: Running report handlers
Running handlers complete
[2014-08-14T12:36:05-07:00] INFO: Report handlers complete
Chef Client finished, 5/5 resources updated in 2.354730576 seconds
```

Notice that `chef-client` printed out the relevant information about your node. Your data should be similar, but some of the details, such as the `IP Address`, will most likely be slightly different. Chef collects a great deal of information about the state of a target machine in the node object. This node information is used to make intelligent decisions about how to automatically place the node into a desired configuration.

Run the `exit` command to get back to the host prompt, then run `kitchen destroy default-centos65`. This will shut down the VM and destroy the instance in your virtualization software, as you are done with this instance for now:

```
[vagrant@default-centos65 ~]$ exit
logout
Connection to 127.0.0.1 closed.
$ *kitchen destroy default-centos65*
-----> Starting Kitchen (v1.2.2.dev)
-----> Destroying <default-centos65>...
       ==> default: Forcing shutdown of VM...
       ==> default: Destroying VM and associated drives...
       Vagrant instance <default-centos65> destroyed.
       Finished destroying <default-centos65> (0m2.98s).
-----> Kitchen is finished. (0m3.24s)
```

Summary

In this chapter, we introduced the concept of a node. Because Chef can manage things other than personal computers, such as network switches and embedded storage systems, Chef uses the more generic term *node* to refer to the entities managed by Chef instead of *server* or *host*.

Any entity managed by Chef must have Chef Client installed. We showed you how to use Test Kitchen to install Chef Client on a node while writing Chef code. In "Bootstrap the Node with Knife" on page 171, we'll show you how the `knife bootstrap` command is used to install Chef Client on production nodes, as Test Kitchen isn't intended for production use.

You learned how to use the `chef-client` tool to perform a *Chef run*. This is how Chef manages a node. `chef-client` reads recipes during a *Chef run*. Recipes indicate a *desired configuration* through *resources*, and Chef determines the optimal sequence of steps in order to put the node into the desired state. Chef is able to reason intelligently about the node configuration, because it collects detailed information about the state of a node in an associated `node attribute` based on the information collected by `ohai`. We also showed you how you can access the information in your Chef recipes.

In the next chapter, we'll show you how to organize multiple recipe files into a cookbook. We'll also show you how you can run `chef-client` on a node using Test Kitchen on your host instead of hopping back and forth between the host and the guest.

## CHAPTER 7

Cookbook Authoring and Use

Cookbooks are the fundamental component of infrastructure management with Chef. Think of a cookbook as a package for your recipes. Each cookbook represents the set of instructions required to configure or deploy a single *unit* of infrastructure such as a web server, database, or application. The recipes with code are only a small part of the entire equation. A cookbook also contains any supporting components, such as archives, images, or libraries. In addition, a cookbook holds configuration information, platform-specific implementations, and resource declarations required to manage a piece of infrastructure with Chef.

Your First Cookbook: Message of the Day

For your first cookbook, let's automate the configuration of a *message of the day* on our guest node running CentOS 6. Let's make it unambiguous that you have logged in to the guest node, by using Chef to configure a message on login stating that this is the guest node.

The command to generate an initial cookbook directory structure will differ, depending on whether you installed the Chef Development Kit or Chef Client on your host.

Even More Choices: Chef Versus Knife

Prior to the Chef Development Kit, developers were required to use many different command-line tools to perform routine actions. We hope that once the Chef Development Kit reaches its 1.0 release (which had not yet occurred at the time of this writing), all commands related to cookbook development will be unified under one umbrella `chef` command-line tool.

Before the Chef Development Kit, `knife`, the primary command-line tool for working with a Chef Server, could also be used to create a cookbook directory structure for development.

Now, with the advent of the Chef Development Kit, the `chef generate` command is the recommended way to manage a cookbook's directory structure. The `knife` tool won't be going away. It continues to be the primary command-line tool for interacting with Chef Server in production, which we'll see later in Chapter 9.

However, there is some new functionality in the `chef generate` subcommand that doesn't exist in `knife`. `chef generate` allows you to customize the recipe and cookbook templates that are generated. Also, `chef generate` lets you create the directory structure incrementally in a progressive fashion, adding just the features you need for your cookbook. `knife` generates only one type of structure, with everything at once, creating many more files than you might need. It doesn't hurt anything, but many people prefer the incremental approach of `chef generate`.

We'll cover both the `chef` and `knife` approaches to cookbook creation in this chapter.

If you have the Chef Development Kit installed, continue on to the next section, "Your First Cookbook: Message of the Day (Chef Development Kit)" on page 100, to learn how to create a cookbook using the `chef` utility. If you have the Chef Client installed, skip ahead to "Your First Cookbook: Message of the Day (Chef Client)" on page 103 to learn how to create a cookbook using the `knife` utility.

Your First Cookbook: Message of the Day (Chef Development Kit)

You'll be using a tool called `chef` to generate an initial directory structure for a message of the day cookbook (motd). `chef` is a new common utility command that debuted with the Chef Development Kit. On a command line, run the `chef generate cookbook motd` command to create the cookbook directory scaffolding. `chef generate` will create a main directory for your cookbook called *motd* as part of the process:

```
$ chef generate cookbook motd
Compiling Cookbooks...
Recipe: code_generator::cookbook
  * directory[/Users/misheska/learningchef/motd] action create
    - create new directory /Users/misheska/learningchef/motd
...
  * template[/Users/misheska/learningchef/motd/recipes/default.rb] action create
    - create new file /Users/misheska/learningchef/motd/recipes/default.rb
    - update content in file /Users/misheska/learningchef/motd/recipes/default
    .rb from none to 9cc885
    (diff output suppressed by config)
```

Make the *motd* directory you just created the current directory:

```
$ cd motd
```

As demonstrated in Example 7-1, modify the *.kitchen.yml* file to use the CentOS 6 image we've tailored for the book.

Example 7-1. chefdk/motd/.kitchen.yml

```
---
driver:
  name: vagrant

provisioner:
  name: chef_zero

platforms:
  - name: centos65
    driver:
      box: learningchef/centos65
      box_url: learningchef/centos65

suites:
  - name: default
    run_list:
      - recipe[motd::default]
    attributes:
```

 As of this writing, there is a bug in the Chef Development Kit 0.1.0 where the chef command generates an incorrect reference to recipe[bar::default]. It should be recipe[motd::default] instead, matching the name of the cookbook. This bug is fixed in the Chef Development Kit 0.2.0-2 release, and should be available by the time you read this. If not, fix the recipe line in the *.kitchen.yml* accordingly.

Check to make sure there are no syntax errors in your *kitchen.yml* file by running kitchen list. If you see a stack trace error instead of the following output, you likely made a typo, inadvertently used tabs instead of spaces, or didn't line up entries correctly:

```
$ kitchen list
Instance          Driver   Provisioner  Last Action
default-centos65  Vagrant  ChefZero     <Not Created>
```

On CentOS, in order to update the message of the day, we need to create a static text file called */etc/motd* on the node. The */etc/motd* file will contain the text with our message of the day. We'll create a copy of the *motd* file we want created in our cookbook. This is how Chef manages files. Then we'll add code to our recipe to ensure that the file will be copied from the cookbook to the node in the appropriate location in the */etc* directory.

Use the `chef generate file motd` command to generate the directory structure required for the *motd* file we will be creating on the node. We need only use the name of the file we want to create, not the path:

```
$ chef generate file motd
Compiling Cookbooks...
Recipe: code_generator::cookbook_file
  * directory[/Users/misheska/learningchef/motd/files/default] action create
    - create new directory /Users/misheska/learningchef/motd/files/default
  * template[/Users/misheska/learningchef/motd/files/default/motd] action create
    - create new file /Users/misheska/learningchef/motd/files/default/motd
    - update content in file /Users/misheska/learningchef/motd/files/default
    /motd from none to e3b0c4
    (diff output suppressed by config)
```

With your handy programmer's text editor, edit the file *files/default/motd* you just created in your motd cookbook. We think all messages are more effective when spoken by a friendly warning cow, so we added a bit of ASCII art to our file, as shown in Example 7-2.

Example 7-2. chefdk/motd/files/default/motd

```
 _____
< YOU ARE ON A SIMULATED CHEF NODE ENVIRONMENT! >
 ----------------------------------------------
        \   ^__^
         \  (oo)_____
            (__)\/\      \
                ||----w |
                ||     ||
```

Introducing the Cookbook_file Resource

We'll use Chef to help us more easily determine that we are running on a guest virtual machine node by writing some automation to change the Linux *message of the day*. On Linux, the message of the day is displayed when a user logs in. The message of the day is used by Linux administrators to communicate with users. You can change the message of the day by editing the file */etc/motd*. When a user successfully logs in, the contents of the */etc/motd* file will be displayed as the message of the day.

`chef cookbook generate` created a *recipes/default.rb* file for you. By convention, this is the default location for your Chef code. All recipe *.rb* files containing Chef code are expected to be in the *recipes/* subdirectory of a cookbook.

At the moment, *recipes/default.rb* doesn't have very much in it, just some comments:

```
#
# Cookbook Name:: motd
# Recipe:: default
#
```

```
# Copyright (C) 2014
#
#
#
```

Add some Chef code to change the */etc/motd* on your node by editing *recipes/ default.rb* to resemble Example 7-3 (we'll leave it as an exercise to the reader to modify the copyright text).

Example 7-3. chefdk/motd/recipes/default.rb

```
#
# Cookbook Name:: motd
# Recipe:: default
#
# Copyright (C) 2014
#
#
#

cookbook_file "/etc/motd" do
  source "motd"
  mode "0644"
end
```

Here's an explanation of what each line of code in Example 7-3 does:

- `cookbook_file` is a Chef *resource*. The `cookbook_file` resource is used to transfer files from the *files/* subdirectory in a cookbook to the node.
- do/end clauses note that the Chef resource definition spans multiple lines.
- The `"/etc/motd"` string passed to `cookbook_file` is the `name`. `name` that defines the path the file should be copied to on the node.
- `source` defines the name of the file in the *files/* subdirectory.
- `mode` defines the octal permissions to set on the file after it is copied. In this case it is octal 644, "world readable." If you don't set the file mode appropriately, other users might not be able to read the contents of this file.

Now that you have created a cookbook directory structure using `chef generate cook book`, skip ahead to "Performing Your First Converge" on page 107 to use Chef to configure your node.

Your First Cookbook: Message of the Day (Chef Client)

You'll be using a tool called *knife* to generate an initial cookbook directory structure for the message of the day cookbook (motd). `knife` is a basic utility command for working with Chef that you installed with Chef Client. On a command line, run the `knife cook` book create subcommand to create the cookbook directory scaffolding. *knife* will create a main directory for your cookbook called *motd* as part of the process:

```
$ knife cookbook create motd --cookbook-path .
WARNING: No knife configuration file found
** Creating cookbook motd
** Creating README for cookbook: motd
** Creating CHANGELOG for cookbook: motd
** Creating metadata for cookbook: motd
```

Next, overlay all the files needed for your cookbook to enable Test Kitchen support, just like you did in Chapter 5:

```
$ cd motd
$ kitchen init --create-gemfile
      create  .kitchen.yml
      create  test/integration/default
      create  Gemfile
      append  Gemfile
      append  Gemfile
You must run `bundle install' to fetch any new gems.
```

Run bundle install to handle the extra Ruby dependencies:

```
$ bundle install
Fetching gem metadata from https://rubygems.org/.........
Resolving dependencies...
Using mixlib-shellout (1.4.0)
Using net-ssh (2.9.1)
Using net-scp (1.2.1)
Using safe_yaml (1.0.3)
Using thor (0.19.1)
Using test-kitchen (1.2.1)
Installing kitchen-vagrant (0.15.0)
Using bundler (1.5.3)
Your bundle is complete!
Use `bundle show [gemname]` to see where a bundled gem is installed.
```

Modify the *.kitchen.yml* file to use the CentOS 6 image we've tailored for the book as seen in Example 7-4.

Example 7-4. knife/motd/.kitchen.yml

```
---
driver:
  name: vagrant

provisioner:
  name: chef_solo

platforms:
  - name: centos65
    driver:
      box: learningchef/centos65
```

```
        box_url: learningchef/centos65

suites:
  - name: default
    run_list:
      - recipe[motd::default]
    attributes:
```

Check to make sure there are no syntax errors in your *kitchen.yml* file by running
`kitchen list`. If you see a stack trace error instead of the following output, you likely
made a typo, inadvertently used tabs instead of spaces, or didn't line up entries correctly:

```
$ kitchen list
Instance          Driver   Provisioner  Last Action
default-centos65  Vagrant  ChefSolo     <Not Created>
```

Because you will be copying a file from the cookbook *files/* subdirectory to the Chef
node, you will need to create the file as well. Again, with your handy programmer's text
editor, create the file *files/default/motd* in your `motd-knife` cookbook. When a cow
udders your message of the day (pun intended), any day becomes a celebration. Liven
up your message with some ASCII art.

Example 7-5. knife/motd/files/default/motd

```
 _____
< YOU ARE ON A SIMULATED CHEF NODE ENVIRONMENT! >
 ------------------------------------------------
        \   ^__^
         \  (oo)_____
            (__)\/\      \
               ||----w |
               ||     ||
```

Introducing the Cookbook_file Resource

We'll use Chef to help us more easily determine that we are running on a guest virtual
machine node by writing some automation to change the Linux *message of the day*. On
Linux, the *message of the day* is displayed when a user logs in. The *message of the day* is
used by Linux administrators to communicate with users. You can change the *message
of the day* by editing the file */etc/motd*. When a user successfully logs in, the contents of
the */etc/motd* file will be displayed as the message of the day.

`knife cookbook create` generates a *recipes/default.rb* file for you. By convention, this
is the default location for your Chef code. All recipe *.rb* files containing Chef code are
expected to be in the *recipes/* subdirectory of a cookbook.

```
#
# Cookbook Name:: motd
# Recipe:: default
#
```

```
# Copyright 2014, YOUR_COMPANY_NAME
#
# All rights reserved - Do Not Redistribute
#
```

Add some Chef code to change the */etc/motd* on your node by editing *recipes/default.rb* to resemble Example 7-6 (we'll leave it as an exercise to the reader to modify the copyright and licensing text in the comments later).

Example 7-6. knife/motd/recipes/default.rb

```
#
# Cookbook Name:: motd
# Recipe:: default
#
# Copyright 2014, YOUR_COMPANY_NAME
#
# All rights reserved - Do Not Redistribute
#

cookbook_file "/etc/motd" do
  source "motd"
  mode "0644"
end
```

Here's an explanation of what each line in Example 7-6 does:

- `cookbook_file` is a Chef *resource*. The `cookbook_file` resource is used to transfer files from the *files/* subdirectory in a cookbook to the node.

- do/end clauses note that the Chef *resource* definition spans multiple lines.

- The `"/etc/motd"` string passed to `cookbook_file` is the name. name defines the path the file should be copied to on the node.

- source defines the name of the file in the *files/* subdirectory.

- mode defines the octal permissions to set on the file after it is copied. In this case it is octal 644, "world readable." If you don't set the file mode appropriately, other users might not be able to read the contents of this file.

Now that you have created a cookbook directory structure using `knife cookbook create`, continue on to "Performing Your First Converge" on page 107 to use Chef to configure your node. This is where the `chef generate cookbook` and `knife cookbook create` instructions in this chapter come together. The instructions that follow are the same for both tools.

Performing Your First Converge

Chef uses the term *converge* to refer to the process of deploying a cookbook to a node, running chef_client on the node, and applying a run list to put the node into a desired state. This is also referred to as *converging* a node. Let's use Test Kitchen to perform a converge on the node using the kitchen converge command.

Convergence Introduced

Chef can dynamically adjust how it brings a node into a desired state depending on the current state of the node. For example, if the Chef run is aborted for any reason, Chef will merely pick up where it left off the next time it runs. Key to this fault-tolerant approach is that the plan for the steps Chef uses to configure a node are entirely data-driven, based on the results produced by ohai, which we covered in Chapter 6.

Another example of a *convergence-based* tool is the make command. It behaves in a similar fashion. The make tool assesses the current state of the components used to produce an application, and it only builds what hasn't been built before. You can run make as many times as you like, and it will only perform the necessary build steps that haven't been successfully performed already.

Make sure you run the kitchen converge command *inside* the *motd* cookbook directory.

If you entered in the code correctly so far, the output of kitchen converge should resemble the following:

```
$ kitchen converge default-centos65
-----> Starting Kitchen (v1.2.2.dev)
-----> Creating <default-centos65>...
       Bringing machine 'default' up with 'virtualbox' provider...
...
-----> Converging <default-centos65>...
       Preparing files for transfer
       Resolving cookbook dependencies with Berkshelf 3.1.3...
       Removing non-cookbook files before transfer
-----> Installing Chef Omnibus (true)
...

       Starting Chef Client, version 11.14.2
       [2014-08-14T13:22:37-07:00] INFO: *** Chef 11.14.2 ***
       [2014-08-14T13:22:37-07:00] INFO: Chef-client pid: 2004
       Creating a new client identity for default-centos65 using the validator
```

key.
[2014-08-14T13:22:40-07:00] INFO: Client key /tmp/kitchen/client.pem is
not present - registering
[2014-08-14T13:22:40-07:00] INFO: HTTP Request Returned 404 Not Found
: Object not found: http://localhost:8889/nodes/default-centos65
[2014-08-14T13:22:40-07:00] INFO: Setting the run_list to ["recipe
[motd::default]"] from CLI options
[2014-08-14T13:22:40-07:00] INFO: Run List is [recipe[motd::default]]
[2014-08-14T13:22:40-07:00] INFO: Run List expands to [motd::default]
[2014-08-14T13:22:40-07:00] INFO: Starting Chef Run for default-centos65
[2014-08-14T13:22:40-07:00] INFO: Running start handlers
[2014-08-14T13:22:40-07:00] INFO: Start handlers complete.
[2014-08-14T13:22:40-07:00] INFO: HTTP Request Returned 404 Not Found :
Object not found: /reports/nodes/default-centos65/runs
resolving cookbooks for run list: ["motd::default"]
[2014-08-14T13:22:40-07:00] INFO: Loading cookbooks [motd@0.1.0]
Synchronizing Cookbooks:
[2014-08-14T13:22:40-07:00] INFO: Storing updated cookbooks/motd
/recipes/default.rb in the cache.
[2014-08-14T13:22:40-07:00] INFO: Storing updated cookbooks/motd/
README.md in the cache.
[2014-08-14T13:22:40-07:00] INFO: Storing updated cookbooks/motd/
metadata.json in the cache.
  - motd
Compiling Cookbooks...
Converging 1 resources
Recipe: motd::default
  * cookbook_file[/etc/motd] action create[2014-08-14T13:22:40-07:00]
  INFO: Processing cookbook_file[/etc/motd] action create (motd::default
  line 10)
[2014-08-14T13:22:40-07:00] INFO: cookbook_file[/etc/motd] backed up to
/tmp/kitchen/backup/etc/motd.chef-20140814132240.562727
[2014-08-14T13:22:40-07:00] INFO: cookbook_file[/etc/motd] updated file
contents /etc/motd

    - update content in file /etc/motd from a7620c to 07a3b1
    --- /etc/motd   2014-07-04 07:47:33.211269359 -0700
    +++ /tmp/.motd20140814-2004-ky1c1j   2014-08-14 13:22:40.561072174
    -0700
    @@ -1,2 +1,9 @@
    -Welcome to your Packer-built virtual machine.
    + _____
    + < YOU ARE ON A SIMULATED CHEF NODE ENVIRONMENT! >
    + --
    +   \   ^__^
    +   \ (oo)_____
    +   (__)\/\   \
    + ||----w |
    + || ||

[2014-08-14T13:22:40-07:00] INFO: Chef Run complete in 0.117514782 seconds

```
      Running handlers:
      [2014-08-14T13:22:40-07:00] INFO: Running report handlers
      Running handlers complete
      [2014-08-14T13:22:40-07:00] INFO: Report handlers complete
      Chef Client finished, 1/1 resources updated in 2.729471192 seconds
      Finished converging <default-centos65> (0m28.88s).
-----> Kitchen is finished. (1m4.31s)
```

As of this writing, there is a bug in the current Chef Development Kit 0.2.0 on Windows when you run `kitchen converge`. You'll get an "SSL certificate verify failed" because the Chef Development Kit installation is not pointing at the correct certificate file. This issue is being tracked here: *https://github.com/opscode/chef-dk/issues/106*.

As a workaround, set the %SSL_CERT_FILE% environment variable before running `kitchen converge`:

Windows command prompt:

```
> set SSL_CERT_FILE=C:\opscode\chefdk\embedded\ssl\certs\cacert.pem
> kitchen converge
```

Windows PowerShell:

```
PS> Set-Item -Path env:SSL_CERT_FILE -Value \
C:\opscode\chefdk\embedded\ssl\certs\cacert.pem
PS> kitchen converge
```

Our output shows that Test Kitchen ran `chef-client` on the node. It reported `Chef Run complete`, how many resources were updated, and that `Kitchen is finished` with no errors.

`kitchen converge` will automatically run `kitchen create` and `kitchen setup` for you if they are needed. In the preceding output, notice that the virtual machine was created, and `chef-client` was installed on the node, indicating that Test Kitchen automatically ran these two steps.

Validate Your Results

Use `kitchen login` to verify that your new message of the day is installed on the node:

```
$ kitchen login default-centos65
Last login: Thu Aug 14 13:22:36 2014 from 10.0.2.2
 _____
< YOU ARE ON A SIMULATED CHEF NODE ENVIRONMENT! >
 ------------------------------------------------
        \   ^__^
         \  (oo)_____
            (__))\/\    \
               ||----w |
               ||     ||
```

Now we hope things are more clear when you are logged in to your simulated Chef node
environment.

The kitchen login command requires the ssh program to be installed on your host. On Windows, ssh is not installed by default. If
you get an error with the text "No such file or directory -ssh" when
running kitchen login, make sure you have ssh installed, according to "Install Unix Tools for Windows" on page 32.

We're done with the sandbox environment we created to verify the motd cookbook. Run
the exit command on the guest to restore your command prompt back to the host:

```
[vagrant@default-centos65 ~]$ exit
logout
Connection to 127.0.0.1 closed.
```

Now run the kitchen destroy command to shut down the virtual machine and release
all the associated system resources:

```
$ kitchen destroy default-centos65
-----> Starting Kitchen (v1.2.2.dev)
-----> Destroying <default-centos65>...
       ==> default: Forcing shutdown of VM...
       ==> default: Destroying VM and associated drives...
       Vagrant instance <default-centos65> destroyed.
       Finished destroying <default-centos65> (0m2.91s).
-----> Kitchen is finished. (0m3.37s)
```

We will be creating a lot of different sandbox environments in this
book. Don't forget to kitchen destroy your environments when they
are done so they won't take up memory and disk space when you
aren't using them. (But just in case you forget to run kitchen de
stroy, we'll keep reminding you.)

If you'd like to get a global overview of all the sandbox environments running on your machine from the command line, run va
grant global-status.

Anatomy of a Chef Run

`kitchen converge` performs a *Chef run* on your test node from your host. Pretty convenient! You can still use `kitchen login` to ssh into the node and poke around if you like, but the `kitchen converge` command is designed to give you fast feedback as you develop your cookbook. We'll rely on `kitchen converge` for the rest of the hands-on exercises in this book.

In production, `chef-client` is typically run in daemonized mode as a service on the node, performing Chef runs at regular intervals; for example, once every 15 minutes. It checks in with Chef Server for any changes to cookbooks or the list of recipes to run on the node, which are stored on Chef Server. We'll discuss this more in Chapter 9.

It is helpful to understand the steps involved in executing a Chef run. We've touched on some of them in Chapter 6, when we mentioned the node object and ohai, but we've yet to go over the steps explicitly, as shown in Figure 7-1.

1. Start the Chef Client

    The `chef-client` process starts on the remote node. The process may be started by a service, cron job, or manually triggered by a user. The `chef-client` is the process responsible for evaluating Chef cookbooks containing recipes with Chef code on the target node.

2. Build the node

    The `chef-client` process constructs the node object in memory. It runs ohai and gathers all the node's automatic attributes (such as the hostname, fqdn, platform, users, etc.)

3. Synchronize

    A run list is sent to the node. The run list contains a list of recipes to execute on the target node. A run list is the ordered, decomposed list of recipes to execute on the target node. The node may also be sent a list of URLs of cookbooks to download that are required by the run list. The target node will download and cache the required cookbooks in a local file cache.

4. Load

    The cookbooks and Ruby components are loaded in this step. Cookbook-level attributes are merged with the automatic attributes generated by ohai in #2. The various components of a cookbook are loaded in this order:

    a. **Libraries.** All files in the *libraries/* folder from every cookbook are loaded so that any language extensions or alterations are available for the remainder of the Chef run.

b. **Attributes.** All files in the *attributes/* folder from every cookbook are loaded and merged with the automatic `ohai` attributes.

c. **Definitions.** All files in the *definitions/* folder from every cookbook are loaded because definitions create resources and must be loaded before recipes.

d. **Resources.** All files in the *resources/* folder from every cookbook are loaded because resources must be loaded before the recipes.

e. **Providers.** All files in the *providers/* folder from every cookbook are loaded so the resources reference the proper provider.

f. **Recipes.** All files in the *recipes/* folder from every cookbook are loaded and evaluated. At this point, the recipes are *not* executed to place the node in the desired configuration, but the Ruby code is executed and each resource is added to the resource collection.

5. Converge

The converge phase is the most critical phase of a Chef run. This is when the Chef recipes are executed on the target node—packages are installed, templates are written, files are copied, and so on.

6. Report

If the Chef Client run is performed successfully, any new values in the node object are saved; otherwise, an exception is raised without updating the node object. Then notification and exception handlers are executed. Notification and exception handlers can perform a variety of functions, such as sending emails, posting to IRC, or sending messages to PagerDuty.

The *run list* is a key component used in a Chef run. As mentioned earlier, the run list contains a list of recipes to execute on the target node. It is not very common to pass a list of recipe *.rb* files, as we've done so far when running `chef-client`. Real-world chef runs typically involve dozens of cookbooks with possibly hundreds of recipes and associated files. There needs to be a succinct way of referring to all the files in a cookbook. That's the purpose of a run list.

A run list is used to specify the cookbook recipes to be evaluated on a node. A run list specifies recipes in the form `recipe['<cookbook_name>::<recipe_name>']`; for example, `recipe['motd::default']`. When the Chef code is contained in the *recipes/default.rb* file of a cookbook, the recipe name is optional as the `default` is implied. `recipe['motd']` is equivalent to `recipe['motd::default']`. Note that the *.rb* file extension is omitted when referring to a recipe, as this is assumed.

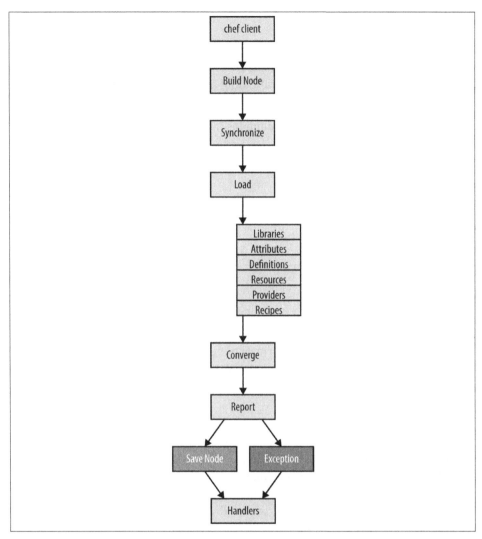

Figure 7-1. Anatomy of a Chef run

In the case of Test Kitchen, the run list is specified in the *.kitchen.yml* file and passed to `chef-client` on the command line via the `-o` parameter. In production, the run list is maintained on Chef Server as a node attribute.

We've just described how a Chef run works in more detail when you run `kitchen con verge`. Now, let's also cover the structure of a cookbook in more detail.

Cookbook Structure

A Chef cookbook is expected to have a specific file and directory structure. You could create these files and directories by hand with your editor and filesystem, but most people find it convenient to use the scaffolding generators Chef provides to lay down the directory structure: `chef generate cookbook` or `knife cookbook create`.

A basic cookbook directory structure contains the following files:

```
cookbook
├── .kitchen.yml
├── README.md
├── attributes
│   └── default/
├── chefignore
├── files/
│   └── default/
├── metadata.rb
├── recipes/
│   └── default.rb
└── templates/
    └── default/
```

\.*kitchen.yml*

> The .*kitchen.yml* file is a YAML-format configuration file for Test Kitchen. You can use Test Kitchen to create sandbox environments to verify and validate your cookbook while you develop it.

README.md

> Every cookbook should come with documentation. The *README.md* is a text file that contains documentation in markdown format. Markdown is a simple way of adding formatting to plain text so that you have the option of converting it to HTML. Markdown is a popular format for README files because the text files are readable as is, without the clutter of HTML tags and formatting instructions. Many popular source control tools will render *README.md* in HTML when viewing source, including GitHub (*https://www.github.com*), GitLib (*https://about.gitlab.com*), Stash (*https://www.atlassian.com/software/stash*), and Bitbucket (*https://bitbucket.org*).

attributes

> You can provide your own custom attributes in a cookbook to complement (or override) the attributes generated automatically by `ohai`. Attributes are commonly used to define application distribution paths, platform-specific values, or software versions to install on a given node. The *attributes/* directory can contain multiple .*rb* files with attribute definitions in them. When there is more than one attribute file, they are evaluated in alphabetical order. By convention, if it makes sense to store your attributes in one file, the file should be named *default.rb*.

chefignore

> This file contains a list of files that should be ignored when uploading the cookbook to a Chef Server, when a Chef server is being used. By default, all files in a cookbook directory are uploaded to the Chef Server. There is no need, however, to upload things such as editor swapfiles or source control tracking files to a Chef Server. References to these files are commonly placed in a *chefignore* file so they won't be uploaded.

files

> The *files* folder is a centralized store in the cookbook for files to be distributed to nodes. Files can be plain text, images, zip files, and so on. These files can be deployed to a target node using the `cookbook_file` resource. A directory structure underneath *files/* controls whether files are copied to particular nodes. For more information on this structure, refer to *http://docs.opscode.com/essentials_cook book_files.html*. When files should be distributed to all nodes, they are expected to be in the *files/default/* subdirectory.

metadata.rb

> The *metadata.rb* file contains all the information (metadata) about a cookbook. Every cookbook must have a *metadata.rb* file containing the name of the cookbook, version, dependencies, and other helpful information.

recipes

> The *recipes* folder contains Chef recipes. A recipe file contains Chef code. There can be multiple *.rb* recipe files in the *recipes/* folder. By convention, the main recipe file is called *default.rb*. For each node, Chef evaluates only recipe files that are specified on the node's *run list*. The run list is specified in the *.kitchen.yml* file or on the `chef-client` command line, or stored on a Chef Server.

templates

> The *templates* directory holds Chef templates. The *templates* directory is similar to *files* in that it contains a set of files to be distributed to nodes. However, the files used are Embedded Ruby templates. A template is plain text that can contain Ruby code, which is evaluated by the Embedded Ruby template engine before being rendered on a node. Templates are useful when you want to generate files with variable or selective content. *templates* follows the same directory-naming structure scheme as *files* to control whether the generated template files are copied to particular nodes.

We will cover all these structures in the next cookbook we write in this chapter. There are several more components to a Chef cookbook structure that are used by more advanced Chef cookbook coders. The additional components are `Berksfile`, `defini tions`, `libraries`, `providers`, and `resource`. We won't be covering these components as this book is intended for beginners, and all but the `Berksfile` are components used to customize Chef. Beginners usually need to spend time using Chef and discovering the limits of the built-in components before trying to tackle customization. Jon Cowie's *Customizing Chef* book is the perfect resource when you are ready to tackle Chef customization.

 We really wanted to cover the `Berksfile` and its accompanying `Berk shelf` tool in this book, but the current 2.0 and 3.0 releases of Berkshelf are far too difficult for Ruby beginners to install using the Chef Client. Beginners basically must use the Chef Development Kit to install the Berksfile tool, but as we've already discussed, the Chef Development Kit isn't available on all platforms at the time of this writing.

For more information on Berkshelf, refer to *http://berkshelf.com* and Jamie Winsor's blog post on The Environment Cookbook Pattern (*http://blog.vialstudios.com/the-environment-cookbook-pattern/*). Jamie Winsor is the creator of the Berkshelf tool.

The Four Resources You Need to Know

If the full list of resources (*http://docs.getchef.com/resource.html#resources*) seems daunting, don't worry: there are really only four types of resources you'll find yourself using over and over:

package
> Installs a package using the appropriate platform-native installer/package manager (`yum`, `apt`, `pacman`, etc.).

service
> Manages the lifecycle of any daemons/services installed by the `package` resource.

cookbook_file
> Transfers a file from the cookbook repository to a path on the node. We introduced the `cookbook_file` resource earlier in this chapter to manage the */etc/motd* file on our node.

template
> A variant of the `cookbook_file` resource that lets you create file content from variables using an Embedded Ruby (ERB) template.

That's it, just four resources. You'll find yourself using these resources over and over again to install and configure apps and services. Let's make this idea more concrete by writing one more cookbook to close out this chapter, a cookbook that will configure a web server to host our home page.

Apache Cookbook: A Step-By-Step Primer for Creating a Cookbook

We've formally introduced the steps in a Chef run and all the components of a cookbook directory structure. Now we will walk you through the step-by-step process we recommend to create cookbooks.

Before creating a cookbook, it's important to define the purpose and scope of the cookbook. This step ensures each cookbook is truly a unit of your infrastructure. It also defines the vision and organization for the cookbook. A cookbook without a clear vision will likely become a source of difficulty in the future.

Completing "Define Prerequisites" on page 117 might help focus your thoughts when you are creating a new cookbook. As you gain more experience writing Chef recipes, the thought process involved in developing a plan for your cookbook will become second nature without the need to formalize the plan in a checklist.

Define Prerequisites

Table 7-1. Cookbook authoring checklist

Name
Purpose
Success criteria
App/Service
Required steps

Name

Although it might seem trivial, choosing a proper and descriptive name for a cookbook is absolutely critical. Because a cookbook's name must be unique across your organization, you only have one chance to name it properly. For example, you can only have one "mysql" cookbook in your organization. A cookbook's name is also an abbreviated statement of work and should follow the principle of least surprise. For example, the "mysql" cookbook should deal exclusively with MySQL.

Purpose

The purpose or goal of a cookbook is the second-most important prerequisite when creating a cookbook. A cookbook without a proper vision is certain to fail, if not immediately, then in the long term due to scope creep resulting in untestable code. The following is a vision statement for our mysql cookbook:

To install and configure the MySQL server and MySQL client on a target machine.

The vision is sometimes closely tied to the metadata's `description` attribute, but this is not a requirement.

Success criteria

Once you have a goal, you need to have some way to determine that you have achieved the goal. Success criteria describe the things we need to evaluate about the cookbook to determine that it meets its intended purpose. The following is an example of success criteria for the mysql cookbook:

Do just enough to get MySQL running and expose a way to create MySQL users, databases, and tables.

App/service

Each cookbook should manage a single application or service (a unit of your infrastructure). You should identify that application or service before creating the cookbook. If you are unable to identify a single application or service, you should consider narrowing the vision from the previous step. For example, our narrowed "App/Service" would be "MySQL."

Required steps

If you don't know the required steps to accomplish your goal, it's going to be difficult to automate the process with a cookbook. Automation first requires a grasp of what steps are needed to install and configure the application manually (along with any prerequisites), then you can start tackling the process of making the installation repeatable without human intervention via automation.

In this section, we will create and author a cookbook named "apache" to configure our web server. Table 7-2 is the completed table for our "apache" cookbook.

Table 7-2. Apache cookbook checklist

Name	apache
Purpose	To configure a web server to serve up our home page.
Success Criteria	We can see the home page in a web browser.
App/Service	Apache HTTP server
Required Steps	1) Install apache, 2) Start the service, 3) Configure service to start when machine boots, 4) Write out the home page

With this cookbook, our goal is to teach you the three remaining Chef resource primitives not yet covered and to outline the steps involved in creating a cookbook, not web server management. These are not the exact steps required to configure the Apache HTTP server configuration in production, but they're perfectly fine for this example. Configuring a real-world Apache HTTP server would involve more configuration steps, but it would still involve these four basic resources.

Now that we have a clear vision for the apache cookbook, we can generate the cookbook skeleton.

Generate the Cookbook Skeleton

We've already been through the steps to generate the scaffolding for a cookbook using `chef generate cookbook` or `knife cookbook create`, depending on whether you have the Chef Development Kit or Chef Client installed on your development workstation. In this case, you'll want to create a cookbook named `apache`.

First, you need to create the cookbook skeleton with Test Kitchen support. We're going to go quickly through the cookbook creation commands this time without showing you the tool output. Refer back to "Your First Cookbook: Message of the Day (Chef Development Kit)" on page 100 if you're using the Chef Development Kit, or "Your First Cookbook: Message of the Day (Chef Client)" on page 103 if you are using Chef Client for a refresher on the steps involved.

Chef Development Kit:

```
$ chef generate cookbook apache
$ cd apache
```

Chef Client:

```
$ knife cookbook create apache --cookbook-path .
$ cd apache
$ kitchen init --create-gemfile
$ bundle install
```

Edit the *.kitchen.yml* to use CentOS image tailored for use in this book.

 From this point forward, we'll provide listings only for the Chef Development Kit versions of the source files, and not Chef Client. There are no functional differences between the two versions. You'll just notice that `knife` creates a few more file types by default that aren't covered in this book, and some of the comments are different. Having the extra generated files doesn't hurt anything as they all are just blank stubs we won't be using.

Example 7-7. chefdk/apache/.kitchen.yml

```
---
driver:
  name: vagrant

provisioner:
  name: chef_zero

platforms:
  - name: centos65
    driver:
      box: learningchef/centos65
      box_url: learningchef/centos65
```

```
suites:
  - name: default
    run_list:
      - recipe[apache::default]
    attributes:
```

Example 7-7 shows how the *run list* is defined in the `suites:` stanza of the *.kitchen.yml*. Chef Development Kit users, remember to make sure this is correct, due to the current bug that incorrectly sets the *run list* to `recipe[bar::default]`.

Now you know that the run list `recipe[apache::default]` is just shorthand indicating that Chef code needs to be executed in the *recipes/default.rb* file of the apache cookbook. `Chef-client` executes the code when we run `kitchen converge`.

To make sure your *.kitchen.yml* has no syntax errors, run `kitchen list`. If there are issues, correct them:

```
$ kitchen list
Instance          Driver   Provisioner  Last Action
default-centos65  Vagrant  ChefZero     <Not Created>
```

Edit the *README.md* File

Your *README.md* file should drive the cookbook development, based on the prerequisites you defined in "Define Prerequisites" on page 117. Example 7-8 shows a suggested *README.md* for your apache cookbook.

Example 7-8. chefdk/apache/README.md

```
# apache cookbook

This cookbook installs and configures a simple web site using the Apache HTTPD server.

Requirements
============
Supports only CentOS or other RHEL variants that use the +httpd+ package.

Usage
=====
Add `apache` to your node's `run_list`.

Testing
=======
A `.kitchen.yml` file is provided.  Run +kitchen converge+ to verify this cookbook.
```

Update *Metadata.rb*

Here's the *metadata.rb* file that was generated in your cookbook skeleton:

```
name              'apache'
maintainer        ''
maintainer_email  ''
license           ''
description       'Installs/Configures apache'
long_description  'Installs/Configures apache'
version           '0.1.0'
```

Note the *apache* string in the name field. This is how Chef determines the name of your cookbook in the run list. It *does not* look at the name of the directory in which the cookbook files reside. For your own sanity, the name field in the *metadata.rb* and your cookbook directory should match, but they aren't required to.

Edit the *metadata.rb* file, adding your name and e-mail address in the maintainer and maintainer_email fields. Because you will want to share your cookbooks, it is also a good idea to indicate how you intend to make your code sharable by listing one of the standard open source license types. Refer to the site *http://choosealicense.com* for more information on open source software licensing.

Example 7-9 shows how I filled out my *metadata.rb* file. When you edit the *metadata.rb* file, use values that are appropriate for you.

Example 7-9. chefdk/apache/metadata.rb

```
name              'apache'
maintainer        'Mischa Taylor'
maintainer_email  'mischa@misheska.com'
license           'MIT'
description       'Installs/Configures apache'
long_description  'Installs/Configures apache'
version           '0.1.0'
```

Introducing the Package Resource

We haven't written any Chef code in our recipe yet, but go ahead and run an initial kitchen converge on your cookbook skeleton to make sure there aren't any syntax errors in the files you have edited so far. We encourage you to run kitchen converge frequently to verify your cookbook code as you write it. The first kitchen converge will take a few minutes, as Test Kitchen needs to set up the sandbox environment and it will also download and install chef-client on the node. But subsequent kitchen converge runs will go pretty quickly. Run kitchen converge now:

```
$ kitchen converge default-centos65
```

Now, let's get to some coding. First, let's use the package resource to install the httpd package using yum install by editing *recipes/default.rb*, as shown in Example 7-10.

Example 7-10. chefdk/apache/recipes/default.rb

```
#
# Cookbook Name:: apache
# Recipe:: default
#
# Copyright (C) 2014
#
#
#


package "httpd" do
  action :install
end
```

Run kitchen converge again to check your work. We also encourage you to use kitchen login to inspect the node to verify that your recipe is doing what you expect. Log in to the node, and verify that the httpd service is installed with the following command. Be sure to exit back out to your host prompt when you are done:

```
$ kitchen converge default-centos65
$ kitchen login default-centos65
Last login: Thu Aug 14 13:48:32 2014 from 10.0.2.2
Welcome to your Packer-built virtual machine.
[vagrant@default-centos65 ~]$ rpm -q httpd
httpd-2.2.15-31.el6.centos.x86_64
[vagrant@default-centos65 ~]$ exit
logout
Connection to 127.0.0.1 closed.
```

The httpd service is indeed installed! The rpm -q command queries the rpm package manager database to see if a package containing the name is present on the system.

If you look at the Chef documentation on the package resource (*http://docs.getchef.com/resource_package.html*), package calls one of many providers based on the platform and platform_family returned by ohai. Because our platform is rhel, the yum_package provider is used.

If you refer to the documentation on the yum_package provider (*http://docs.getchef.com/resource_yum.html*), you'll notice that there are four possible actions: :install, :upgrade, :remove, and :purge. Because :install is the default, we don't need to specify the action. Let's change our recipe accordingly, as shown in Example 7-11.

Example 7-11. chefdk/apache/recipes/default.rb

```
#
# Cookbook Name:: apache
# Recipe:: default
#
# Copyright (C) 2014
#
```

```
#
#

package "httpd"
```

Now the package reference is a lot more concise, and it performs the same action. Look for opportunities to make use of default actions where possible.

Introducing the Service Resource

Next, let's use the service resource to start the httpd service and automatically enable it on restart. The service resource can start a service with the :start action, and it can enable a service at boot with the :enable action.

You can pass more than one action to the service resource by passing them as an array. In Chapter 3 we discussed how an array is a delimited list of comma-delimited items contained within square brackets ([]).

Add the service resource to *recipes/default.rb* as shown in Example 7-12.

Example 7-12. chefdk/apache/recipes/default.rb

```
#
# Cookbook Name:: apache
# Recipe:: default
#
# Copyright (C) 2014
#
#
#

package "httpd"

service "httpd" do
  action [ :enable, :start ]
end
```

This is the first time we've encountered multiple resources in one recipe. Chef evaluates the recipes as you would expect—in the order they are listed in the file.

Let's run kitchen converge again and log in to verify that our cookbook produced the intended result:

```
$ kitchen converge default-centos65
$ kitchen login default-centos65
Last login: Thu Aug 14 13:50:39 2014 from 10.0.2.2
Welcome to your Packer-built virtual machine.
[vagrant@default-centos65 ~]$ chkconfig --list httpd | grep 3:on
httpd           0:off       1:off   2:on    3:on    4:on    5:on    6:off
[vagrant@default-centos65 ~]$ exit
```

```
logout
Connection to 127.0.0.1 closed.
```

Our service is enabled! For CentOS and other Redhat variants, services are enabled in different run levels. Our service should be enabled for runlevel 3, which is multi-user text mode with networking enabled—the default for a working CentOS server running in text mode. In our `grep` statement, we verified that the service is set to be on for runlevel 3.

Introducing the Template Resource

We'll introduce the `template` resource by showing you how to generate the file containing the content for our website. The template resource is similar to *cookbook_file* in that it creates a file on the node. However, a template has the additional ability to expand variable references to the file and other statements in the form of Embedded RuBy (ERB).

Let's add the `resource` statement to *recipes/default.rb* as shown in Example 7-13.

Example 7-13. chefdk/apache/recipes/default.rb

```
#
# Cookbook Name:: apache
# Recipe:: default
#
# Copyright (C) 2014
#
#
#

package "httpd"

service "httpd" do
  action [ :enable, :start ]
end

template "/var/www/html/index.html" do
  source 'index.html.erb'
  mode '0644'
end
```

By default, the `httpd` server looks for web pages in the directory */var/www/html*. The file for the default website is expected to be in the file */var/www/html/index.html*. We also still have to set the file mode to be world-readable. What's probably new to you, compared to the `file` resource, is this `source` attribute.

The `source` attribute specifies the file containing a template with ERB statements. This template is expected to be located underneath the *templates* folder in the cookbook, following the same subdirectory convention as *files*. So to copy the template to all nodes (which is the default), make sure that template files are located in the *templates/ default* directory.

What's with "Default" Subdirectory?

What's with the "default" subdirectory in *files/default* and *template/default*? Chef allows you to select the most appropriate file (or template) within a cookbook according to the node's platform. Chef requires you to create a directory underneath "files" or "templates" with your filter name. Options include filtering files and templates by

- host node name (e.g., foo.bar.com)
- platform-version (e.g., redhat-6.5.1)
- platform-version_components (e.g., redhat-6.5, redhat-6)
- platform (e.g., redhat)
- default

Ninety-nine percent of the time, you'll just use *default* as the directory name, indicating that the file or template should be copied to all nodes.

Let's create an ERB template for our *index.html* file. By convention, an ERB template is expected to have the suffix *.erb* appended to the generated filename. The Chef Development kit does this expansion for you automatically when you run *chef generate template index.html*, creating the file `templates/default/index.html.erb`. With the Chef Client, you must create this file manually.

Chef Development Kit:

```
$ chef generate template index.html
```

Chef Client - Linux/Mac OS X:

```
$ touch templates/default/index.html.erb
```

Chef Client - Windows:

```
$ touch templates\default\index.html.erb
```

Variables get expanded in an ERB file when Chef sees statements bounded by <%= and %>, such as <%= node['hostname'] %> in the following *index.html.erb* file. Chef evaluates the node['hostname'] variable and replaces the contents of the <%= node['hostname'] %> block with the resultant value when the file is written out to the node. Edit *templates/default/index.html.erb* as shown in Example 7-14.

Example 7-14. chefdk/apache/templates/default/index.hmtl.erb

```
This site was set up by <%= node['hostname'] %>
```

Run `kitchen converge`, then run `kitchen login` to verify that our `template` resource created the file. Check to make sure the file exists at */var/www/html/index.html*, and use the `curl` to see the web page rendered on the command line. Note that when the */var/www/html/index.html* file was created, the `<%= node['hostname'] %>` string in our template was replaced by the value of the `node['hostname']`:

```
$ kitchen converge default-centos65
$ kitchen login default-centos65
Last login: Thu Aug 14 13:52:00 2014 from 10.0.2.2
Welcome to your Packer-built virtual machine.
[vagrant@default-centos65 ~]$ more /var/www/html/index.html
This site was set up by default-centos65
[vagrant@default-centos65 ~]$ curl localhost
This site was set up by default-centos65
[vagrant@default-centos65 ~]$ exit
logout
Connection to 127.0.0.1 closed.
```

While it is great to see this output, we haven't quite yet met our defined success criteria for this cookbook. We need to be able to see the home page in a web browser on your host. Let's do that in the next section.

Verify Success Criteria Are Met

In order to give your host access to the website on your guest, you'll need to assign a known, static IP to your node in your *.kitchenl.yml*. This is done by adding a `driver: network:` block to your .kitchen.yml in the following form:

```
driver:
  network:
  - ["private_network", {ip: "192.168.33.7"}]
```

The static IP address should be chosen from the TCP/IP reserved private address space (*https://en.wikipedia.org/wiki/Private_network#Private_IPv4_address_spaces*) that does not conflict with other machines on the same network. The IP address `192.168.33.7` should work for nearly everyone, as most routers don't use this subnet by default, so modify your *.kitchen.yml* file accordingly, as shown in Example 7-15.

Example 7-15. chefdk/apache/.kitchen.yml

```
---
driver:
  name: vagrant

provisioner:
  name: chef_zero

platforms:
  - name: centos65
    driver:
```

```
box: learningchef/centos65
box_url: learningchef/centos65
network:
  - ["private_network", {ip: "192.168.33.7"}]

suites:
  - name: default
    run_list:
      - recipe[apache::default]
    attributes:
```

Unfortunately, Test Kitchen will apply network configuration settings in the *.kitchen.yml* only when running kitchen create the first time, when the sandbox environment is created. Because we have already created the sandbox environment, we'll need to run kitchen destroy first, before running kitchen converge, so it will create a new sandbox environment. Otherwise, Test Kitchen will ignore the networking change we just added to the *kitchen.yml*:

```
$ kitchen destroy default-centos65
$ kitchen converge default-centos65
```

Now that the sandbox environment has been created with an IP address accessible from our host, try it out in your web browser using the address *http://192.168.33.7*. You should see the template file we just created, as in Figure 7-2. Success criteria met!

Figure 7-2. Your apache site on 192.168.33.7

If you get an error, check the following:

1. Make sure you created the file *apache/templates/default/index.html.erb* and it has the correct content.

2. Run kitchen login, then run curl localhost to make sure that Chef run completed properly and the web server is working *within the virtual machine*.

3. Scrutinize the `kitchen converge` output to make sure there was no error when `vagrant` configured the `private_network` address when it set up the virtual network adapters on the virtual machine.

4. There is no possibility that another machine on the local network has the same IP address. If so, modify the *.kitchen.yml* and recreate the virtual machine.

We are now done with this cookbook and virtual machine. Run the `kitchen destroy` command to shut down the virtual machine and release all the associated system resources:

```
$ kitchen destroy default-centos65
-----> Starting Kitchen (v1.2.2.dev)
-----> Destroying <default-centos65>...
       ==> default: Forcing shutdown of VM...
       ==> default: Destroying VM and associated drives...
       Vagrant instance <default-centos65> destroyed.
       Finished destroying <default-centos65> (0m2.95s).
-----> Kitchen is finished. (0m3.43s)
```

Summary

In this chapter, we introduced the concept of a cookbook. Chef needs more than recipe files with code to automate the configuration of nodes. A cookbook contains all the other associated information, packing everything together into a single unit of deployment. We covered three of these additional components of a cookbook in this chapter: the *metadata.rb* file, the *files* folder, and the *templates* folder. We also showed you that Chef code resides in the *recipes* folder.

We introduced you to the four essential resources you'll find yourself using over and over again in your recipe code:

package
Installs a package using the system package manager

service
Manages the lifecycle of any daemons/services installed by the package resource

cookbook_file
Transfers a file from the *files* folder of a cookbook to a path on the node

template
A variant of the cookbook_file resource that lets you create file content from variables using an Embedded Ruby (ERB) template. Templates are located in the *templates* folder of a cookbook

Finally, we walked you through a process we recommend you use when creating a cookbook:

1. Define prerequisites and goals.

2. Generate the cookbook skeleton.

3. Let the documentation you write in the *README.md* file guide development.

4. Define metadata in the *metadata.rb* file.

5. Verify cookbook code as you write it using `kitchen converge` and `kitchen login`.

6. Verify conditions of success are met.

In the next chapter, we'll delve a bit more deeply into attributes. You can create your own custom attributes. We'll cover where and how attributes are set in more detail.

## CHAPTER 8

Attributes

Attributes represent information about your node. In addition to the information that can be automatically generated by ohai, you can set attributes in Chef recipes or in separate attribute files.

Attribute files are located in the *attributes* folder of a cookbook. Similar to recipes, the default attribute file is called:

```
<cookbook>
└─ attributes
    └─ default.rb
```

Figure 8-1 shows the format of an attribute when it is specified in a cookbook attribute file.

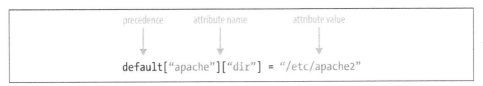

Figure 8-1. Setting attributes in attribute files

Attributes can also be set directly in recipes. Figure 8-2 shows the format of an attribute when it is set in a recipe. You must precede the attribute name with node. when you set an attribute directly in a recipe.

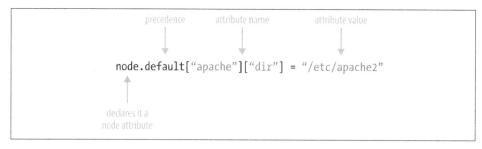

Figure 8-2. Setting attributes in recipes

Because attributes can be defined in multiple places, all attribute values are composed together during a Chef run according to the priority levels as shown in Figure 8-3. Attributes defined by ohai have the highest priority, followed by attributes defined in a recipe, then attributes defined in an attribute file. In other words, recipe attributes have a higher priority than those defined in attribute file, and will override them by default. Attributes defined by ohai trump everything else.

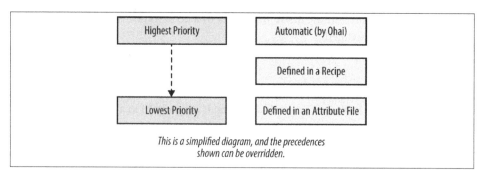

Figure 8-3. Attribute priority

We'll talk more about precedence levels later in this chapter. However, when setting an attribute in a cookbook, it should (almost) always be a *default* attribute with *default* precedence.

Motd-Attributes Cookbook

Let's experiment with attributes in a cookbook called motd-cookbook. This is an attribute-driven version of the motd cookbook we created in Chapter 7. We're going to go through the cookbook creation steps quickly in this chapter. If you need a refresher on what each of these commands mean and the expected output, refer back to Chapter 7.

First, generate the `motd-attributes` cookbook using either the `chef generate cook` book command in the Chef Development Kit or the `knife cookbook create` command in Chef Client, depending on which is installed on your Chef Development workstation.

Chef Development Kit:

```
$ chef generate cookbook motd-attributes
$ cd motd-attributes
```

Chef Client:

```
$ knife cookbook create motd-attributes --cookbook-path .
$ cd motd-attributes
$ kitchen init --create-gemfile
$ bundle install
```

Next, modify the *.kitchen.yml* file to use our favorite box image, as shown in Example 8-1.

Example 8-1. chefdk/motd-attributes/.kitchen.yml

```
---
driver:
  name: vagrant

provisioner:
  name: chef_zero

platforms:
  - name: centos65
    driver:
      box: learningchef/centos65
      box_url: learningchef/centos65

suites:
  - name: default
    run_list:
      - recipe[motd-attributes::default]
    attributes:
```

Create a recipe that uses the `template` resource to generate a */etc/motd* file, but this time, we'll use some attributes in the template file. The initial *recipes/default.rb* file you create should resemble Example 8-2.

Example 8-2. chefdk/motd-attributes/recipes/default.rb

```
#
# Cookbook Name:: motd-attributes
# Recipe:: default
#
# Copyright (C) 2014
#
#
```

```
#

template '/etc/motd' do
  source 'motd.erb'
  mode '0644'
end
```

Generate a template file to generate */etc/motd*.

Chef Development Kit:

```
$ chef generate template motd
```

Chef Client - Linux/Mac OS X:

```
$ touch templates/default/motd.erb
```

Chef Client - Windows:

```
$ touch templates\default\motd.erb
```

Create a template /etc/motd that uses some node attributes generated by ohai, as shown in Example 8-3.

Example 8-3. chefdk/motd-attributes/templates/default/motd.erb

```
The hostname of this node is <%= node['hostname'] %>
The IP address of this node is <%= node['ipaddress'] %>
```

Perform a kitchen converge to apply the cookbook to your node, and then when you run kitchen login it should display the following, with the expected values for node["ipaddress"] and node["hostname"]. (Reminder: Once you have issued these commands and verified the output is correct, make sure you run the exit command to get back to the host prompt directory with your cookbook source.)

```
$ kitchen converge
$ kitchen login
Last login: Sun Jul 20 19:40:55 2014 from 10.0.2.2
The hostname of this node is default-centos65
The IP address of this node is 10.0.2.15
[vagrant@default-centos65 ~]$ exit
logout
Connection to 127.0.0.1 closed.
```

If the last line with the IP address is missing, even though it is clear-ly in the *motd.erb*, add an extra newline in your text editor at the end of the file. The message of the day won't display the last line if it does not have a carriage return in the text.

Setting Attributes

Now, let's try setting some attributes in our cookbook. First, generate a default attributes file.

Chef Development Kit:

```
$ chef generate attribute default
```

Chef Client - Linux/Mac OS X:

```
$ touch attributes/default.rb
```

Chef Client - Windows:

```
$ touch attributes\default.rb
```

By default, the Chef Development Kit does not create an *attributes* directory until you tell it to generate an attribute file. Chef Client, on the other hand, always creates the directory, but leaves it up to you to create the *default.rb* attribute file by hand.

Now, let's set an attribute in our *attributes* file following the form outlined in Figure 8-1. Before you edit *attributes/default.rb* the file will have no content, as shown in Example 8-4.

Example 8-4. chefdk/motd-attributes/attributes/default.rb

```
default['motd-attributes']['company'] = 'Chef'
```

By convention, when attributes are set in a cookbook's attribute file, the values are expected to be *namespaced* under a top-level key matching the cookbook name. Then all the key/value pairs are contained within the top-level key; for example, the default['motd-attributes']['company'] value is the string 'Chef' in this example, as the cookbook name in the *metadata.rb* file is motd-attributes. Also, following the form outlined in Figure 8-1, the attribute uses the default precedence level.

Let's also set an attribute value in our recipe, as seen in Example 8-5, following the form in Figure 8-2.

Example 8-5. chefdk/motd-attributes/recipes/default.rb

```
node.default['motd-attributes']['message'] = "It's a wonderful day today!"

template '/etc/motd' do
  source 'motd.erb'
  mode '0644'
end
```

Update the *motd.erb* template as shown in Example 8-6. You can access attributes from any source under the node object: attribute file values, values set in recipes, or values set automatically by ohai. They're all just the corresponding node values.

Example 8-6. chefdk/motd-attributes/templates/default/motd.erb

```
Welcome to <%= node['motd-attributes']['company'] %>
<%= node['motd-attributes']['message'] %>
The hostname of this node is <%= node['hostname'] %>
The IP address of this node is <%= node['ipaddress'] %>
```

Performing another Chef run and checking the message of the day should produce the following output (again, make sure to exit back out to the host prompt):

```
$ kitchen converge
$ kitchen login
Last login: Sun Jul 20 19:52:53 2014 from 10.0.2.2
Welcome to Chef
It's a wonderful day today!
The hostname of this node is default-centos65
The IP address of this node is 10.0.2.15
[vagrant@default-centos65 ~]$ exit
logout
Connection to 127.0.0.1 closed.
```

Basic Attribute Priority

Now let's experiment with the basics of attribute priorities by trying to reset values set elsewhere. As shown in Example 8-7, modify the *recipe/default.rb* so that it tries to reset the value of a higher priority automatic attribute set by ohai, and a lower priority attribute defined in the attribute file.

Example 8-7. chefdk/motd-attributes/recipes/default.rb

```
node.default['ipaddress'] = '1.1.1.1'
node.default['motd-attributes']['company'] = 'My Company'
node.default['motd-attributes']['message'] = "It's a wonderful day today!"

template '/etc/motd' do
  source 'motd.erb'
  mode "0644"
end
```

Perform a Chef run and check to see the resulting values:

```
$ kitchen converge
$ kitchen login
Last login: Sun Jul 20 20:05:38 2014 from 10.0.2.2
Welcome to My Company
It's a wonderful day today!
The hostname of this node is default-centos65
The IP address of this node is 10.0.2.15
[vagrant@default-centos65 ~]$ exit
logout
Connection to 127.0.0.1 closed.
```

You should notice:

- The node['motd-attributes']['company'] value set in the recipe 'My Company' has a *higher priority* than the value 'Chef' set in the attribute file, so this is the value displayed in the template.
- The node['ipaddress'] value set in the recipe '1.1.1.1' has a *lower priority* than the automatic value *10.0.2.15* set by ohai, so the value set in the recipe is ignored, and the template displays the higher priority value.

These priorities represent how the variables are intended to be used. Values set in an attribute file are intended to be defaults that can be overridden by a recipe. On the other hand, the automatic values set by ohai should never be overridden as they represent important information about a system, such as the fact that it shouldn't be easy to reset the node's IP address, for example.

Include_Recipe

You might wonder why there is a need for this priority mechanism with Chef attributes. It's because like in most other programming languages, a Chef recipe can reference other Chef recipe files using an "include" statement: include_recipe. So when your Chef code is processed during a Chef run, it could possibly include a chain of references to multiple recipe files that might even be in other cookbooks, as shown in Figure 8-4. Because you can use include_recipe, Chef code might contain conflicting attribute assignments, and there needs to be some guidelines for how these conflicts are resolved.

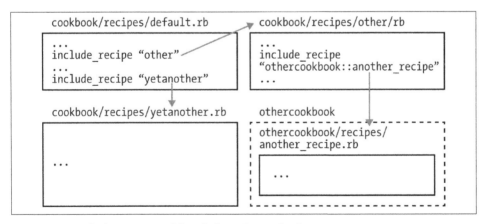

Figure 8-4. include_recipe could include a chain of references

A rule of thumb many Chef coders find useful is that a recipe file shouldn't be longer than a "screenful" of code—between one dozen and two lines. Anything longer gets difficult to understand at a glance because you have to scroll up or down to see all the code. When your recipe code starts getting this long, consider breaking it up into multiple recipe files, stitching them together with `include_recipe` statements.

In order to use `include_recipe`, you reference a recipe in the exact same form that you reference a recipe in a run list, in the form `"<cookbook>::<recipe>"`. For example, `"motd-attributes::message"`.

Let's add an `include_recipe` statement to our `motd-attributes` cookbook. Generate a new recipe called `message`.

Chef Development Kit:

```
$ chef generate recipe message
```

Chef Client - Linux/Mac OS X:

```
$ touch recipes/message.rb
```

Chef Client - Windows:

```
$ touch recipes\message.rb
```

Now edit the *recipes/message.rb* file containing the recipe as shown in Example 8-8. The message recipe will be used to set additional values related to the message of the day.

Example 8-8. chefdk/motd-attributes/recipes/message.rb

```
node.default['motd-attributes']['company'] = 'the best company in the universe'
```

Note that our *.kitchen.yml* file includes only a reference to the `de fault` recipe in its run list. We never intend for external consumers of our cookbook to refer to this `message` recipe directly. We're just using the `message` recipe to organize our code, and it is assumed that `include_recipe` will be used inside the `default` recipe to include any other necessary code:

```
...
  run_list:
    - recipe[motd-attributes::default]
...
```

Some Chef coders use the convention of putting an underscore prefix ("_") in the name of recipes that are "private"—recipes used merely to organize Chef code into smaller, more understandable chunks. They name the recipe file `"_message.rb"` to make this intent more clear in the cookbook file structure.

Also, you need to add an `include_recipe` statement to your *default.rb*. The `in clude_recipe` statement ensures that the *message.rb* file gets processed during the Chef run. Otherwise, only the recipe file *default.rb* will be evaluated when the run list is `motd-attributes::default`. We won't remove any of the attribute values we set earlier, in order to illustrate a few more attribute priority concepts.

Example 8-9. chefdk/motd-attributes/recipes/default.rb

```
#
# Cookbook Name:: motd-attributes
# Recipe:: default
#
# Copyright (C) 2014
#
#
#

node.default['ipaddress'] = '1.1.1.1'
node.default['motd-attributes']['company'] = 'My Company'
node.default['motd-attributes']['message'] = "It's a wonderful day today!"

include_recipe 'motd-attributes::message'

template '/etc/motd' do
  source 'motd.erb'
  mode '0644'
end
```

`include_recipe` statements can be present anywhere in a recipe file. When the Chef code is evaluated, the `include_recipe` statement is replaced with an expansion of the recipe code that is referenced, as shown in Figure 8-5.

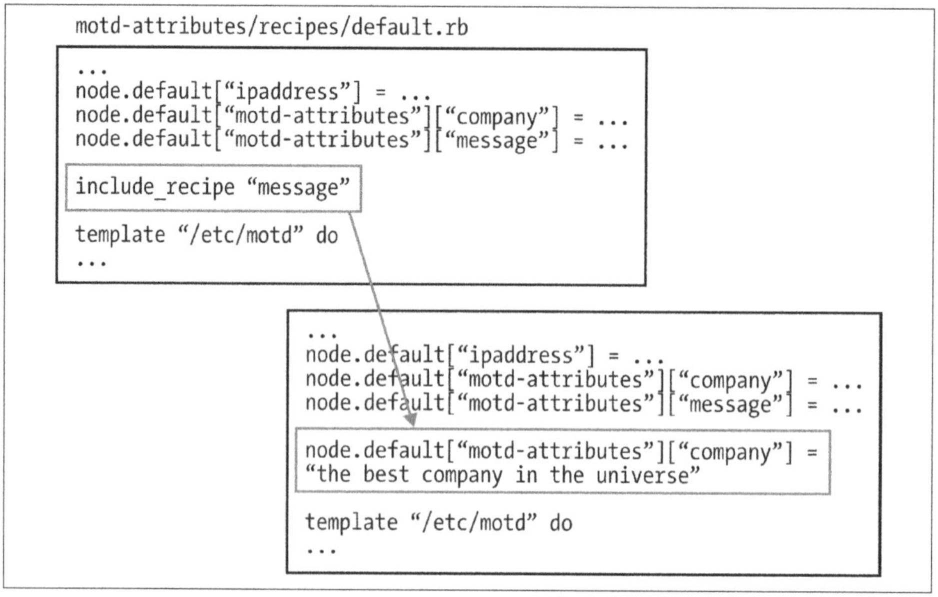

Figure 8-5. Chef expands any include_recipe references

Perform a `kitchen converge` and inspect the resulting message. When there is a duplicate attribute value set at the same priority level, the last attribute value setting wins. In this case, with the `include_recipe` expansion, `node.default["motd-attributes"]` `["company"]` is set twice; the last value set before the `template` resource is what is used—"the greatest company in the universe":

```
$ kitchen converge
$ kitchen login
Last login: Mon Jul 21 11:34:05 2014 from 10.0.2.2
Welcome to the best company in the universe
It's a wonderful day today!
The hostname of this node is 10.0.2.15
The IP address of this node is default-centos65
[vagrant@default-centos65 ~]$ exit
logout
Connection to 127.0.0.1 closed.
```

Attribute Precedence

Figure 8-6 shows the three most commonly used levels of precedence that can be used in attribute definitions:

Automatic
    attributes are those discovered by `ohai`.

Default
> attributes are typically set in cookbooks and attribute files.

Override
> attributes are the strongest way to set an attribute—use sparingly.

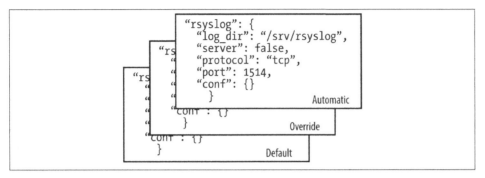

Figure 8-6. Precedence levels

When setting an attribute in a cookbook, it should (almost) always be a *default* attribute. There is one exception to this rule, where it makes sense to use override precedence with environments. We'll explore the reasoning behind this in Chapter 15.

Other than the special case of Chef environments, attribute precedence is most frequently used when you want to customize Chef, which is beyond the scope of this book. When you want to implement a new feature in Chef, such as a custom resource, being able to tinker with Chef's powerful attribute precedence engine lets you add new features to the language that follow the general expectations for basic attribute priority outlined in this chapter. For more information on this topic, refer to *Customizing Chef*, by Jon Cowie.

Debugging Attributes

If you need to debug where attributes are being set, the node object exposes a helpful node.debug_value() method. Let's say, for example, you did not know that ohai set node['ipaddress'] using automatic precedence. You could determine this by using node.debug_value().

Modify *recipes/default.rb* as shown in Example 8-10. Because we have access to the full power of the Ruby language in a Chef recipe, we also make use of the "pretty printer for Ruby objects" function included with the core Ruby library. This function will print out the contents of a Ruby object in a more readable format. The node.debug_value() returns the raw contents of an object; pp just makes the output look nicer.

Example 8-10. chefdk/motd-attributes/recipes/default.rb

```
#
# Cookbook Name:: motd-attributes
# Recipe:: default
#
# Copyright (C) 2014
#
#
#

require 'pp'

node.default['ipaddress'] = '1.1.1.1'
pp node.debug_value('ipaddress')

node.default['motd-attributes']['company'] = 'My Company'
node.default['motd-attributes']['message'] = "It's a wonderful day today!"

include_recipe 'motd-attributes::message'

template '/etc/motd' do
  source 'motd.erb'
  mode '0644'
end
```

When you run `kitchen converge`, you should see the following output:

```
$ kitchen converge
-----> Starting Kitchen (v1.2.2.dev)
...
        [["set_unless_enabled?", false],
         ["default", "1.1.1.1"],
         ["env_default", :not_present],
         ["role_default",
         :not_present],
         ["force_default", :not_present],
         ["normal", :not_present],
         ["override", :not_present],
         ["role_override", :not_present],
         ["env_override", :not_present],
         ["force_override", :not_present],
         ["automatic", "10.0.2.15"]]
    ...
```

From here, you could sort out that the node['ipaddress'] attribute was set to the value of "10.0.2.15" at the automatic precedence level and set to the value "1.1.1.1" at the default precedence level. So Chef did register that you set the value to "1.1.1.1", but the override took precedence.

You might notice that there are more precedence levels in the node.de bug_level() output than we have discussed so far in this book. We are intentionally simplifying attribute precedence in this book. If you follow the guideline of using *default* precedence, unless there is a specific need, you rarely have to deal with the full complexity of attribute precedence with basic Chef cookbook code.

A lot of the complexity of attributes arose as the precedence feature was introduced in Chef and cookbooks needed to be written to be backward-compatible with older versions. With Chef 11, most cookbooks follow the *default* precedence guideline.

If you'd like to learn more about the details of attribute precedence, refer to the aforementioned *Customizing Chef.*

Debugging when an attribute is set in two or more places at the same precedence level is a little more difficult to trace, but still not too complicated. You just need to sprinkle node.debug_value() statements before and after include_recipe calls.

For example, say we didn't know that the motd-attributes::message recipe set node.default['motd-attributes']['message']. We could figure this out by sprinkling more node.debug_value() calls in our code. Change *recipes/default.rb* as shown in Example 8-11, adding a call to node.debug_value('motd-attributes', 'message') before and after include_recipe.

Example 8-11. chefdk/motd-attributes/recipes/default.rb

```
#
# Cookbook Name:: motd-attributes
# Recipe:: default
#
# Copyright (C) 2014
#
#
#

require 'pp'

node.default['ipaddress'] = '1.1.1.1'
pp node.debug_value('ipaddress')

node.default['motd-attributes']['company'] = 'My Company'
node.default['motd-attributes']['message'] = "It's a wonderful day today!"

pp node.debug_value('motd-attributes', 'company')
include_recipe 'motd-attributes::message'
pp node.debug_value('motd-attributes', 'company')

template '/etc/motd' do
```

```
  source 'motd.erb'
  mode '0644'
end
```

Run kitchen converge again, and the output of node.debug_value() should resemble
the output shown in Figure 8-7, with the second-to-last dump of node.debug_val
ue() being before include_recipe and the last being after include_recipe.

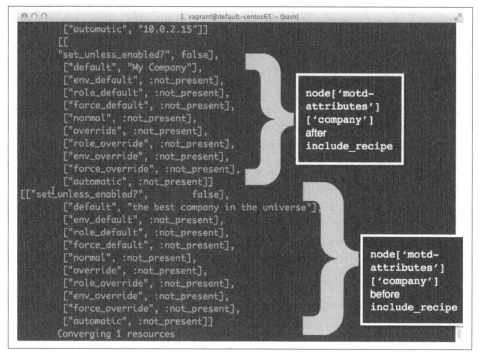

Figure 8-7. node.debug_value() output before and after include_recipe

From this output, you could sort out that something in motd-attributes::message
recipe set the attribute node['motd-attributes']['company'] to "the best company
in the universe" using the default precedence, overriding what was set earlier.

Now we're done with this cookbook and virtual machine in this chapter. Run the kitch
en destroy command to shut down the virtual machine and release all the associated
system resources:

```
$ kitchen destroy
-----> Starting Kitchen (v1.2.2.dev)
-----> Destroying <default-centos65>...
       ==> default: Forcing shutdown of VM...
       ==> default: Destroying VM and associated drives...
       Vagrant instance <default-centos65> destroyed.
```

```
             Finished destroying <default-centos65> (0m2.95s).
    -----> Kitchen is finished. (0m3.43s)
```

Summary

In this chapter, we presented an overview of attributes and how Chef uses attributes to capture the state of a node. Attributes can be defined in multiple places:

- Automatically via ohai
- Attribute files
- Recipes
- Other cookbooks

Because attributes can be defined in multiple places, Chef defines a *priority* scheme for how attribute values are composed from multiple sources. You can tweak this priority scheme by manually providing different levels of *precedence*, including *automatic*, *default*, and *override*. In general, you should use the *default* precedence, unless there is a specific need to extend or customize Chef, letting Chef choose the default priority in which attribute values are merged together.

In the next chapter, we'll be introducing Chef Server. Chef Server is a useful central repository for all shared information necessary to manage multiple nodes effectively.

## CHAPTER 9

Manage Multiple Nodes at Once with Chef Server

We've shown you how much you can do with Chef without ever needing to install its server component. However, to get the full benefits of Chef, you need to set up a Chef Server in your production environment. Using a Chef Server is recommended when you need to manage more than one machine at a time with Chef, which is typically how Chef is used. Chef Server adds more capabilities that can be used in your cookbooks, including roles, environments, data bags, and powerful search.

As of this writing, there are three flavors of Chef Server, as detailed in Table 9-1. Although there are subtle differences, they all contain common features, including an API endpoint, data bags, environments, node objects, roles, and search. Some of these terms are new; we will cover them in the remaining chapters of the book.

Table 9-1. Types of Chef Server

Flavor	Details
Hosted Enterprise Chef	Formerly called Hosted Chef, Hosted Enterprise Chef is "Chef as a Service"—software as a service. It is cloud-based and highly scalable, and comes with an industry-standard service-level agreement. It requires no setup or configuration of the server itself.
Enterprise Chef On-Premises	Enterprise Chef On-Premises, formerly called Private Chef, is a Chef Server inside an organization's firewall. It is designed to be deployed inside an organization's infrastructure, and includes additional features on top of Hosted Enterprise Chef. Enterprise Chef On-Premises is most useful to organizations that must comply with HIPAA or PCI compliance issues, large organizations that wish to manage their own servers, and companies that require tight control and auditing of data.
Open Source Chef Server	As the name suggests, Open Source Chef Server is a free, open source version of Chef Server that includes a subset of premium Chef Server features available in Enterprise Chef, most useful to small organizations.

Chef Server is the centralized store for configuration data in your infrastructure. It stores and indexes cookbooks, environments, templates, metadata, files, and distribution policies. Chef Server is aware of all machines it manages, and in this way, Chef Server also acts as an inventory management system.

As of Chef 11, Chef Server is written in Erlang, a programming language designed with *concurrency* in mind. Chef Server is also composed of a web server, cookbook store, web interface, messaging queue, and backend database. Figure 9-1 shows how each of these pieces interact.

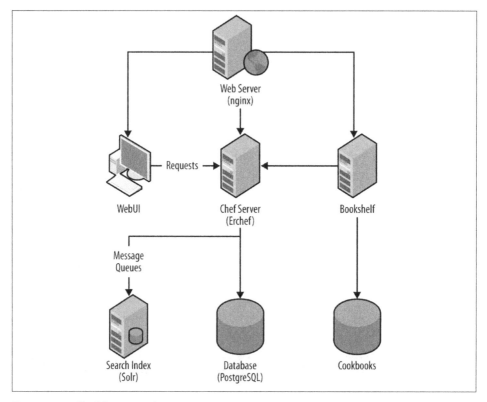

Figure 9-1. Chef Server architecture

Web server
> The nginx web server is a simple reverse proxy server that acts as the front-end interface for Chef Server (Erchef). It also performs load balancing for Chef Server. All requests to the Chef Server API are routed through the nginx web server.

WebUI
> The WebUI is the consumer-facing web application. It is a Ruby on Rails application that provides a web-guided user interface for interacting with Chef Server.

Chef Server

Erchef is the component of Chef Server that processes API requests. As its name suggests, Chef Server is written in Erlang for high concurrency and reliability. Even though Chef Server is written in Erlang, it is still capable of running Ruby code. In fact, writing Erlang Chef recipes is not supported at this writing. Erchef is the core API for Chef Server.

Bookshelf

The Bookshelf is the central store for all Chef cookbooks and cookbook contents (such as files, templates, definitions, metadata, and recipes). Each cookbook is automatically checksummed and versioned. Bookshelf is a flat-file database and is intentionally stored outside of Chef Server's index.

Search Index

The Search Index is an Apache Solr server that handles the indexing and searching mechanism for various API calls, both internally and externally. The server is wrapped by `chef-solr`, which exposes a RESTful API.

Message queues

The queues handle all messages that are sent to the Search Index for parsing. The queues are managed by RabbitMQ, an open source queuing system. `chef-expander` pulls messages from the message queues, formats the messages, and then sends the messages to the Search Index.

Database

The database is a PostgreSQL persistent data store. Prior to Chef 11, the data store was CouchDB, but was moved to PostgreSQL due to CouchDB's inability to scale.

In the first part of this chapter, we'll install Enterprise Chef On-Premises Server in a sandbox environment using Test Kitchen. In order to set up the server in a virtual machine, you'll need at least 2 GB of free memory on your machine—1.5 GB for Chef Server itself plus 512 MB for the accompanying node.

With Enterprise Chef On-Premises, you can manage up to five nodes for free, more than enough for learning all the enterprise capabilities of Chef Server. Appendix A covers the installation of Open Source Chef Server, should you not wish to provide contact information and don't currently need the advanced capabilities of Enterprise Chef in your organization. With Open Source Chef Server, you can manage an unlimited number of nodes for free. Appendix B presents a similar overview of Hosted Enterprise Chef, should you wish to explore the Chef—it also offers the ability manage up to five nodes with its free tier.

How to Install Enterprise Chef Server Manually

As shown in Figure 9-2, go to *http://www.getchef.com/contact/on-premises* and provide your contact information to receive download details and installation instructions for Enterprise Chef Server.

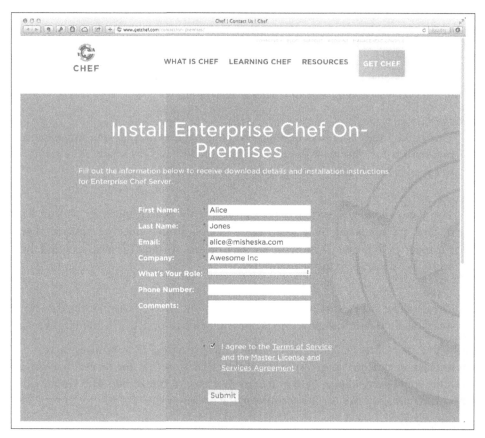

Figure 9-2. Register to receive On-Premise Enterprise Chef download details

Once you accept the agreement, you'll be presented a download link page as shown in Figure 9-3. Bookmark this download link page in your web browser for future reference. Copy the link for the Red Hat Enterprise Linux 6 download, as shown.

Figure 9-3. Enterprise Chef Download links

To manually replicate a basic Enterprise Chef install in a cookbook, we first need to download the Enterprise Chef Server install package for Red Hat Enterprise Linux 6, as we'll be installing on CentOS 6.5. To match the exercises in the book, use version 11.1.8 (*https://s3.amazonaws.com/opscode-private-chef/el/6/x86_64/private-chef-11.1.8-1.el6.x86_64.rpm*). Use the *Copy Link Address* option on the download link to copy the full download URL to your clipboard.

> The download page may not match the images presented in this book exactly. The download and install procedure should be similar even if the web presentation is different.

The rest of the steps necessary to install Chef Server are displayed below the download link:

1. Install the chef-server package.
2. Run `sudo private-chef-ctl reconfigure`.

Install Enterprise Chef Server

Assuming you have sufficient resources to install Enterprise Chef Server locally along with a test node, let's create an `enterprise-chef` cookbook that will install Enterprise Chef Server. To maintain consistency with Hosted Enterprise Chef, create the directory *chef-repo/cookbooks* and create the `enterprise` cookbook in that directory. Having a top-level `chef-repo` directory will help you handle the additional files necessary to manage Enterprise Chef beyond the cookbooks themselves. You'll definitely be using more than one cookbook in your organization, so we suggest putting them in a *chef-repo/cookbooks* subdirectory.

Create the *chef-repo/cookbooks* directory and make it the current working directory.

Linux/Mac OS X:

```
$ mkdir -p chef-repo/cookbooks
$ cd chef-repo/cookbooks
```

Windows:

```
> mkdir chef-repo\cookbooks
> cd chef-repo\cookbooks
```

Then generate the `enterprise-chef` cookbook with `chef generate cookbook` or `knife cookbook create`, depending on whether you are using the Chef Development Kit or the Chef Client. We're going to go through the cookbook creation steps quickly in this chapter. If you need a refresher on what each of these commands mean and the expected output, refer back to Chapter 7.

Chef Development Kit:

```
$ chef generate cookbook enterprise-chef
$ cd enterprise-chef
```

Chef Client:

```
$ knife cookbook create enterprise-chef --cookbook-path .
$ cd enterprise-chef
$ kitchen init --create-gemfile
$ bundle install
```

As shown in Example 9-1, edit the *.kitchen.yml* file to use the CentOS 6.5 basebox we prepared specifically for this book. Also, assign a private network address like we did in Chapter 7. This time, we're going to use the IP address 192.168.33.34. If this conflicts with an address already being used on your local network, change it to a nonconflicting one. We also need more memory than the default 512 MB allocated, so add a `custom ize:` block with a `memory:` statement to increase the memory to 1.5 GB (memory is specified in megabytes only).

Make sure that you use the `chef_solo` provisioner for this cookbook, as the in-memory Chef Server the `chef_zero` provisioner spawns will cause a conflict with the hands-on exercises coming up in Chapter 10. As of this writing, if you want to automate the installation of a Chef Server with Chef cookbooks, using Chef Solo is recommended so that the deployment code doesn't get confused by the presence of the in-memory Chef Server used in Chef Zero.

Example 9-1. chefdk/chef-repo/cookbooks/enterprise-chef/.kitchen.yml

```
---
driver:
  name: vagrant

provisioner:
  name: chef_solo

platforms:
  - name: centos65
    driver:
      box: learningchef/centos65
      box_url: learningchef/centos65
      network:
      - ["private_network", {ip: "192.168.33.34"}]
      customize:
        memory: 1536

suites:
  - name: default
    run_list:
      - recipe[enterprise-chef::default]
    attributes:
```

Generate a default attributes file in *attributes/default.rb*.

Chef Development Kit:

    $ **chef generate attribute default**

Chef Client:

    $ **touch attributes/default.rb**

Add an attribute specifying the download URL for the Chef Server package that you obtained from the Enterprise Chef download link page. We recommend using the 11.1.8 version URL as shown in Example 9-2, as we wrote the examples for this chapter for this version of Chef.

Example 9-2. chefdk/chef-repo/cookbooks/enterprise-chef/attributes/default.rb

```
default['enterprise-chef']['url'] = \
'https://s3.amazonaws.com/opscode-private-chef/el/6/x86_64/'\
'private-chef-11.1.8-1.el6.x86_64.rpm'
```

Let's take an initial stab at coding a recipe to replicate the manual steps to install Chef Server outlined in "How to Install Enterprise Chef Server Manually" on page 150. Enter in the first version of the code as shown in Example 9-3. Let's go over some of the highlights of the code in the following paragraphs.

Rather than typing in long variable names like node['enterprise-chef']['url'], feel free to use temporary local variables in a recipe with shorter names, such as:

```
package_url = node['enterprise-chef']['url']
```

Remember that you have the full power of Ruby classes and methods available to you in your Chef recipes, so don't be afraid to use it. For example, you can use the ::File.basename() method to extract the package name from the URL. The package name is the last component of the URL after the forward slash ("/"): private-chef-11.1.8-1.el6.x86_64.rpm. Refer to the Ruby core API documentation (*http://bit.ly/common_functionality*) for more information on the ::File class:

```
package_name = ::File.basename(package_url)
```

Unfortunately, the package resource does not work with URLs, so we're introducing a new resource, the remote_file resource. The remote_file resource will download files from a remote location. Rather than hardcoding a path like "/tmp" for the package download, Chef provides a variable you should use instead: Chef::Config[:file_cache_path]. Let Chef choose the best place to store temporary files for you. Pass the local path where you want to store the file as a string parameter to remote_file or as a name attribute; in this case, we use the package_local_path variable. The download URL should be passed to remote_file as the source attribute.

The package resource should be familiar to you by now, as we used it in Chapter 7.

In order to execute the chef-server-ctl reconfigure, we need to introduce another new resource, the execute resource. When you fail to find a resource that meets your needs, you can use the execute resource to run arbitrary shell commands. Pass the shell command you want to execute as a string parameter to the execute resource.

Here's the full code listing shown in Example 9-3.

Example 9-3. chefdk/chef-repo/cookbooks/enterprise-chef/recipes/default.rb

```
#
# Cookbook Name:: enterprise-chef
# Recipe:: default
#
```

```
# Copyright (C) 2014
#
#
#

package_url = node['enterprise-chef']['url']
package_name = ::File.basename(package_url)
package_local_path = "#{Chef::Config[:file_cache_path]}/#{package_name}"

# omnibus_package is remote (i.e., a URL) let's download it
remote_file package_local_path do
  source package_url
end

package package_local_path

# reconfigure the installation
execute 'private-chef-ctl reconfigure'
```

Run kitchen converge to install Enterprise Chef Server, and use kitchen login to verify that the private-chef package was installed. The kitchen converge will take some time, perhaps as long as 10 to 15 minutes, as it needs to download an 800-MB installation package for Enterprise Chef:

```
$ kitchen converge default-centos65
$ kitchen login default-centos65
[vagrant@default-centos65 ~]$ rpm -q private-chef
private-chef-11.1.8-1.el6.x86_64
[vagrant@default-centos65 ~]$ exit
logout
Connection to 127.0.0.1 closed.
```

Introducing Idempotence

Although the recipe we created in Example 9-3 is a good first attempt, it is not *idempotent*. When Chef code is *idempotent*, it can run multiple times on the same system and the results will always be identical, without producing unintended side effects. All Chef default resources are guaranteed to be *idempotent* with the exception of the exe cute resource.

execute resources are generally not idempotent, because most command-line utilities can be run only once. They assume that a human being is interacting with the system and understands the state of the system. For example, assuming the file */learningchef/ file1.txt* exists, the following mv command will work the first time it is run, but it will fail the second time:

```
$ mv /learningchef/file1.txt /file1.txt
```

A great way to test to see if your recipe is idempotent is to run `kitchen converge` *twice*. When a recipe has no unintended side effects, there should be 0 resources updated on the second run.

Does our recipe pass the idempotency test? Sadly, no. Here's a sampling of the output from an initial `kitchen converge`:

```
$ kitchen converge
-----> Starting Kitchen (v1.2.2.dev)
-----> Creating <default-centos65>...
       ...
       Starting Chef Client, version 11.14.2
       [2014-08-14T19:25:13-07:00] INFO: *** Chef 11.14.2 ***
       [2014-08-14T19:25:13-07:00] INFO: Chef-client pid: 2387
       [2014-08-14T19:25:15-07:00] INFO: Setting the run_list to
       ["recipe[enterprise-chef::default]"] from CLI options
       [2014-08-14T19:25:15-07:00] INFO: Run List is
       [recipe[enterprise-chef::default]]
       [2014-08-14T19:25:15-07:00] INFO: Run List expands to
       [enterprise-chef::default]
       [2014-08-14T19:25:15-07:00] INFO: Starting Chef Run for default-centos65
       [2014-08-14T19:25:15-07:00] INFO: Running start handlers
       [2014-08-14T19:25:15-07:00] INFO: Start handlers complete.
       Compiling Cookbooks...
       Converging 3 resources
       ...

       [2014-08-14T19:36:22-07:00] INFO: Chef Run complete in 666.814045747
       seconds

       Running handlers:
       [2014-08-14T19:36:22-07:00] INFO: Running report handlers
       Running handlers complete
       [2014-08-14T19:36:22-07:00] INFO: Report handlers complete
       Chef Client finished, 3/3 resources updated in 668.536290312 seconds
       Finished converging <default-centos65> (11m59.64s).
-----> Kitchen is finished. (12m33.89s)
```

Here's the output from the second run. Chef mistakenly thinks there's still stuff it needs to do—2/3 resources updated in this second run. If the recipe were truly idempotent, we'd see 0/3 resources updated. Chef would inspect the state of the system, recognize that nothing had changed since the last run—no one touched the node between the two runs—and perform no resource updates:

```
$ kitchen converge
-----> Starting Kitchen (v1.2.2.dev)
-----> Converging <default-centos65>...
       ...
       Converging 3 resources
       Recipe: enterprise-chef::default
         * remote_file[/tmp/kitchen/cache/private-chef-11.1.8-1.el6.x86_64.rpm]
           action create[2014-08-14T19:41:13-07:00] INFO: Processing
           remote_file[/tmp/kitchen/cache/private-chef-11.1.8-1.el6.x86_64.rpm]
```

```
      action create (enterprise-chef::default line 15)
      (up to date)
      * package[/tmp/kitchen/cache/private-chef-11.1.8-1.el6.x86_64.rpm]
      action install[2014-08-14T19:41:20-07:00] INFO: Processing
      package[/tmp/kitchen/cache/private-chef-11.1.8-1.el6.x86_64.rpm]
      action install (enterprise-chef::default line 19)

        - install version 11.1.8-1.el6 of package /tmp/kitchen/cache/
        private-chef-11.1.8-1.el6.x86_64.rpm

      * execute[private-chef-ctl reconfigure] action
      run[2014-08-14T19:41:28-07:00] INFO: Processing
      execute[private-chef-ctl reconfigure] action run
      (enterprise-chef::default line 22)
      [2014-08-14T19:41:39-07:00] INFO: execute[private-chef-ctl reconfigure]
      ran successfully

        - execute private-chef-ctl reconfigure

      [2014-08-14T19:41:39-07:00] INFO: Chef Run complete in 26.305913778
      seconds

      Running handlers:
      [2014-08-14T19:41:39-07:00] INFO: Running report handlers
      Running handlers complete
      [2014-08-14T19:41:39-07:00] INFO: Report handlers complete
      Chef Client finished, 2/3 resources updated in 27.930367706 seconds
      Finished converging <default-centos65> (0m30.94s).
  -----> Kitchen is finished. (0m31.41s)
```

As mentioned earlier, most default Chef resources are *idempotent*. Notice that the *remote_file* resource is idempotent. It is reporting (up to date). The *package* resource is normally idempotent. We specifically crafted this example to show you a platform-specific quirk related to idempotency when it is used on RedHat-variant platforms, such as CentOS, which we'll show you how to address.

There are some issues with the package and execute resources, however, as on the second kitchen converge run Chef:

1. Reinstalled the rpm package, unnecessarily
2. Executed chef-server-ctl reconfigure a second time

Let's fix these idempotency issues in our code now. Example 9-4 has the final idempotent version of the code.

The first issue is a common one that Chef developers encounter with the package resource when they try to install from a downloaded rpm instead of using a package repository. Instead of using a package one-liner for a downloaded rpm, you need to tell the package resource to explicitly use the Chef::Provider::Package::Rpm provider using the `provider` attribute. You also need to specify the string representing the package name using the `source` attribute, like so:

```
package package_name do
  source package_local_path
  provider Chef::Provider::Package::Rpm
end
```

You can use the `rpm_package` short name to specify `Chef::Provid er::Package::Rpm` to the package resource, if you prefer. The following code is equivalent to the preceding code:

```
rpm_package package_name do
  source package_local_path
end
```

Fixing the second issue with the `execute` resource is a little more involved. That's why you should prefer built-in Chef resources over using the `execute` resource, because it's up to you to make the execute resources idempotent.

One way to fix this issue is with a `not_if` *guard* to the `execute` resource. Guards are used to make a resource idempotent by allowing the resource to test for a desired state, and if the desired state is present, the resource should do nothing. In this case, we'll test to see if the chef-server package is already installed, by adding a `not_if` clause to the `execute` resource as follows. `not_if` will test to see if the exit code of the command is 0; if so, the resource does nothing.

If you need to test the opposite logic of `not_if`, there is also an on ly_if guard. It's more typical to use `only_if` on Windows, given that a successful exit code for Windows commands is frequently the value 1 instead of 0. Take a look at *http://bit.ly/common_functionality* for more information.

```
execute "chef-server-ctl reconfigure" do
  not_if "rpm -q chef-server"
end
```

Although this is a reasonable way to address the issue, it's a little clunky. You have to figure out a way to detect whether Chef Server is installed, and the method used in the previous example is not very reliable. A better approach is to trigger the execute when the package resource installs the package. You can trigger events in other resources with a *notifies* statement.

In order to use `notifies`, we'll need to change the `execute` resource statement a bit. First, you'll want to change the resource so it does nothing by default when `execute` is evaluated during the Chef run; we do this by adding an `action :nothing` attribute.

Also, you'll want to move the actual command line explicitly to the command attribute, so you can use a short name to trigger the execute block. By default, the name passed to the execute resource as a string parameter is used as the command attribute, which is great for a self-documenting one-liner. but not so great when you want to trigger the command by name. So let's transform the execute resource like so:

```
# reconfigure the installation
execute 'reconfigure-chef-server' do
  command 'chef-server-ctl reconfigure'
  action :nothing
end
```

Then add the notifies attribute as follows. The notifies attribute takes three parameters: an action, the name of the resource to notify, and a timer indicating when the action should be perform. As shown in the following code block, we want to perform the :run action on the execute[reconfigure-chef-server] resource, and we want the action performed :immediately. For more information on notifies parameters, refer to the Chef documentation (*http://docs.opscode.com/resource_common.html*):

```
package package_name do
  source package_local_path
  provider Chef::Provider::Package::Rpm
  notifies :run, 'execute[reconfigure-chef-server]', :immediately
end
```

Example 9-4 shows what the final version of our idempotent code looks like.

Example 9-4. chefdk/chef-repo/cookbooks/enterprise-chef/recipes/default.rb

```
# Cookbook Name:: enterprise-chef
# Recipe:: default
#
# Copyright (C) 2014
#
#
#

package_url = node['enterprise-chef']['url']
package_name = ::File.basename(package_url)
package_local_path = "#{Chef::Config[:file_cache_path]}/#{package_name}"

# omnibus_package is remote (i.e., a URL) let's download it
remote_file package_local_path do
  source package_url
end

package package_name do
  source package_local_path
  provider Chef::Provider::Package::Rpm
  notifies :run, 'execute[reconfigure-chef-server]', :immediately
end
```

```
# reconfigure the installation
execute 'reconfigure-chef-server' do
  command 'private-chef-ctl reconfigure'
  action :nothing
end
```

Try running kitchen converge against this revised recipe, and note that it reports 0/2 resources updated, which is the result we are looking for; no resources are updated after running kitchen converge for the second time:

```
$ kitchen converge
-----> Starting Kitchen (v1.2.2.dev)
-----> Converging <default-centos65>...
       ...
       Converging 3 resources
       Recipe: enterprise-chef::default
         * remote_file[/tmp/kitchen/cache/private-chef-11.1.8-1.el6.x86_64.rpm]
         action create[2014-08-14T19:46:12-07:00] INFO: Processing
         remote_file[/tmp/kitchen/cache/private-chef-11.1.8-1.el6.x86_64.rpm]
         action create (enterprise-chef::default line 15)
         (up to date)
         * package[private-chef-11.1.8-1.el6.x86_64.rpm] action
         install[2014-08-14T19:46:20-07:00] INFO: Processing
         package[private-chef-11.1.8-1.el6.x86_64.rpm] action install
         (enterprise-chef::default line 19)
         (up to date)
         * execute[reconfigure-chef-server] action
         nothing[2014-08-14T19:46:20-07:00] INFO: Processing
         execute[reconfigure-chef-server] action nothing
         (enterprise-chef::default line 26)
         (skipped due to action :nothing)
         [2014-08-14T19:46:20-07:00] INFO: Chef Run complete in 8.771936095
         seconds

         Running handlers:
         [2014-08-14T19:46:20-07:00] INFO: Running report handlers
         Running handlers complete
         [2014-08-14T19:46:20-07:00] INFO: Report handlers complete
         Chef Client finished, 0/2 resources updated in 10.423184134 seconds
         Finished converging <default-centos65> (0m12.31s).
-----> Kitchen is finished. (0m12.86s)
```

Always check your recipes to see if they are idempotent before deploying them to production. If we had deployed the first version of this recipe in production, given that the chef-client usually runs on a periodic timer performing Chef runs, all our nodes would have been reinstalling the Chef Server package and reconfiguring the server every 15 minutes!

Configure Enterprise Chef Server

If your Enterprise Chef Server installed properly, you should be able to access the web admin console using the `private_network` IP address you configured in your *.kitchen.yml*. In our case, we used the address 192.168.33.34. After you dismiss a warning about the use of a self-signed SSL certificate, click on the Sign up link, as shown in Figure 9-4.

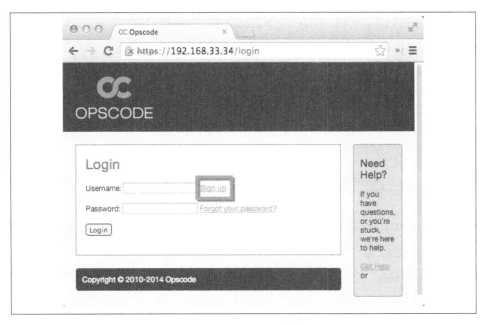

Figure 9-4. Sign up

You will be prompted to create a user account. Enter in the required values, then click on the Submit button. Figure 9-5 shows the values we used for our user account; yours will be different, of course.

Once you click on the Submit button, the Enterprise Chef web UI indicates that the next step you should perform is to create an organization. Click on the *Create* link to create an organization, as shown in Figure 9-6.

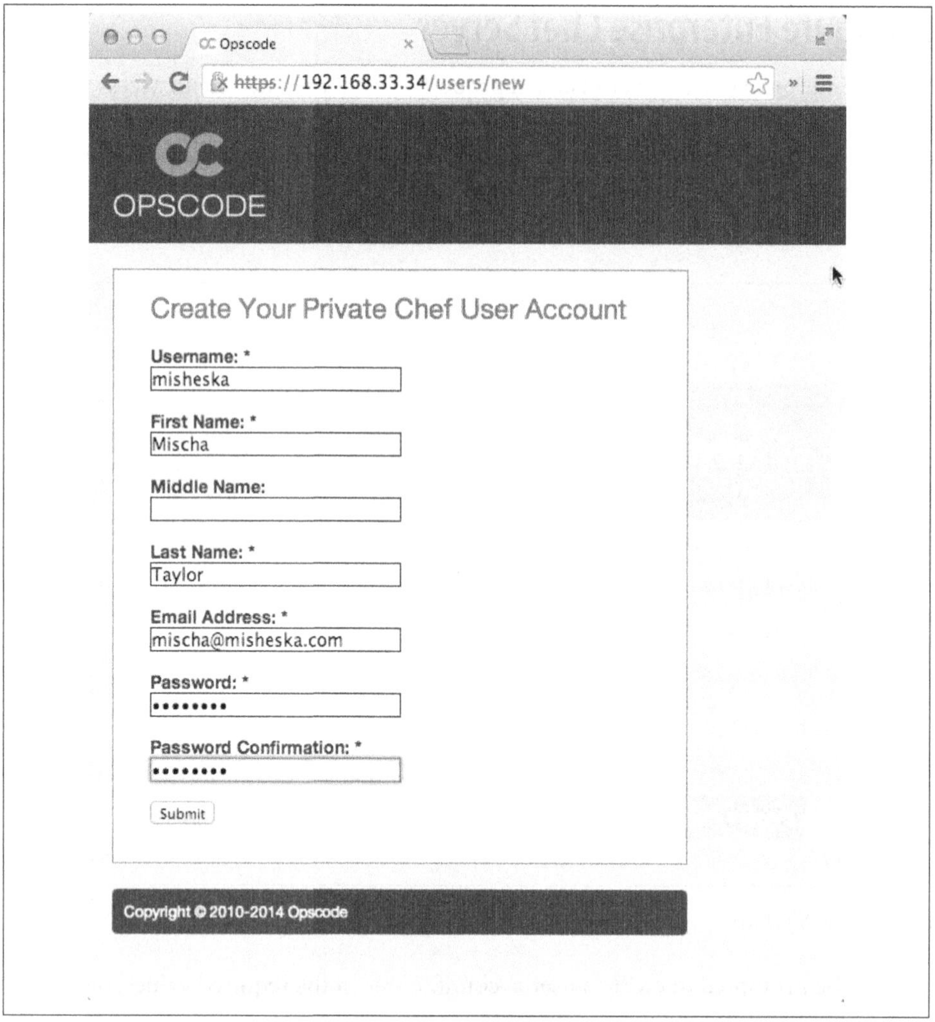

Figure 9-5. Create a user

An *<organization>* is the name of your company or organization. It is used as a unique identifier to authenticate *your organization* against Chef Server. Figure 9-7 shows how we filled out the organization fields in our setup.

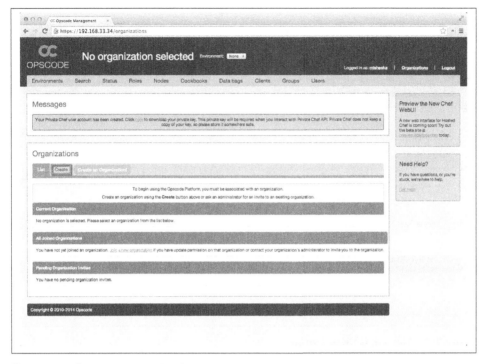

Figure 9-6. Create an organization

Once you click on the Create Organization button, you will be prompted to save two files: the validation key and the knife configuration file, as shown in Figure 9-8:

- *<organization>-validator.pem*
- *knife.rb*

After you've download the *<organization>-validator.pem* and *knife.rb* files, click on your username link on the upper right-hand side of the web page as shown in Figure 9-9. Our username is `misheska`; yours will be different.

As shown in Figure 9-10, click on the *Regenerate Private Key* link to download the third and final configuration file you need *<username>.pem*.

Once you have these three files downloaded, go back to the root directory where you created *chef-repo*. Make it the current working directory. Then create a *chef-repo/.chef* directory.

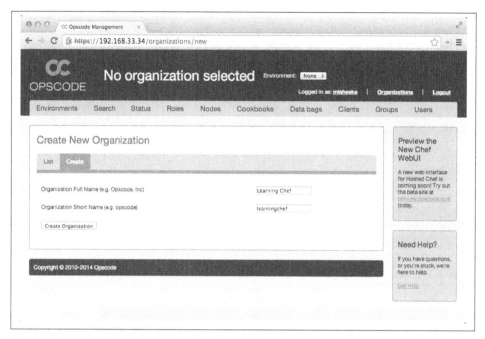

Figure 9-7. Create new organization

Copy the *<username>.pem*, *<organization>-validator.pem*, and *knife.rb* files to the *chef-repo/.chef* directory. Once you've copied these files, the *chef-repo* directory should resemble the following:

```
chef-repo/
├── .chef
│   ├── knife.rb
│   ├── <organization>-validator.pem
│   └── <username>.pem
└── cookbooks
    └── enterprise-chef
        ├── .kitchen
        ├── .kitchen.yml
        ├── Berksfile
        ├── Berksfile.lock
        ├── README.md
        ├── attributes
        │   └── default.rb
        ├── chefignore
        ├── metadata.rb
        └── recipes
            └── default.rb
```

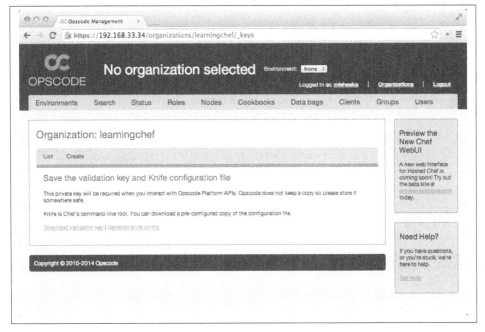

Figure 9-8. Save the validation key and Knife configuration file

Because we registered with the username "misheska" and the organization "learningchef," our *.chef* directory contains the following:

- *misheska.pem*
- *learningchef-validator.pem*
- *knife.rb*

The *<username>.pem* file is a unique identifier used to authenticate *you* against Chef Server. This should be treated like a password—do not share it with anyone and do not alter the contents of the file.

The *<organization>.pem* file is a unique identifier used to authenticate *your organization* against Chef Server. This should be treated like a password, but it must also be shared among all your Chef developers. Anyone needing access to your Chef organization will also need a copy of this file. Do not alter the contents of this file.

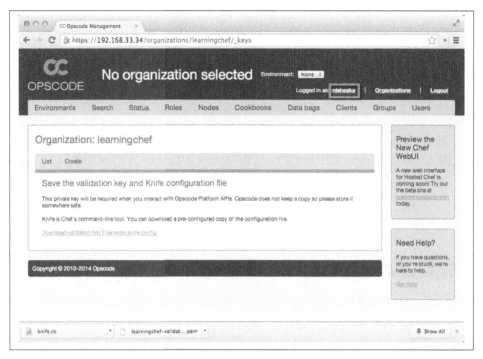

Figure 9-9. Click on your username link

RSA Key-Pairs

Chef *.pem* files contain the RSA private key generated during the signup process. Chef generates an RSA key-pair for your organization for you to download. The associated public key is stored on the Enterprise Chef Server and used to authenticate your organization when programs make requests to the server.

Unlike a *.pem* file, the *knife.rb* file is meant to be edited, altered, and customized. The *knife.rb* file is recognized as Ruby and read by Chef when it issues commands:

```
current_dir = File.dirname(__FILE__)
log_level                :info
log_location             STDOUT
node_name                "<username>"
client_key               "#{current_dir}/<username>.pem"
validation_client_name   "<organization>-validator"
validation_key           "#{current_dir}/<organization>-validator.pem"
chef_server_url          "https://default-centos65.vagrantup.com/\
organizations/learningchef"
cache_type               'BasicFile'
```

```
cache_options( :path => "#{ENV['HOME']}/.chef/checksums" )
cookbook_path           ["#{current_dir}/../cookbooks"]
```

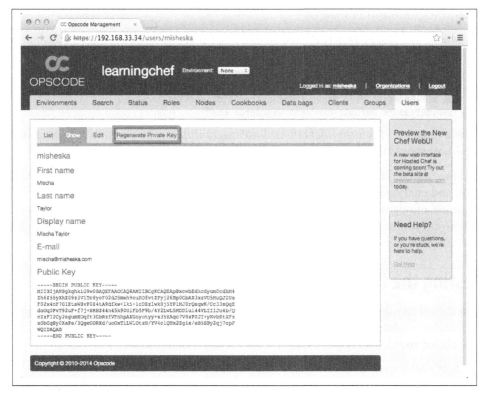

Figure 9-10. Regenerate private key

Note that the `chef_server_url` field in our example uses a fake DNS hostname of `default-centos65.vagrantup.com` because that's the hostname vagrant set up. If you try to visit the URL *https://default-centos65.vagrantup.com/organizations/learningchef*, you will discover that it is not valid.

Chef Server requires that hosts have valid fully qualified domain names set up in your local domain name service (DNS). In production, you would have your Chef Server hostname configured in your Domain Name System (DNS) server before installing Chef Server. Let's add a temporary host entry for `default-centos65.vagrantup.com` in your local host database in lieu of making a DNS change, as we are just doing a book exercise.

Run one of the following commands to add a host entry. Following are the commands we ran on our machine. If you used an IP address other than `192.168.33.34`, make sure it matches when you run the command.

Linux/Mac OS X:

```
$ sudo sh -c "echo '192.168.33.34 default-centos65.vagrantup.com' >> /etc/hosts"
```

Windows Command Prompt:

```
> echo 192.168.33.34 default-centos65.vagrantup.com >> \
%WINDIR%\System32\Drivers\Etc\Hosts
```

Windows PowerShell:

```
PS> ac -Encoding UTF8 $env:windir\system32\drivers\etc\hosts \
"192.168.33.34 default-centos65.vagrantup.com"
```

Now if you try to visit *https://default-centos65.vagrantup.com* in your web browser, your local host should think that this is a valid hostname.

You may add additional values to the *knife.rb*, such as EC2 credentials, proxy information, and encrypted data bag settings. Although certain pieces of the *knife.rb* will be common among your team members, the contents of the generally file should be unique to you and your machine. However, unless you have access keys and passwords in your *knife.rb*, you do not need to treat it like a password.

Testing the Connection

You should run the following commands from inside the Chef repository. Open your terminal or command prompt, and make *chef-repo* the current working directory. If you placed your Chef repo in a different location, use that instead:

```
$ cd ~/chef-repo
```

Now you can use knife, the command-line tool for Chef Server, to test your connection and authentication against Chef Server. At the time of this writing, Chef does not provide a "connection test" command. However, asking Chef Server to list the clients will verify

- Your network can connect to Chef Server.
- The authentication files are in the correct location.
- The authentication files can be read by Chef.
- The response from Chef Server is received by your workstation.

Issue the knife client list command on your terminal. You should see the following:

```
$ knife client list
learningchef-validator
```

If you get an error, check the following:

1. You can access *https://default-centos65.vagrantup.com:443* from a web browser.

2. You are running commands from inside the *chef-repo* directory.

3. The *.chef* directory contains two *.pem* files and a *knife.rb*.

4. Your authentication files have the correct file permissions (they should be only user-readable).

If you have confirmed the preceding steps and are still unable to connect to Chef Server, please consult the Chef online documentation (*http://docs.opscode.com*).

Now that you have verified that your host can connect to Chef Server, let's create another cookbook for a node instance and register it to be managed by Chef Server.

Bootstrapping a Node

In Chef, the term "bootstrapping" refers to the process by which a remote system is prepared to be managed by Chef. This process includes installing Chef Client and registering the target node with Chef Server.

Create a Node in a Sandbox Environment

Let's use Test Kitchen to define a project that spins up a node in a sandbox environment, similar to what we did back in Chapter 5 before we learned how to create cookbooks.

Create a node directory alongside the chef-server cookbook you created in this chapter. This technically isn't a cookbook—it's just a Test Kitchen project—but putting it beside the chef-server cookbook directory makes it convenient to go back and forth between the two.

Create the directory *~/chef-repo/cookbooks/node*, and make it the current working directory:

```
$ cd ~/chef-repo/cookbooks
$ mkdir node
$ cd node
```

The knife client list command should work even in this subdirectory. Verify this now:

```
$ knife client list
learningchef-validator
```

This node directory will just be a test kitchen project, not a cookbook, so run the following commands to create a *.kitchen.yml* file for Test Kitchen:

```
$ kitchen init --create-gemfile
$ bundle install
```

Edit the *.kitchen.yml* file, as in Example 9-5, to use the CentOS 6.5 basebox we prepared specifically for this book. Also assign a private network address like we did in Chapter 7. This time, we're going to use the IP address 192.168.33.35. Make sure this address does not conflict with the IP address of your Chef Server, which should be 192.168.33.34.

Note that we also changed the suite name to be node, as this sandbox environment will be running our node, but we also have another sandbox environment running our Chef Server. Having different names will disambiguate the two environments.

Also, we've configured a synced folder pointing at the root *chef-repo* directory. As shown in Figure 9-11, Vagrant can keep directories on your host Chef development workstation synchronized with directories in the sandbox environment running on the guest.

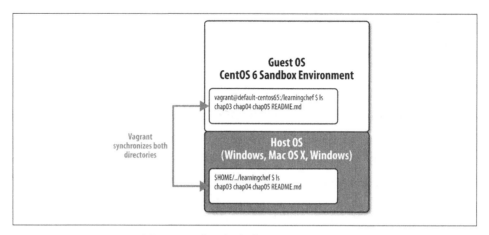

Figure 9-11. Overview of the Virtualized Chef Training Environment

The following synced_folders: stanza in a *.kitchen.yml* file ensures that the *chef-repo* directory on the host is kept in sync with the */chef-repo* directory on the guest:

```
...
    synced_folders:
    - ["../../../chef-repo", "/chef-repo"]
...
```

The */chef-repo* synced folder will be used later in Chapter 10 when we configure SSL verification with the server.

Example 9-5. chefdk/chef-repo/cookbooks/node/.kitchen.yml

```
---
driver:
  name: vagrant

provisioner:
  name: shell

platforms:
```

```
- name: centos65
  driver:
    box: learningchef/centos65
    box_url: learningchef/centos65
    network:
    - ["private_network", {ip: "192.168.33.35"}]
    synced_folders:
    - ["../../../chef-repo", "/chef-repo"]

suites:
- name: node
  attributes:
```

Spin up the node environment with `kitchen create`:

```
$ kitchen create
```

Bootstrap the Node with Knife

Figure 9-12 is an overview of the setup we've configured so far in this chapter. We've configured a Chef server (or used Hosted Enterprise Chef), and we configured a *knife.rb* with the appropriate keys so we can communicate with the Chef server from our host, the administrator's workstation. We've established that this communication channel works by verifying that `knife client list` produces the expected output.

Now let's set up our node like we would in production by "bootstrapping" the node with `knife bootstrap`. (((("Test Kitchen","in production environments")))We won't be able to use Test Kitchen in production!) When we run `knife bootstrap` on the our host, it will install Chef Client on the node and register it to be managed by Chef Server.

Nodes must have valid fully qualified domain names set up in your local domain name service (DNS) as well. Let's add an entry to our local host database for the node just like we did for Chef Server.

Run one of the following commands to add a node entry. Following are the commands we ran on our machine. If you used an IP address other than `192.168.33.35`, make sure it matches when you run the command.

Linux/Mac OS X:

```
$ sudo sh -c "echo '192.168.33.35 node-centos65.vagrantup.com' >> /etc/hosts"
```

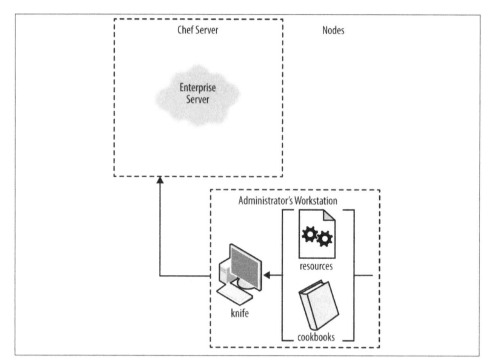

Figure 9-12. Overview of our setup so far, before nodes

Windows Command Prompt:

```
> echo 192.168.33.35 node-centos65.vagrantup.com >> \
%WINDIR%\System32\Drivers\Etc\Hosts
```

Windows PowerShell:

```
PS> ac -Encoding UTF8 $env:windir\system32\drivers\etc\hosts \
"192.168.33.35 node-centos65.vagrantup.com"
```

You also need to `kitchen login` to the node and configure the local host database on the node to provide it the name of the server when you run `chef-client`. Once complete, `exit` back out to your host prompt. As mentioned before, in production, you'd just make sure the DNS was configured with these hostnames before installing Chef Server and any nodes:

```
$ kitchen login node-centos65
Last login: Sat Aug 16 01:50:02 2014 from 192.168.33.1
Welcome to your Packer-built virtual machine.
[vagrant@node-centos65 ~]$ sudo sh -c "echo \
'192.168.33.34 default-centos65.vagrantup.com' >> /etc/hosts"
[vagrant@node-centos65 ~]$ exit
logout
Connection to 127.0.0.1 closed.
```

If you get the error "No instances for regex `node-centos65`," you forgot to change the suite name to *node*. Run `kitchen destroy` to clear the node instance with the incorrect name. Then refer to Example 9-5 and make sure the `suites` stanza resembles the following:

```
suites:
  - name: node
```

Run `kitchen create` again after making the correction.

Run the following command to bootstrap your node:

```
$ knife bootstrap --sudo --ssh-user vagrant --ssh-password \
vagrant --no-host-key-verify node-centos65.vagrantup.com
Connecting to node-centos65.vagrantup.com
node-centos65.vagrantup.com Installing Chef Client...
...
node-centos65.vagrantup.com Thank you for installing Chef!
node-centos65.vagrantup.com Starting first Chef Client run...
...
node-centos65.vagrantup.com Starting Chef Client, version 11.14.2
node-centos65.vagrantup.com Creating a new client identity for
node-centos65.vagrantup.com using the validator key.
node-centos65.vagrantup.com resolving cookbooks for run list: []
node-centos65.vagrantup.com Synchronizing Cookbooks:
node-centos65.vagrantup.com Compiling Cookbooks...
node-centos65.vagrantup.com [2014-08-16T01:56:43-07:00] WARN: Node
node-centos65.vagrantup.com has an empty run list.
node-centos65.vagrantup.com Converging 0 resources
node-centos65.vagrantup.com
node-centos65.vagrantup.com Running handlers:
node-centos65.vagrantup.com Running handlers complete
node-centos65.vagrantup.com Chef Client finished, 0/0 resources updated in
2.646571561 seconds
```

You can tell from the output that it successfully installed Chef Client, and even performed a courtesy Chef Client run.

To verify that the node is now registered on Chef Server, log into the web interface and click on the *Nodes* tab. Now you should see that you have a node registered with your Chef Server, as shown in Figure 9-13.

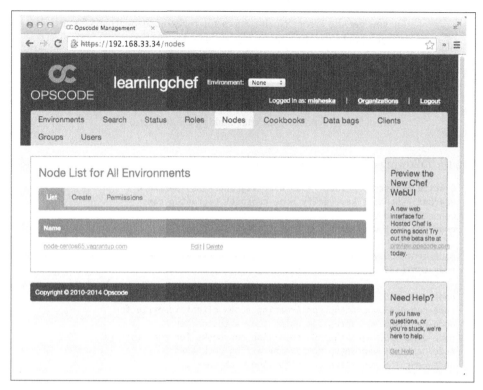

Figure 9-13. Node is registered with Chef Server

If you click on the link to the node, you should see that Chef Server displays information about the node as shown in Figure 9-14. The values you see under attributes should look familiar; these are the attributes generated automatically by ohai. They are stored on Chef Server for each node, and the data is searchable by all clients.

We'll be using both Chef Server and node sandbox instances in the next chapter, so don't kitchen destroy them just yet, as you don't want to have to go through all the setup steps you performed in this chapter. If you need to stop the virtual machines temporarily because you plan on powering off your machine before tackling the next chapter, you can use the vagrant halt command. Unfortunately, as of this writing, Test Kitchen doesn't have a way to halt or suspend virtual machines with the kitchen command, so you have to use the vagrant tool that Test Kitchen uses behind the scenes instead.

Figure 9-14. Node detail

In order to run `vagrant halt` to perform a graceful shutdown of your virtual machines, you'll need to make sure the *Vagrantfile* directory that is used by `vagrant` to configure the virtual machine is the current working directory. As of this writing, the associated Vagrantfiles are located in the *.kitchen* directory that Test Kitchen uses for temporary files in a directory matching the suite name in the *.kitchen.yml*. To halt both virtual machines, run the following commands:

```
$ cd ~/chef-repo/cookbooks/enterprise-chef/.kitchen/kitchen-vagrant/
$ default-centos65 vagrant halt
==> default: Attempting graceful shutdown of VM...
$ cd ~/chef-repo/cookbooks/node/.kitchen/kitchen-vagrant/node-centos65
$ vagrant halt
==> default: Attempting graceful shutdown of VM...
```

When you want to restart them, run `vagrant reload` against both Vagrantfiles:

```
$ cd ~/chef-repo/cookbooks/enterprise-chef/.kitchen/kitchen-vagrant/
$ default-centos65 vagrant reload
==> default: Checking if box 'learningchef/centos65' is up to date...
...
==> default: Booting VM...
==> default: Waiting for machine to boot. This may take a few minutes...
...
$ cd ~/chef-repo/cookbooks/node/.kitchen/kitchen-vagrant/node-centos65
$ vagrant reload
==> default: Checking if box 'learningchef/centos65' is up to date...
...
==> default: Booting VM...
==> default: Waiting for machine to boot. This may take a few minutes...
...
$ cd ~/chef-repo
```

Bootstrap Chef Server with Chef Solo

Before we conclude this chapter, it is worth mentioning that you can use Chef Solo outside of Test Kitchen to automate the deployment of Chef Server in production. We expect to see most Chef Solo-based software migrate to Chef Local/Chef Zero, as we covered in "Chef Client Modes" on page 92. However, Chef Solo is still singularly useful for bootstrapping Chef Server itself, as some scripts get confused about which server to communicate with when you try to set up Chef Server using Chef Local/Chef Zero, because Chef Zero launches a second in-memory Chef Server.

 Although we expect Chef coders to transition to Chef Local/Chef Zero, there are some truly amazing systems still built on Chef Solo. One tool worth checking out if you use Mac OS X is SoloWizard (*http://www.solowizard.com*), by Pivotal Labs. By filling out a simple web form you can have it automatically generate a Chef Solo-based script to auto-generate a Mac OS X development workstation. As of this writing, there is no Chef Local equivalent of this tool, but there might be one by the time you read this.

Here's an overview of the steps required to use Chef Solo to bootstrap Chef Server:

1. Install Chef Client (which includes `chef-solo`).

2. Create */var/chef/cache* and */var/chef/cookbooks* directories. These are the default locations where `chef-solo` stores state information and looks for cookbooks, respectively. (You can override these settings by supplying a *.json* file with configuration settings on the command line. See *http://docs.getchef.com/chef_solo.html* for more information.)

3. Copy any necessary cookbooks down to the host.

4. Run chef-solo.

Although we won't go through another hands-on exercise bootstrapping Chef Server with Chef Solo, as you've done this already with Test Kitchen, here are the commands you would use to perform the preceding steps:

```
# install chef-solo
$ curl -L https://www.getchef.com/chef/install.sh | sudo bash
# create required directories
$ sudo mkdir -p /var/chef/cache /var/chef/cookbooks
# copy your cookbook code to create a Chef Server - Chef Software
# provides a cookbook for open source Chef Server
$ sudo mkdir /var/chef/cookbooks/chef-server
$ wget -qO- https://github.com/opscode-cookbooks/chef-server/archive/\
master.tar.gz | sudo tar xvzC /var/chef/cookbooks/chef-server \
--strip-components=1
# Run chef-solo to bootstrap Chef Server
$ sudo chef-solo -o 'recipe[chef-server::default]'
```

 As of this writing, there is no Windows version of Chef Server. It is available on the Linux platform exclusively. That is why you see only Linux commands in the preceding code block.

Summary

In this chapter, we've covered the basics of installing Chef Server. We showed you how to install a test Chef Server setup driven by Chef recipes in both sandbox environments using Test Kitchen, and on production servers using chef-solo.

We also introduced the concept of idempotence when we covered how to write Chef code to install Chef Server. Chef code is idempotent when it can run multiple times on the same system and the results will always be identical, without producing unintended side effects.

Although nearly all the default Chef resources are guaranteed to be *idempotent*, the execute resource is not. We showed you how to test that Chef code is *idempotent* by performing a Chef run twice in succession, such as with kitchen converge. On the second run, idempotent Chef code should display no resource updates.

In the next chapter, we'll talk about the Chef Community Cookbook. We'll highlight the chef-client cookbook, an oft-used community cookbook people find useful in bootstrapping nodes in production.

## CHAPTER 10

Community and the Chef-Client Cookbook

In this chapter we'll be talking about the Chef community and community cookbooks. The Chef community site provides access to great Chef resources, including cookbooks, knife plug-ins, and the ability to connect to amazing people who create wonderful things built on Chef.

Before we get started, make sure you are running Chef Server and the node you created in Chapter 9. We'll be making heavy use of the `knife` command line tool in this chapter, and it requires a Chef Server setup to function.

Using Community Cookbooks

Although we've been writing all the cookbooks and recipes we've used so far in this book, so you can learn Chef coding, there is an easier way. There are hundreds of freely available prewritten Chef cookbooks to install and configure a variety of commonly used services and applications in production environments. For instance, there are cookbooks to help you set up Apache, Nginx, and IIS web servers and MySQL, PostgreSQL, Microsoft SQL Server, and Oracle databases. There are cookbooks to support the deployment of apps written in Java, Ruby, Python, PHP, node.js, and much, much more!

You can browse and download these community cookbooks from Chef Software's Chef Supermarket (*https://community.opscode.com/*) community hub, and from a variety of other locations including GitHub. Some of these cookbooks were created and are maintained by Chef Software, but the majority are developed by Chef users. In general, as with any third-party software, you should always independently verify the behavior and flexibility of a community cookbook in an isolated environment before using it in production.

Always verify that the cookbook's license is suitable for your organization!

What *is* a Community Cookbook?

A community cookbook is a tarball (`.tar.gz`) package of the cookbook structure discussed Chapter 7. It is packaged in this manner for easy cross-platform distribution. At its core, a community cookbook is exactly the same as an internally authored cookbook.

The best place to find free community cookbooks is the Chef Supermarket (*https://supermarket.getchef.com/*). This site is a Ruby on Rails application hosted and maintained by Chef Software where you can share, contribute, download, use, rate, and review community cookbooks. Chef Supermarket is akin to rubygems.org, cpan.org, and other focused distribution sites. You can log in to Chef Supermarket using the same credentials as your Hosted Enterprise Chef account. Once you have logged in, you will be able to comment on and follow cookbooks of interest and contribute your own cookbooks to the community.

You do *not* need to log in to the Chef Marketplace to *download* or *use* its community cookbooks.

The Chef Supermarket lets you search for cookbooks by name or description as shown in Figure 10-1.

Chef Supermarket will query cookbook names, descriptions, platforms, categories, and other metadata. You can even sort results by *most downloaded* or *most followed*. Take time exploring to find the best cookbooks for you.

If you do not find the cookbook you are looking for at Chef Supermarket, your next obvious bet is a good old-fashioned Internet search. Chef Supermarket is not the sole authority on cookbooks; GitHub also has good cookbooks, such as Fletcher Nichol's rvm cookbook.

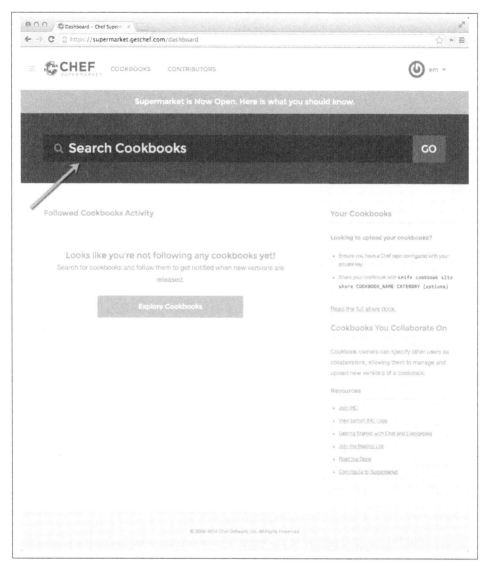

Figure 10-1. Search for free cookbooks on the Chef Supermarket site

Chef-Client Cookbook

One community cookbook you should be aware of is the chef-client cookbook. Go ahead and search for it now at Chef Supermarket. Figure 10-2 shows the search results you should get for chef-client.

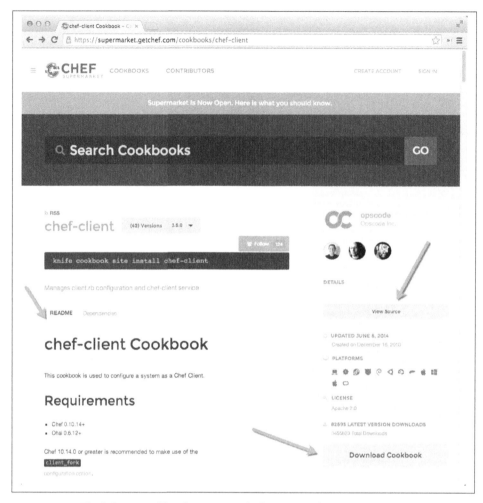

Figure 10-2. Chef-client cookbook entry at Chef Supermarket

The arrows in Figure 10-2 point out the most important components on the page when a cookbook is displayed in the Chef Supermarket. Front and center (well, actually, a little to the left) is a rendered version of the *README.md* file. Well-written *README* files, like the one in the chef-client cookbook, tell you what problem the cookbook is trying to solve, plus how to use the cookbook.

On the right are two big buttons, *View Source* and *Download Cookbook*. The View Source button will take you to the cookbook source code. (Usually it's some link on the GitHub source hosting service.) From there you can inspect the cookbook more closely. Finally there is the Download Cookbook button, which lets you download a tarball containing the cookbook source.

The chef-client cookbook is a popular cookbook because it makes two things easy:

1. Configuring chef-client to run as a service or a cron job
2. Deleting the *validation.pem* file

Because one of the design goals for Chef Server is scalability, the server tries to offload as much processing as it can onto the nodes. So by default, the node is responsible for scheduling and initiating a chef-client run and performing all the related processing, not Chef Server. Chef Server itself is really just a dumb artifact repository for cookbooks and other associated metadata about your infrastructure.

When you bootstrap a node with knife in order to install chef-client, as we did in "Bootstrap the Node with Knife" on page 171, the bootstrap process does not configure chef-client to download any cookbook updates or perform Chef runs at regular intervals. You'll definitely want to configure all your nodes to do this on a regular basis, say, every 15 to 30 minutes. The chef-client cookbook makes it easy to configure chef-client to run as a service or a cron job.

Also, it's important to delete the *validation.pem* file after the first Chef run. With Enterprise Chef, this file is called *<organization-validator>.pem* by default. With Open Source Chef Server, the file is called *validation.pem* by default. To explain why deleting the *validation.pem* file is important, we need to provide a quick explanation of how requests by nodes are verified by Chef Server.

Chef Server requires that every request chef-client makes to the server be authenticated using a client public/private key pair. Every node has its own special public/private key pair. You have already seen this because users have their own special public/private key pair as well—you needed to download the *<username.pem>* file to configure knife to make requests against Chef Server. The *<username>.pem* file you downloaded contains the private portion of the key pair. The public portion of this key is stored on Chef Server, and the key is used to authenticate you as a valid Chef Server user.

Similarly, there is a *.pem* for each node that runs chef-client containing a private key. We'll call this *client.pem* for the sake of discussion. Figure 10-3 presents an overview of how this key is used to verify that requests come from a node. In this example, Node A has a private key, which is a unique *client.pem* file that lives on the node. When the *client.pem* file was created, an associated public key was generated and stored on the Chef server. Node A signs all HTTP requests it makes to Chef Server with its private key. When Chef Server receives a request, it verifies that the signature is from Node A by using Node A's public key to ensure it is a legitimate request from Node A.

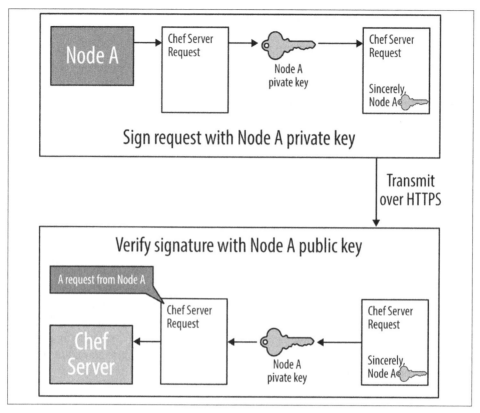

Figure 10-3. How Chef Server verifies a request from a node

When you run `chef-client` for the first time, there is a problem—you don't have a *client.pem* file for your node yet, and a corresponding public key for the node does not exist on the Chef server. To solve this bootstrapping issue, a node uses a company-wide, well-known key when it generates the request to register the node as a client. That's what the *validation.pem* key is for. The *validation.pem* is an organization-wide private key used specifically to sign the request to register a new node with Chef Server on the first `chef-client` run.

Chef Server performs a validation of a signature using the *validator.pem* similar to the one it performs with the *client.pem*. During the bootstrap process, the *validator.pem* is created with the name */etc/chef/validation.pem* on the node.

Although the */etc/chef/validation.pem* is secured with root privileges, it's a good idea to delete it once the node has a proper client key to run `chef-client`. Anyone who obtains the */etc/chef/validation.pem* file can create new nodes. Once the node has a client key, it no longer needs the */etc/chef/validation.pem*. It's a good idea to leave the */etc/chef/*

validation.pem key on the node only during the time it actually needs to create a client public/private key pair for itself and send its client public key to Chef Server.

You can verify that the *validation.pem* file is still present on the node you bootstrapped in Chapter 9. Make sure the *chef-repo/cookbooks/node* directory is the current working directory by running one of the following commands. If the parent of your `chef-repo` tree is not $HOME, change the command to reflect the correct parent.

Linux/Mac OS X:

```
$ cd $HOME/chef-repo/cookbooks/node
```

Windows Command Prompt:

```
> cd %USERPROFILE%\chef-repo\cookbooks\node
```

Windows PowerShell:

```
> cd $HOME\chef-repo\cookbooks\node
```

Use `kitchen login` to ssh into the node, as follows. Check the contents of the directory with */etc/chef/validation.pem*. Note that it is still there. Then make sure you exit back out to your host prompt:

```
$ kitchen login
Last login: Thu Aug 14 20:14:59 2014 from 192.168.33.1
Welcome to your Packer-built virtual machine.
[vagrant@default-centos65 ~]$ ls /etc/chef
client.pem  client.rb  first-boot.json  validation.pem
[vagrant@default-centos65 ~]$ exit
logout
Connection to 127.0.0.1 closed.
```

We'll talk more about the use of the `chef-client` recipe later, in "Chef-Client Recipes" on page 190. First, we need to talk about the `knife cookbook site` plugin.

Knife Cookbook Site Plugin

While the Chef Supermarket's *Download Cookbook* link is very helpful, you still need to upload the cookbook source to your Chef Server in order to use it in production. Also, although a website is great for discovery, you'll find yourself wanting to use a command-line tool for day-to-day community cookbook management because it is faster. All recent versions of both the Chef Client and the Chef Development Kit ship with a cookbook site plugin for knife designed to enable command-line interaction with the Chef Supermarket.

Let's walk you through the most commonly use subcommands now. Feel free to type them in if you like. Make sure your current working directory is the *chef-repo* from Chapter 9. Assuming that the *chef-repo* is located in your home directory, run one of the following commands, depending on your platform. Change the root path to suit where you created *chef-repo*.

Linux/Mac OS X:

```
$ cd $HOME/chef-repo
```

Windows Command Prompt:

```
> cd %USERPROFILE%\chef-repo
```

Windows PowerShell:

```
> cd $HOME\chef-repo
```

Search for Community Cookbooks Using Knife Cookbook Site

You can use the `knife cookbook site search` command to search the Chef Supermarket for cookbooks. You will need to specify a search string as a parameter. `knife cookbook site` will search the following fields in the cookbook metadata at Chef Supermarket:

- name
- URL
- description
- maintainer

The `knife cookbook site` plugin will perform simple substring matching using your search string. Try it now with a `chef-client` query:

```
$ knife cookbook site search chef-client
chef:
  cookbook:              http://cookbooks.opscode.com/api/v1/cookbooks/chef
  cookbook_description: Installs and configures Chef for chef-client and
  chef-server
  cookbook_maintainer:  chef
  cookbook_name:        chef
chef-client:
  cookbook:              http://cookbooks.opscode.com/api/v1/cookbooks/
  chef-client
  cookbook_description: Manages client.rb configuration and chef-client service
  cookbook_maintainer:  chef
  cookbook_name:        chef-client
  ...
```

There's also a related `knife cookbook site show` command to display more detailed information about a cookbook, when you can provide a cookbook name. Try it now for the `chef-client` cookbook:

```
$ knife cookbook site show chef-client
average_rating:
category:       Other
created_at:     2010-12-16T23:00:45.000Z
deprecated:     false
description:    Manages client.rb configuration and chef-client service
external_url:   http://github.com/opscode-cookbooks/chef-client
latest_version: http://cookbooks.opscode.com/api/v1/cookbooks/chef-client
                /versions/3.7.0
maintainer:     chef
...
name:           chef-client
updated_at:     2014-08-13T17:18:54.109Z
...
```

Manage Chef Supermarket Cookbooks on Your Chef Server Using Knife Cookbook Site

Although the search/show capabilities of `knife cookbook site` are helpful, you'll use this plugin most often to download cookbooks from Chef Supermarket and upload community cookbooks to your local Chef Server. In order to download a cookbook from Chef Supermarket and upload it to your Chef Server, you must perform three steps:

1. Download the cookbook using `knife cookbook site download`.
2. Extract the cookbook package with tar.
3. Upload the cookbook using `knife cookbook upload`.
4. Repeat steps 1-3 for any cookbook dependencies.

Let's go through this process now for the `chef-client` cookbook. Download the `chef-client` with `knife cookbook site download` as follows:

```
$ knife cookbook site download chef-client 3.7.0
Downloading chef-client from the cookbooks site at version 3.7.0 to
/Users/misheska/learningchef/chef-repo/chef-client-3.7.0.tar.gz
Cookbook saved: /Users/misheska/learningchef/chef-repo/chef-client-3.7.0.tar.gz
```

 I've specified the version in all these commands because cookbooks change frequently, even though you don't have to specify a version to get the very latest cookbook.

The downloaded cookbook package is a `.tar.gz` file (a gzip-compressed `.tar` file). You'll need to extract it with the `tar` command. Use the `-C` option to make sure the cookbook is extracted as *chef-repo/cookbooks/chef-client*. You'll want to store all downloaded cookbooks in *chef-repo/cookbooks*. Use the `tar` command to extract the archive.

Linux/Mac OS X:

```
$ tar xvf chef-client*.tar.gz -C cookbooks/
x chef-client/README.md
x chef-client/CHANGELOG.md
x chef-client/metadata.json
x chef-client/metadata.rb
x chef-client/attributes/default.rb
x chef-client/files/default
x chef-client/files/default/tests
...
```

Windows:

```
$ bash tar xvf .\chef-client-3.7.0.tar.gz -C cookbooks
x chef-client/README.md
x chef-client/CHANGELOG.md
x chef-client/metadata.json
x chef-client/metadata.rb
x chef-client/attributes/default.rb
x chef-client/files/default
x chef-client/files/default/tests
...
```

 The `tar` program provided with Chef on Windows does not correctly expand filenames that include wildcards, such as `chef-client*.tar.gz`. On Windows, the easiest workaround is to provide the full file name. Thankfully, all the Windows shell programs support tab-completion. So you need only type in the first few letters of `chef-client-3.7.0.tar.gz`, then hit the Tab key and the shell should expand to use the full filename.

Unfortunately, if you try to upload the `chef-client` cookbook to your Chef Server right now, you'll get an error that resembles the following:

```
$ knife cookbook upload chef-client —cookbook-path cookbooks
Uploading chef-client [3.7.0]
ERROR: Cookbook chef-client depends on cookbooks which are not currently
ERROR: being uploaded and cannot be found on the server.
ERROR: The missing cookbook(s) are: 'cron' version '>= 1.2.0', 'logrotate'
version '>= 1.2.0'
```

If you recall when we introduced `include_recipe` in "Include_Recipe" on page 137 cookbooks can contain a chain of references to other cookbooks. These references are called *dependencies*, and are noted in the *metadata.rb* of a cookbook using the *de-*

pends statement. If you take a look at the *metadata.rb* (*http://bit.ly/metadata_rb*) file for the chef-client cookbook, you'll see that it resembles the following:

```
name                'chef-client'
maintainer          'Opscode, Inc.'
maintainer_email    'cookbooks@opscode.com'
license             'Apache 2.0'
description         'Manages client.rb configuration and chef-client service'
long_description    IO.read(File.join(File.dirname(__FILE__), 'README.md'))
version             '3.7.0'
...
depends 'cron', '>= 1.2.0'
depends 'logrotate', '>= 1.2.0'
```

There are depends statements at the bottom of the *metadata.rb* file that state chef-client is dependent on the cron and logrotate cookbooks. Exactly the two cookbooks mentioned in the error message! This is where you will need to repeat the knife cookbook site > un-tar > knife cookbook upload cycle for any cookbook dependencies.

So, download these two additional cookbooks with the knife cookbook site command, like so:

```
$ knife cookbook site download cron 1.4.0
$ knife cookbook site download logrotate 1.6.0
```

Extract them to *chef-repo/cookbooks/* using the tar command, like you did for the chef-client cookbook.

Linux/Mac OS X:

```
$ tar xvf cron*.tar.gz -C cookbooks/
$ tar xvf logrotate*.tar.gz -C cookbooks/
```

Windows:

```
$ tar xvf cron-1.4.0.tar.gz -C cookbooks
$ tar xvf logrotate-1.6.0.tar.gz -C cookbooks
```

Finally, upload all the cookbooks, cron, logrotate, and chef-client, using knife cookbook upload, taking care to upload chef-client *after* its dependencies:

```
$ knife cookbook upload cron --cookbook-path cookbooks
Uploading cron          [1.4.0]
Uploaded 1 cookbook.
$ knife cookbook upload logrotate --cookbook-path cookbooks
Uploading logrotate     [1.6.0]
Uploaded 1 cookbook.
$ knife cookbook upload chef-client --cookbook-path cookbooks
Uploading chef-client   [3.7.0]
Uploaded 1 cookbook.
```

Chef-Client Recipes

Now let's perform a Chef run adding two recipes to the run-list we touched on in "Chef-Client Cookbook" on page 181:

1. `chef-client::default` recipe—Configures `chef-client` to run as a service
2. `chef-client::delete_validation` recipe—Deletes the */etc/chef/validation.pem* file

Use `knife node run_list add` to add the `chef-client::delete_validation` recipe to the node's run list. For all `knife` command lines, recipes are referenced in a run list in the form `"recipe[<cookbook>::<recipe>]"`; for example, `"recipe[chef-client::delete_validation]"`.

Run the following `knife node run_list add` command to add `"recipe[chef-client::delete_validation]"` to the `node-centos65.vagrantup.com` node's run list that we bootstrapped in Chapter 9:

```
$ knife node run_list add node-centos65.vagrantup.com \
"recipe[chef-client::delete_validation]"
node-centos65.vagrantup.com:
  run_list: recipe[chef-client::delete_validation]
```

> If you need a reminder of what the node name is, run the following command:
>
> ```
> $ knife node list
> node-centos65.vagrantup.com
> ```

Also add the `chef-client::default` recipe to the run list. Note that you can use a shorthand notation using just the cookbook name, when you want to use the `default` recipe. Run the following command now:

```
$ knife node run_list add node-centos65.vagrantup.com "recipe[chef-client]"
node-centos65.vagrantup.com:
  run_list:
    recipe[chef-client::delete_validation]
    recipe[chef-client]
```

Both the `chef-client::delete_validation` and `chef-client::default` recipes have been added to the node's run list, and will be processed in the order provided.

> You can add more than one recipe at a time to a run list—just separate the recipe names with commas:
>
> ```
> $ knife node run_list add <node> \
> "recipe[<cookbook>::<recipe>],recipe[<cookbook>::<recipe>]"
> ```

Make sure the *chef-repo/cookbooks/node* directory is the current working directory, by running one of the following commands. If the parent of your *chef-repo* tree is not $HOME, change the command to reflect the correct parent.

Linux/Mac OS X:

```
$ cd $HOME/chef-repo/cookbooks/node
```

Windows Command Prompt:

```
> cd %USERPROFILE%\chef-repo\cookbooks\node
```

Windows PowerShell:

```
> cd $HOME\chef-repo\cookbooks\node
```

Perform an initial chef-client run by using kitchen login to ssh into the node, and then run sudo chef-client as follows:

```
$ kitchen login
Last login: Sat Jul 26 01:17:10 2014 from 192.168.33.1
Welcome to your Packer-built virtual machine.
[vagrant@node-centos65 ~]$ sudo chef-client
...
  * service[chef-client] action enable
    - enable service service[chef-client]

  * service[chef-client] action start
    - start service service[chef-client]

  * service[chef-client] action restart
    - restart service service[chef-client]


Running handlers:
Running handlers complete

Chef Client finished, 10/11 resources updated in 8.137774709 seconds
```

While you are still on the node, verify that the *validation.pem* was deleted and that the chef-client is now running as a daemon:

```
[vagrant@node-centos65 ~]$ ls /etc/chef
client.pem  client.rb  first-boot.json
[vagrant@node-centos65 ~]$ ps awux | grep chef-client
root      2184  0.0  7.9 217180 40152 ?        Sl   21:52
0:00 /opt/chef/embedded/bin/ruby /usr/bin/chef-client -d -c
/etc/chef/client.rb -L /var/log/chef/client.log -P /var/run/chef/client.pid
-i 1800 -s 300
```

Return back to the host prompt now:

```
[vagrant@node-centos65 ~]$ exit
```

Configure Knife to Use a Production SSL Setup

In Chapter 6, we mentioned the SSL warning you get running `chef-client` on the node when HTTPS connections are not validated. Before we end this chapter, let's go over how you would configure SSL in a production environment.

On the node, SSL verification is controlled through settings in the file */etc/chef/ client.rb*, the file that configures `chef-client`. You can enable this setting by setting attributes in the `chef-client` cookbook. Nearly everything in the `chef-client` cookbook is controllable through attributes.

Cookbooks Should Change Behavior Based on Attributes

Well-written cookbooks change behavior based on attributes. Ideally, you shouldn't have to modify the contents of a cookbook to accommodate your needs.

Look at the attributes directory for things you can override to change the behavior of a cookbook. Well-written cookbook also have sane defaults, and a *README.md* file to describe how the attributes influence cookbook behavior.

SSL setups can be quite complex to set up. So it is recommended that you first validate the setup with `knife` on your development workstation, before trying to configure your nodes to use verified SSL connections. Let's do that now. We'll use a simple setup that makes use of the self-signed certificate that was generated when you installed Chef Server in Chapter 9.

You will need to make sure that Chef Server is configured to use a certificate you intend to be used to verify communication over HTTPS. By default, Chef Server automatically generates a self-signed certificate during the installation. If you want to use the self-signed certificate, everything is already set up for you. In this exercise, we'll use the self-signed certificate.

Refer to the Chef documentation (*http://bit.ly/chef_security*) for more information on how to configure ChefServer with a certificate authority-verified certificate.

Also, a Chef community member, Mislav Marohnić, wrote an excellent blog post on troubleshooting Chef Server SSL issues (*http://bit.ly/ ruby_openssl*) and published a set of scripts to help troubleshoot connection issues (*http://bit.ly/ssl-tools*).

Once the certificate is configured on Chef Server, run `knife ssl check` on your development workstation to find out what you need to do next. You should see output similar to the following:

```
$ knife ssl check
Connecting to host 192.168.33.34:443
ERROR: The SSL certificate of 192.168.33.34 could not be verified
Certificate issuer data: /C=US/ST=WA/L=Seattle/O=YouCorp/OU=Operations/CN
=default-centos65.vagrantup.com/emailAddress=you@example.com

Configuration Info:

OpenSSL Configuration:
* Version: OpenSSL 1.0.1h 5 Jun 2014
* Certificate file: /opt/chefdk/embedded/ssl/cert.pem
* Certificate directory: /opt/chefdk/embedded/ssl/certs
Chef SSL Configuration:
* ssl_ca_path: nil
* ssl_ca_file: nil
* trusted_certs_dir:
"/Users/misheska/learningchef/chef-repo/.chef/trusted_certs"

TO FIX THIS ERROR:

If the server you are connecting to uses a self-signed certificate, you must
configure chef to trust that server's certificate.

By default, the certificate is stored in the following location on the host
where your chef-server runs:

  /var/opt/chef-server/nginx/ca/SERVER_HOSTNAME.crt

Copy that file to your trusted_certs_dir (currently:
/Users/misheska/learningchef/chef-repo/.chef/trusted_certs)
using SSH/SCP or some other secure method, then re-run this command to confirm
that the server's certificate is now trusted.
```

The `knife ssl check` command says that you need to copy the certificate to your `trusted_certs_dir`. Run the command `knife ssl fetch` to automatically download the certificate and place it in your `trusted_certs_dir`:

```
$ knife ssl fetch
WARNING: Certificates from 192.168.33.34 will be fetched and placed in your
trusted_cert directory
(/Users/misheska/learningchef/chef-repo/.chef/trusted_certs).

Knife has no means to verify these are the correct certificates. You should
verify the authenticity of these certificates after downloading.

Adding certificate for default-centos65.vagrantup.com in /Users/misheska
/learningchef/chef-repo/.chef/trusted_certs/default-centos65_vagrantup_com.crt
```

Run `knife ssl check` one final time, and it should verify successfully. If not, double-check to make sure the local hosts entry is correct, and that the hostname matched the expected name/IP when you ran `knife ssl check` in the previous step:

```
$ knife ssl check
Connecting to host default-centos65.vagrantup.com:443
Successfully verified certificates from `default-centos65.vagrantup.com'
```

Configure Chef-Client to Use a Production SSL Setup

The `chef-client` cookbook includes a recipe `chef-client::config`, which can be used to automatically generate the */etc/chef/client.rb* config file with the SSL settings we need. In this way you can automate the configuration of SSL on your nodes.

Log in to the node and check the */etc/chef/client.rb* file. The *client.rb* file was created to configure `chef-client` settings when you ran `knife bootstrap` on the node. Notice that it resembles the following. Make sure you log back out to the exist prompt when you are done.

```
$ kitchen login
Last login: Sat Aug 16 09:06:12 2014 from 10.0.2.2
Welcome to your Packer-built virtual machine.
[vagrant@node-centos65 ~]$ cat /etc/chef/client.rb
log_location      STDOUT
chef_server_url
"https://default-centos65.vagrantup.com/organizations/learningchef"
validation_client_name "learningchef-validator"
# Using default node name (fqdn)

[vagrant@node-centos65 ~]$ exit
logout
Connection to 127.0.0.1 closed.
```

In order to enable verification of the SSL certificate on the server, we need to add the following setting to */etc/chef/client.rb* (the default setting is `:verify_none`):

```
ssl_verify_mode :verify_peer
```

To enable this setting and have the `chef-client::config` recipe generate the appropriate configuration setting, we need to set the following attribute:

```
node.default['chef_client']['config']['ssl_verify_mode'] = ':verify_peer'
```

We'll do this by using Chef Server's management site (*https://default-centos65.vagrantup.com/*). Once you log in, click on the *Nodes* tab, then click on the *Edit* link for `node-centos65.vagrantup.com` as shown in Figure 10-4.

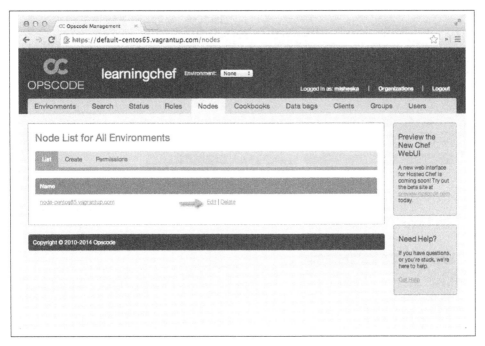

Figure 10-4. Node actions

The node editing page will be displayed. We'll be using the node attributes portion of the page at the bottom, as shown in Figure 10-5.

Click on the *source* tab for attributes. Enter in the text as shown in Figure 10-6. This is the attribute setting `node.default['chef_client']['config']['ssl_veri fy_mode'] = ':verify_peer'` in JSON format. If you are reading this book in electronic format, feel free to copy and paste the following text into the *json* edit box:

```
{
  "chef_client": {
    "config": {
      "ssl_verify_mode": ":verify_peer"
    }
  }
}
```

Once you are done typing in the attribute value, click on the *Load JSON from Source* icon in the editing pane as shown in Figure 10-7. This will update the attribute setting in the `json` tree on the left. Then click on the *Save Node* button. If there is no syntax error, you should see this message: *The node was updated successfully.*

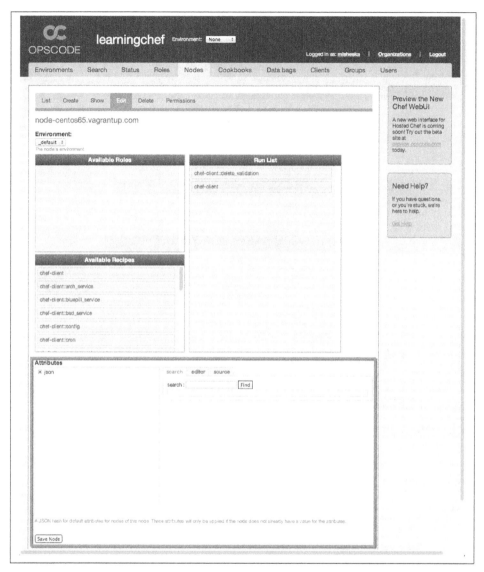

Figure 10-5. Edit node attributes web tool

You can also edit node attributes on the command line with the `knife node edit` command.

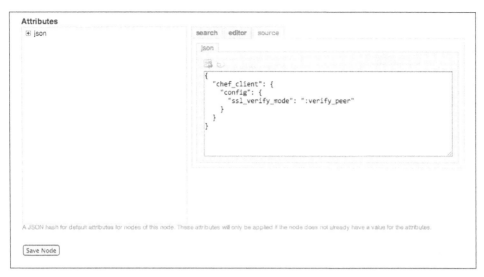

Figure 10-6. Set node.default['chef_client']['config']['ssl_verify_mode'] = ':verify_peer'

On the command line, verify that the attribute was set back in your *chef-repo* directory. Use the knife node show --attribute command to display the chef_client.ssl_ver ify_mode attribute for the node, as follows:

```
$ knife node list
node-centos65.vagrantup.com
$ knife node show --attribute "chef_client.config.ssl_verify_mode" \
node-centos65.vagrantup.com
node-centos65.vagrantup.com:
    chef_client.config.ssl_verify_mode: :verify_peer
```

If the output does not match exactly, make sure that you remembered to click on the Save Node button. It is easy to forget because it's at the bottom of the page outside the editing window. Also make sure that you remembered to click on the *Load JSON from Source* button, and make sure the json tree rendered on the left matches the figure exactly.

Because we are using a self-signed certificate, we need to set one more attribute setting. We need to tell the SSL library on the node that we trust the self-signed server certificate. In production, you'd do this by writing a recipe that adds the custom certificate to the certificate store. If you are using OpenSSL on your node, you will need to copy the certificate to the *SSL_CERT_DIR*, the directory where trusted certificates are stored, and run c_rehash to register the self-signed certificate.

Figure 10-7. Click on the icon to update the attribute setting in the json tree, then click on Save Node

In our test setup, we simulate this with the synchronized folder we set up for the node that we configured in Chapter 9. The synchronized folder makes the certificate we have in *chef-repo/.chef/trusted_certs* locally on our host available on the node. This directory was set up when you ran `knife ssl fetch`.

Go back to the Chef Server web interface, and add the `ssl_ca_file` attribute to the node. Copy and paste the following JSON source:

```
{
  "chef_client": {
    "config": {
      "ssl_verify_mode": ":verify_peer",
      "ssl_ca_file":
      "/chef-repo/.chef/trusted_certs/default-centos65_vagrantup_com.crt"
    }
  }
}
```

Double-check to make sure the settings for `chef_client.config.ssl_verify_mode` and `chef_client.config.ssl_ca_file` are correct by checking them with `knife node show --attribute` as follows. Make sure these settings match exactly, and the /chef-repo/.chef/trusted_certs/default-centos65_vagrantup_com.crt is synced to your node before going further:

```
$ knife node show --attribute "chef_client.config.ssl_verify_mode" \
node-centos65.vagrantup.com
node-centos65.vagrantup.com:
  chef_client.config.ssl_verify_mode: :verify_peer
```

```
$ knife node show --attribute "chef_client.config.ssl_ca_file" \
node-centos65.vagrantup.com
node-centos65.vagrantup.com:
  chef_client.config.ssl_ca_file: /chef-repo/.chef/trusted_certs/
  default-centos65_vagrantup_com.crt
$ kitchen login
Last login: Sat Aug 16 10:29:58 2014 from 10.0.2.2
Welcome to your Packer-built virtual machine.
[vagrant@node-centos65 ~]$ ls /chef-repo/.chef/trusted_certs
default-centos65_vagrantup_com.crt
[vagrant@node-centos65 ~]$ exit
logout
Connection to 127.0.0.1 closed.
```

Once you have verified all the settings are correct, add the chef-client::config recipe
to your node's run list:

```
$ knife node run_list add node-centos65.vagrantup.com \
"recipe[chef-client::config]"
node-centos65.vagrantup.com:
  run_list:
    recipe[chef-client::delete_validation]
    recipe[chef-client]
    recipe[chef-client::config]
```

Then log in to the node and perform a Chef run. Because you added the chef-
client::config recipe to your run list, Chef will make sure that the /etc/chef/
client.rb matches the settings corresponding to the attributes you set on the node. You'll
get the SSL warning one more time as chef-client hasn't yet applied your SSL verification settings:

```
$ kitchen login node-centos65
$ sudo chef-client
[2014-08-16T10:45:52-07:00] WARN:
* * * * * * * * * * * * * * * * * * * * * * * * * * * * * * * * * * * *
SSL validation of HTTPS requests is disabled. HTTPS connections are still
encrypted, but chef is not able to detect forged replies or man in the middle
attacks.
...
* * * * * * * * * * * * * * * * * * * * * * * * * * * * * * * * * * * *

Starting Chef Client, version 11.14.2
resolving cookbooks for run list: ["chef-client::delete_validation",
"chef-client", "chef-client::config"]
Synchronizing Cookbooks:
  - cron
  - chef-client
  - logrotate
Compiling Cookbooks...
...
Converging 17 resources
Recipe: chef-client::delete_validation
```

```
    * file[/etc/chef/validation.pem] action delete (up to date)
  Recipe: chef-client::init_service
    * directory[/var/run/chef] action create (up to date)
    * directory[/var/cache/chef] action create (up to date)
    * directory[/var/lib/chef] action create (up to date)
    * directory[/var/log/chef] action create (up to date)
    * directory[/etc/chef] action create (up to date)
    * template[/etc/init.d/chef-client] action create (up to date)
    * template[/etc/sysconfig/chef-client] action create (up to date)
    * service[chef-client] action enable (up to date)
    * service[chef-client] action start (up to date)
  Recipe: chef-client::config
    * directory[/var/run/chef] action create (up to date)
    * directory[/var/cache/chef] action create (up to date)
    * directory[/var/lib/chef] action create (up to date)
    * directory[/var/log/chef] action create (up to date)
    * directory[/etc/chef] action create (up to date)
    * template[/etc/chef/client.rb] action create
      - update content in file /etc/chef/client.rb from 6d6918 to 934e27
      --- /etc/chef/client.rb    2014-08-16 10:45:47.725998848 -0700
      +++ /tmp/chef-rendered-template20140816-5689-wqon53 2014-08-16 10:45:54
      .766997307 -0700
      @@ -1,5 +1,7 @@
       chef_server_url "https://default-centos65.vagrantup.com/organizations
       /learningchef"
       validation_client_name "learningchef-validator"
      +ssl_verify_mode :verify_peer
      +ssl_ca_file "/chef-repo/.chef/trusted_certs/
      default-centos65_vagrantup_com.crt"
       # Using default node name (fqdn)


    * ruby_block[reload_client_config] action create
      - execute the ruby block reload_client_config
    * directory[/etc/chef/client.d] action create (up to date)
    * ruby_block[reload_client_config] action nothing (skipped due to action :nothing)

  Running handlers:
  Running handlers complete
  Chef Client finished, 2/18 resources updated in 2.654285226 seconds
```

Now, if you run chef-client one more time, finally there is no more SSL warning:

```
$ sudo chef-client
Starting Chef Client, version 11.14.2
resolving cookbooks for run list: ["chef-client::delete_validation",
"chef-client", "chef-client::config"]
Synchronizing Cookbooks:
  - cron
  - logrotate
  - chef-client
Compiling Cookbooks...
...
```

```
Converging 17 resources
Recipe: chef-client::delete_validation
  * file[/etc/chef/validation.pem] action delete (up to date)
Recipe: chef-client::init_service
  * directory[/var/run/chef] action create (up to date)
  * directory[/var/cache/chef] action create (up to date)
  * directory[/var/lib/chef] action create (up to date)
  * directory[/var/log/chef] action create (up to date)
  * directory[/etc/chef] action create (up to date)
  * template[/etc/init.d/chef-client] action create (up to date)
  * template[/etc/sysconfig/chef-client] action create (up to date)
  * service[chef-client] action enable (up to date)
  * service[chef-client] action start (up to date)
Recipe: chef-client::config
  * directory[/var/run/chef] action create (up to date)
  * directory[/var/cache/chef] action create (up to date)
  * directory[/var/lib/chef] action create (up to date)
  * directory[/var/log/chef] action create (up to date)
  * directory[/etc/chef] action create (up to date)
  * template[/etc/chef/client.rb] action create (up to date)
  * directory[/etc/chef/client.d] action create (up to date)
  * ruby_block[reload_client_config] action nothing (skipped due to
  action :nothing)

Running handlers:
Running handlers complete
Chef Client finished, 0/17 resources updated in 2.72449843 seconds
```

Go ahead and exit back out to the host prompt now:

```
[vagrant@node-centos65 ~]$ exit
logout
Connection to 127.0.0.1 closed.
```

Your tour of the chef-client cookbook is now complete. We are now done with both our Chef Server and node. Go ahead and kitchen destroy both of them.

Linux/Mac OS X:

```
$ cd $HOME/chef-repo/cookbooks/enterprise-chef
$ kitchen destroy
$ cd $HOME/chef-repo/cookbooks/node
$ kitchen destroy
```

Windows Command Prompt:

```
> cd %USERPROFILE%\chef-repo\cookbooks\enterprise-chef
> kitchen destroy
> cd %USERPROFILE%\chef-repo\cookbooks\node
> kitchen destroy
```

Windows PowerShell:

```
> cd $HOME\chef-repo\cookbooks\enterprise-chef
> kitchen destroy
> cd $HOME\chef-repo\cookbooks\node
> kitchen destroy
```

 Don't forget to remove the entries for *default-centos65.vagrantup.com* and *node-centos65.vagrantup.com* from */etc/hosts* on Linux/Mac OS X or *%WINDIR%\system32\drivers\etc\hosts* on Windows.

Summary

In this chapter we showed you the Chef Supermarket, which is the hub of the Chef community. We showed you how you can download cookbooks from the Chef Supermarket using both the web interface and the command line.

We recommend using the `knife` command line tool, because it makes it easy to not only download a community cookbook, but to upload and manage a cookbook on your Chef server so you can use it in your organization.

We presented an overview of the `chef-client` cookbook and how it is useful for configuring a node after it has been bootstrapped with `chef-client`.

In the next chapter, we'll introduce you to Chef Zero, a small, fast-start, in-memory version of Chef Server, great for local testing.

## CHAPTER 11

Chef Zero

Wouldn't it be nice to be able to spin up a Chef Server locally using a smaller memory footprint than shown in Chapter 9? On many systems, requiring 2 GB of free memory just to simulate a production Chef Server environment is a lot to ask. The Chef Development Kit and Chef Client just so happen to include a stripped-down version of Chef Server for this very purpose, called chef-zero.

chef-zero runs comfortably in as little as 20 MB of memory. Because it is small, it also starts up quickly, which is great for testing. In order to fit into such a small memory footprint, chef-zero sacrifices a few things. There is no web UI, nor is there any persistence; once Chef Zero is stopped, all data is lost. Neither of these two things is needed for testing.

Test Kitchen provides built-in support for chef-zero. Let's go through a simple example of how you can use chef-zero with Test Kitchen. It's great for testing your cookbook in a sandbox environment with chef-client using chef-zero as a simulated Chef Server, so you can test cookbooks that exploit Chef Server-specific features. We'll be covering more of these server-specific features in the remainder of this book, so having a nimbler test environment available will be handy.

For those using Chef Client, you will need to install an additional gem to use Chef Zero. Run the following command to install chef-zero:

```
$ sudo gem install chef-zero --no-ri --no-rdoc
```

If you're using the Chef Development Kit, you're fine, this Ruby gem has already been installed for you.

Test Kitchen and Chef Zero

Generate a cookbook named `zero` with `chef generate cookbook` or `knife cookbook create`, depending on whether you are using the Chef Development Kit or the Chef Client respectively. Also, enable the cookbook to use Test Kitchen. We're going to go through the cookbook creation steps quickly in this chapter. If you need a refresher on what each of these commands mean and the expected output, refer back to Chapter 7.

Chef Development Kit:

```
$ chef generate cookbook zero
$ cd zero
```

Chef Client:

```
$ knife cookbook create zero --cookbook-path .
$ cd zero
$ kitchen init --create-gemfile
$ bundle install
```

Edit the `provisioner:` stanza in the generated *.kitchen.yml* to use `chef_zero`. As of this writing, `chef_zero` is not the default provisioner, but it might be by the time you read this. Also, edit the *.kitchen.yml* file to use the CentOS 6.5 basebox we prepared specifically for this book. Next, assign a private network address like we did in Chapter 7. This time, we're going to use the IP address 192.168.33.34. If this conflicts with an address already being used on your local network, change it to be a nonconflicting one.

Example 11-1. chefdk/zero/.kitchen.yml

```
---
driver:
  name: vagrant

provisioner:
  name: chef_zero

platforms:
  - name: centos65
    driver:
      box: learningchef/centos65
      box_url: learningchef/centos65

suites:
  - name: default
    run_list:
      - recipe[zero::default]
    attributes:
```

Because we just want to present an overview of what `chef-zero` does, we're going to use the default-generated cookbook, which does nothing. Perform a `kitchen converge` to perform a Chef run using chef-zero. You should notice that the output looks a little different than when you used chef-solo:

```
$ kitchen converge
-----> Starting Kitchen (v1.2.2.dev)
-----> Creating <default-centos65>...
-----> Converging <default-centos65>...
-----> Installing Chef Omnibus (true)
       Transferring files to <default-centos65>
       [2014-07-22T10:31:35-07:00] INFO: Starting chef-zero on port 8889 with
       repository at repository at /tmp/kitchen
         One version per cookbook

       [2014-07-22T10:31:35-07:00] INFO: Forking chef instance to converge...
       Starting Chef Client, version 11.12.8
       [2014-07-22T10:31:35-07:00] INFO: *** Chef 11.12.8 ***
       [2014-07-22T10:31:35-07:00] INFO: Chef-client pid: 2004
       Creating a new client identity for default-centos65 using the validator
       key.
       [2014-07-22T10:31:37-07:00] INFO: Client key /tmp/kitchen/client.pem
       is not present - registering
       [2014-07-22T10:31:37-07:00] INFO: HTTP Request Returned 404 Not Found :
       Object not found: http://127.0.0.1:8889/nodes/default-centos65
       [2014-07-22T10:31:37-07:00] INFO: Setting the run_list to
       ["recipe[zero::default]"] from CLI options
       [2014-07-22T10:31:37-07:00] INFO: Run List is [recipe[zero::default]]
       [2014-07-22T10:31:37-07:00] INFO: Run List expands to [zero::default]
       [2014-07-22T10:31:37-07:00] INFO: Starting Chef Run for default-centos65
       [2014-07-22T10:31:37-07:00] INFO: Running start handlers
       [2014-07-22T10:31:37-07:00] INFO: Start handlers complete.
       [2014-07-22T10:31:38-07:00] INFO: HTTP Request Returned 404 Not Found :
       Object not found: /reports/nodes/default-centos65/runs
       resolving cookbooks for run list: ["zero::default"]
       [2014-07-22T10:31:38-07:00] INFO: Loading cookbooks [zero@0.1.0]
       Synchronizing Cookbooks:
       [2014-07-22T10:31:38-07:00] INFO: Storing updated
       cookbooks/zero/recipes/default.rb in the cache.
       [2014-07-22T10:31:38-07:00] INFO: Storing updated
       cookbooks/zero/README.md in the cache.
       [2014-07-22T10:31:38-07:00] INFO: Storing updated
       cookbooks/zero/metadata.json in the cache.
         - zero
       Compiling Cookbooks...
       Converging 0 resources
       [2014-07-22T10:31:38-07:00] INFO: Chef Run complete in 0.043313495 seconds

       Running handlers:
       [2014-07-22T10:31:38-07:00] INFO: Running report handlers
       Running handlers complete

       [2014-07-22T10:31:38-07:00] INFO: Report handlers complete
       Chef Client finished, 0/0 resources updated in 2.396534174 seconds
```

```
      Finished converging <default-centos65> (0m29.51s).
-----> Kitchen is finished. (1m4.76s)
```

Here's an overview of the steps Test Kitchen performed to set up `chef-zero` in the sandbox environment. It:

1. Installed Chef Client

2. Created fake *validation.pem* and *client.pem* keys in */tmp/kitchen*

3. Generated *client.rb* (the configuration file for `chef-client`) in */tmp/kitchen*

4. Generated *dna.json* file with run list in */tmp/kitchen*

5. Synchronized cookbooks on host in */tmp/kitchen/cookbooks*

6. Ran `chef-client` in *local mode*. The full command line used is `chef-client --local-mode --config /tmp/kitchen/client.rb --log_level --chef-zero-port 8889 --json-attributes dna.json`

Destroy the sandbox environment; we're done with it for now:

```
$ kitchen destroy
```

One important thing to remember is that Test Kitchen runs `chef-zero` in the background during the Chef run, then stops `chef-zero` once the Chef run is complete. It does not leave `chef-zero` running, nor does it configure `knife` to run in your sandbox environment. As discussed in Chapter 9, `knife` is the primary tool for interacting with a Chef Server. It is handy to be able to simulate `knife` as well in a test environment. But we need to do a few more things in order to also simulate a Chef Server using `knife`.

Running Chef-Zero on Your Host Using Chef-Playground

You can also run `chef-zero` on your host. The most likely reason you'll want to do this is to simulate a Chef Server so you can run the `knife` tool, like we did in Chapter 9. When you want to interact with a Chef Server, you'll find yourself using `knife` on your host Development Workstation even when you are using Test Kitchen. Also, some Chef Server features such as data bags or search really benefit from being able to use `knife`, even during testing.

We'll be creating a project directory called *chef-playground* which models the `chef-repo` setup we used in Chapter 9, but uses `chef-zero` instead. We'll follow similar steps that we used in "Test Kitchen and Chef Zero" on page 204:

1. Assume Chef Client or the Chef Development Kit is installed.

2. Create fake *validation.pem* and *client.pem* keys.

3. Create *knife.rb* (the configuration file for `knife`).

4. Run chef-zero.

5. Synchronize cookbooks with chef-zero simulated Chef Server.

6. Run knife.

Create a directory called *chef-playground*, and make it the current working directory:

```
$ mkdir chef-playground
$ cd chef-playground
```

Then create another subdirectory called *.chef* (similar to the *chef-repo/.chef* directory we created in Chapter 9), which will contain our fake keys and configuration files:

```
$ mkdir .chef
$ cd .chef
```

Use the ssh-keygen tool to generate some client keys. They don't need to be real keys tied to a user or to Chef, but they do need to contain a readable key. We discussed the purpose of the *client.pem* file in Chapter 10. In this case, we'll name the file *devhost.pem*, which matches the devhost name we'll be using for our Development Workstation. Enter in the following command lines. (The -P option supplies a passphrase for the key. In this case, we don't want a passphrase, so we pass in double quotes [""] to supply a blank password.)

Linux/Mac OS X/Windows Command Prompt:

```
$ ssh-keygen -f devhost.pem -P ""
$ ssh-keygen -f validation.pem -P ""
```

Windows PowerShell:

```
$ ssh-keygen --% -f devhost.pem -P ""
$ ssh-keygen --% -f validation.pem -P ""
```

Create a *knife.rb* file in the *chef-playground/.chef* directory as shown in Example 11-2. This is the final configuration file you need to create.

Example 11-2. chef-playground/.chef/knife.rb

```
chef_repo = File.join(File.dirname(__FILE__), "..")

chef_server_url "http://127.0.0.1:9501"
node_name       "devhost"
client_key      File.join(File.dirname(__FILE__), "devhost.pem")
cookbook_path   "#{chef_repo}/cookbooks"
cache_type      "BasicFile"
cache_options   :path => "#{chef_repo}/checksums"
```

Finally, open up a separate terminal window and run chef-zero alongside the command prompt in which you are doing these hands-on-exercises, as shown in Figure 11-1. Run chef-zero as shown in the following code, passing in a port number besides the default port 8889, so you won't conflict with other Chef tools running on your host in local mode. If you discover a conflict with the suggested port 9501, use another.

```
$ chef-zero --port 9501
```

 You can run chef-zero in "daemonized" mode by passing in the --daemon parameter. Chef-zero will detach itself from the current command line process and run in the background.

As shown in Figure 11-1, when run on a command line, chef-zero will display that it is listening, not returning to the command prompt. This is why we recommend running it in a separate window. Leave chef-zero running for now.

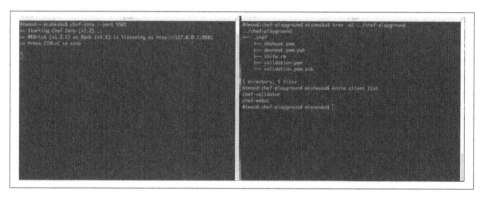

Figure 11-1. Run chef-zero in a window alongside your cookbook

Make sure that the *chef-playground* directory is the current working directory. Assuming everything is configured properly, when you run knife client list, it should return chef-validator and chef-webui as shown in the following code block:

```
$ pwd
/Users/misheska/chef-playground

$ knife client list
chef-validator
chef-webui
```

The knife tool will look for configuration files and credentials in the *$HOME/.chef* directory by default. If knife doesn't find anything in this default location, it will then walk up a directory tree looking for the first *.chef* directory, if it exists. This is a recommended way to arrange your configuration files, if you have to work against multiple Chef servers using the Chef tools in client mode—sprinkle *.chef* directories in root locations that make sense for the project, such as *chef-playground/.chef*.

We won't be using `knife --local-mode` in this book, but it's helpful to mention. Similar to `chef-client`, the `knife` tool supports a *local mode* using the `--local-mode` option. A benefit to using *local mode* with `knife` is that it will automatically start `chef-zero` for you.

You could have run the following to run `knife` in local mode to check clients. A benefit to this approach is that it will automatically start `chef-zero` for you. This doesn't conflict with the `chef-zero` instance you already started because it is running on a different port than the default port 8889.

```
$ knife client list --local-mode
```

However, you'll notice that the output differs compared to when `knife` is running in "client" mode. So we won't be making use of the local mode feature in this book. Jon Cowie's *Customizing Chef* book covers the use of both `chef-client` and `knife` using local mode.

Before we finish with our `chef-playground` project, let's pre-populate `chef-zero` with some node information so we can get more useful test results back from search queries against Chef Server.

Create a directory called *nodes* underneath *chef-playground*, and make it the current working directory:

```
$ mkdir nodes
$ cd nodes
```

Within the *chef-playground/nodes* directory, create three files, as shown in Example 11-3, Example 11-4, and Example 11-5. When you are done, the *chef-playground* directory structure should resemble the following:

```
chef-playground/
├── .chef
│   ├── devhost.pem
│   ├── devhost.pem.pub
│   ├── knife.rb
│   ├── validator.pem
│   └── validator.pem.pub
└── nodes
    ├── atwood.json
    ├── snowman.json
    └── susu.json
```

Example 11-3. chef-playground/nodes/atwood.json

```
{
  "name": "atwood",
  "chef_type": "node",
  "json_class": "Chef::Node",
  "chef_environment": "_default",
```

```
  "run_list": ["recipe[apache]", "recipe[motd]"],
  "automatic": {
    "ipaddress": "192.168.33.31",
    "hostname": "atwood",
    "fqdn": "atwood.playground.local",
    "os": "linux",
    "os_version": "2.6.32-431.el6.x86_64",
    "platform": "centos",
    "platform_version": "6.5",
    "platform_family": "rhel",
    "recipes": ["apache", "motd"]
  }
}
```

Example 11-4. chef-playground/nodes/snowman.json

```
{
  "name": "snowman",
  "chef_type": "node",
  "json_class": "Chef::Node",
  "chef_environment": "_default",
  "run_list": ["recipe[apache]", "recipe[motd]", "recipe[motd-attributes]"],
  "automatic": {
    "ipaddress": "192.168.33.32",
    "hostname": "snowman",
    "fqdn": "snowman.playground.local",
    "os": "linux",
    "os_version": "3.13.0-24-generic",
    "platform": "ubuntu",
    "platform_version": "14.04",
    "platform_family": "debian",
    "recipes": ["apache", "motd", "motd-attributes"]
  }
}
```

Example 11-5. chef-playground/nodes/susu.json

```
{
  "name": "susu",
  "chef_type": "node",
  "json_class": "Chef::Node",
  "chef_environment": "_default",
  "run_list": ["recipe[apache]", "recipe[motd]"],
  "automatic": {
    "ipaddress": "192.168.33.33",
    "hostname": "susu",
    "fqdn": "susu.playground.local",
    "os": "linux",
    "os_version": "2.6.32-431.el6.x86_64",
    "platform": "centos",
    "platform_version": "6.5",
    "platform_family": "rhel",
    "recipes": ["apache", "motd"]
```

```
    }
}
```

Once you have the files in the *nodes/* subdirectory created, make sure that *chef-playground* is the current working directory. Then, run the `knife upload` command to create the node information on the server. We'll use this `knife upload` technique in subsequent chapters of this book to pre-populate the `chef-zero` server with test data before running other `knife` commands:

```
$ pwd
/Users/misheska/chef-playground

$ knife upload nodes
Created nodes/atwood.json
Created nodes/snowman.json
Created nodes/susu.json
```

Now if you run the `knife node list` command, you'll see that `chef-zero` thinks that there are three nodes being managed:

```
$ knife node list
atwood
snowman
susu
```

That's a quick overview of Chef Zero. We'll be using Chef Zero to show you more Chef Server functionality in upcoming chapters. Hit Ctrl-C in the window in which you launched `chef-zero` to stop the Chef Zero server.

Summary

In this chapter, we showed you how Chef Zero provides a complete, in-memory version of Chef Server that is easy to install and great for checking out features of Chef Server locally without needing to have a full Chef Server setup. We'll be using this nimbler implementation of Chef Server for the rest of the exercises in this book.

## CHAPTER 12

Search

Chef search provides the ability to query data indexed on Chef Server. The search query runs on Chef Server and search results are returned to clients. Queries can be invoked by using `knife` on the command line or from within a recipe. Typical queries are usually inventory related, such as a count and system names of all the computers that have particular operating system configurations or software installed. For example, searches for versions of the openssl library vulnerable to the Heartbleed Virus were quite popular as we were writing this book.

Search from the Command Line

Let's start by performing a search query with `knife` on the command line. Use the *chef-playground* directory you created in Chapter 11. Use the same dual command prompt setup you used there. Start the `chef-zero` server on an open port in one window. We will be using port 9501 in the examples in this chapter:

```
$ chef-zero --port 9501
```

Then, in the other window, make the *chef-playground* directory the current working directory and run the `knife upload nodes` command to populate Chef Server with some test data about nodes:

```
$ cd chef-playground
$ knife upload nodes
Created nodes/susu.json
Created nodes/atwood.json
Created nodes/snowman.json
```

Search from the Command Line with Knife

You can also perform searches in production on the command line with the `knife search` command. The search query syntax with `knife` is in the following form:

```
$ knife search <index> <search_query>
```

The index can be one of the following:

- `node`
- `client`
- `environment`
- `role`
- `<name of data bag>`

In this chapter, we'll use `node` for the *index* field. Figure 12-1 shows an example of a search for nodes that have an IP address beginning with 10.1.1.

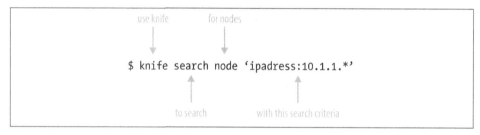

Figure 12-1. Knife search query syntax

Chef uses Apache Solr for searching and search indexing. The following command performs a search query for all nodes and returns the results using the Solr search query string "*:*." The results contain the test data we just populated with `knife upload`, showing three nodes registered to be managed by Chef.

```
$ knife search node "*:*"
3 items found

Node Name:   atwood
Environment: _default
FQDN:        atwood.playground.local
IP:          192.168.33.31
Run List:    recipe[apache], recipe[motd]
Roles:
Recipes:     apache, motd
Platform:    centos 6.5
Tags:
```

```
Node Name:    snowman
Environment:  _default
FQDN:         snowman.playground.local
IP:           192.168.33.32
Run List:     recipe[apache], recipe[motd], recipe[motd-attributes]
Roles:
Recipes:      apache, motd, motd-attributes
Platform:     ubuntu 14.04
Tags:

Node Name:    susu
Environment:  _default
FQDN:         susu.playground.local
IP:           192.168.33.33
Run List:     recipe[apache], recipe[motd]
Roles:
Recipes:      apache, motd
Platform:     centos 6.5
Tags:
```

Chef search queries use the Solr "<attribute>:<search_pattern>" form:

```
knife search node "ipaddress:192.168.33.32"
```

Use an asterisk ("*") within a search query to perform a wildcard search matching 0 or more characters:

```
knife search node "ipaddress:192.*"
knife search node "platfo*:centos"
```

Use a question mark ("?") to match any single character:

```
knife search node "platform_version:14.0?"
```

You can add specific key-value pairs in the query part of the knife search command line. The following query will return the item where node == snowman:

```
$ knife search node "hostname:snowman"
1 items found

Node Name:    snowman
Environment:  _default
FQDN:         snowman.playground.local
IP:           192.168.33.32
Run List:     recipe[apache], recipe[motd], recipe[motd-attributes]
Roles:
Recipes:      apache, motd, motd-attributes
Platform:     ubuntu 14.04
Tags:
```

To obtain a list of attribute names to use in a search, run the `knife <index> show` command using the `--long` option. It will show you all the available attributes. For example, we ran the following command to determine that the attribute for `Node Name:` was `hostname`:

```
knife node snowman --long
```

Note that our test data doesn't include all the possible attributes. You'll need to run `knife node show` against a real Chef Server setup. Another way to collect this information for a node without needing a real setup is to run `ohai` and look through the results. Most of the attributes about a node come from `ohai`.

Multiple key-value pairs can be specified using boolean values, such as OR. For example, the following query would return the items where the id is `alice` OR `bob`:

```
$ knife search node "name:susu OR name:atwood"
2 items found

Node Name:   atwood
Environment: _default
FQDN:        atwood.playground.local
IP:          192.168.33.31
Run List:    recipe[apache], recipe[motd]
Roles:
Recipes:     apache, motd
Platform:    centos 6.5
Tags:

Node Name:   susu
Environment: _default
FQDN:        susu.playground.local
IP:          192.168.33.33
Run List:    recipe[apache], recipe[motd]
Roles:
Recipes:     apache, motd
Platform:    centos 6.5
Tags:
```

Logical AND can be used as well, if you want to return results matching all value criteria:

```
$ knife search node "ipaddress:192* AND platform:ubuntu"
1 items found

Node Name:   snowman
Environment: _default
FQDN:        snowman.playground.local
IP:          192.168.33.32
Run List:    recipe[apache], recipe[motd], recipe[motd-attributes]
Roles:
Recipes:     apache, motd, motd-attributes
```

```
    Platform:    ubuntu 14.04
    Tags:
```

Search results can be filtered with the -a parameter. For example, -a ipaddress only returns the value for the ipaddress attribute:

```
$ knife search node "*:*" -a ipaddress
3 items found

atwood:
  ipaddress: 192.168.33.31

snowman:
  ipaddress: 192.168.33.32

susu:
  ipaddress: 192.168.33.33
```

Search in a Recipe Using Test Kitchen

You can also perform search queries in your Chef code. In this section we'll write a cookbook using Test Kitchen and chef_zero that performs search queries. Create the directory *chef-playground/cookbooks*, and make sure it is the current working directory:

Linux/Mac OS X:

```
$ cd chef-playground/cookbooks
```

Windows:

```
> cd chef-playground\cookbooks
```

Now, generate a nodes cookbook in the *chef-playground/cookbooks* directory.

Chef Development Kit:

```
$ chef generate cookbook nodes
$ cd nodes
```

Chef Client:

```
$ knife cookbook create nodes --cookbook-path .
$ cd nodes
$ kitchen init --create-gemfile
$ bundle install
```

Edit the *.kitchen.yml* to make sure you are using the chef_zero provisioner and our favorite basebox image as shown in Example 12-1. Notice there is a new addition to the provisioner: stanza, the nodes_path:

```
provisioner:
  name: chef_zero
  nodes_path: ../../nodes
```

nodes_path is a relative path pointing to the *chef-playground/nodes* directory we created
with our test data in Chapter 11. Test data is normally located somewhere outside the
main cookbook source code so it doesn't get inadvertently uploaded to the Chef server.

Example 12-1. chefdk/chef-playground/cookbooks/nodes/.kitchen.yml

```
---
driver:
  name: vagrant

provisioner:
  name: chef_zero
  nodes_path: ../../nodes

platforms:
  - name: centos65
    driver:
      box: learningchef/centos65
      box_url: learningchef/centos65

suites:
  - name: default
    run_list:
      - recipe[nodes::default]
    attributes:
```

Let's write a recipe that performs a search query on Chef Server for all nodes, like we
did in the previous section. Chef provides a `search()` method that you can use in your
Chef code. It takes two parameters, similar to the two `command line` parameters used
in `knife search`:

`search(index, search_query)`:

index

> Possible values for index are `node`, `client`, `environment`, `role`, and *<name of data
> bag>*. In this example, we'll be using `node`.

search_query

> Apache Solr search query.

Make sure *recipes/default.rb* matches the code contained in Example 12-2. It contains
Chef code that queries Chef Server for all items in the `users` data bag.

Example 12-2. chefdk/chef-playground/cookbooks/nodes/recipes/default.rb

```
#
# Cookbook Name:: users
# Recipe:: default
#
# Copyright (C) 2014
#
```

```
#
#
# Print every node name matching the search pattern
search("node", "*:*").each do |matching_node|
  log matching_node.to_s
end
```

The `.each` statement in *recipes/default.rb* is a looping construct specific to Ruby. If you are familiar with other programming languages, look at the following code for something that might be a little more familiar. The following code creates a `counter` variable, incrementing it by 1 until it equals 5:

```
counter = 0
while counter < 5
  puts counter
  counter = counter + 1
end
```

Although the preceding is completely valid Ruby, a more idiomatic way is to use the `.each` iterator to return all the elements in an array one-by-one. Ruby shines in having really compact ways to specify common coding constructs.

The `do..end` block construct is more sophisticated than we've covered so far. It can be used to define a method with no name. Also, you can pass this nameless method one or more parameters enclosed by two vertical bars (`||`), such as `|counter|` in the following example.

In the following example, we pass a code block to `(0..5).each`. When you pass a code block to an iterator method, it will execute the specified method for each item. In this case, each item of the range `(0..5)` will be passed to our code block as the `|counter|` variable. The block uses this variable to print out each value in the range:

```
(0..5).each do |counter|
  puts counter
end
```

We're doing something similar in Example 12-2, iterating through each node item returned by `search()` and returning the item content in the `matching_node` variable. `matching_node` is a hash containing the key-value pairs in the node item.

The code just reads these values from the `matching_node` hash and uses the `to_s` method to print a string representation of the object using `log`, which is the node name.

Run `kitchen converge`. If all goes well, you should notice that Test Kitchen uploads the cookbook code to the sandbox environment and creates node entries in a `chef-zero` instance. Then it runs the cookbook code, which performs a query for all nodes, printing out the following results:

```
$ kitchen converge
-----> Starting Kitchen (v1.2.2.dev)
-----> Converging <default-centos65>...
       Preparing files for transfer
       Resolving cookbook dependencies with Berkshelf 3.1.3...
       Removing non-cookbook files before transfer
       Preparing nodes

...

       Converging 4 resources
       Recipe: nodes::default
         * log[node[atwood]] action write
       [2014-07-27T13:05:24-07:00] INFO: Processing log[node[atwood]] action
       write (nodes::default line 12)
       [2014-07-27T13:05:24-07:00] INFO: node[atwood]


           * log[node[default-centos65]] action write[2014-07-27T13:05:24-07:00]
           INFO: Processing log[node[default-centos65]] action write
           (nodes::default line 12)
       [2014-07-27T13:05:24-07:00] INFO: node[default-centos65]


           * log[node[snowman]] action write[2014-07-27T13:05:24-07:00] INFO:
           Processing log[node[snowman]] action write (nodes::default line 12)
       [2014-07-27T13:05:24-07:00] INFO: node[snowman]


           * log[node[susu]] action write[2014-07-27T13:05:24-07:00] INFO:
           Processing log[node[susu]] action write (nodes::default line 12)
       [2014-07-27T13:05:24-07:00] INFO: node[susu]


       [2014-07-27T13:05:24-07:00] INFO: Chef Run complete in 0.068921558
       seconds

       Running handlers:
       [2014-07-27T13:05:24-07:00] INFO: Running report handlers
       Running handlers complete

       [2014-07-27T13:05:24-07:00] INFO: Report handlers complete
       Chef Client finished, 4/4 resources updated in 2.158656241 seconds
       Finished converging <default-centos65> (0m5.12s).
-----> Kitchen is finished. (0m5.57s)
```

Sharp-eyed readers might notice that the search returns four results instead of the three we received running `knife` using the command line. The search result returns the nodes `atwood`, `snowman`, `susu`, and `default-centos65`. The additional node entry is the sandbox node Test Kitchen creates for us. When Test Kitchen performs a `kitchen converge`, it automatically registers the sandbox instance as a node with its own `chef-zero` instance.

You have been introduced to Chef search. We're done with the `chef-zero` instance on your host and the Test Kitchen sandbox environment. Hit Ctrl-C in the window in which you launched `chef-zero` to stop the Chef Zero server. Make sure the *chef-playground/cookbooks/nodes* directory with your cookbook is the current working directory, then run:

```
$ kitchen destroy
```

Summary

In this chapter we introduced you to Chef search. Chef Server uses Apache Solr behind the scenes to add support for searching and indexing. The Apache Solr `"<at tribute>:<query>"` syntax is also used for search queries. You can search from anything that can talk with Chef Server, given that Chef Server's search capability is implemented as an API. We showed you how to search from the command line using `knife node search` and how to search within a recipe using the `search()` method.

In the next chapter, we'll cover data bags. Data bags contain data that can be accessed by more than one node. Data bags were added as a feature in Chef Server to get around the limitation that node attributes can be read only by the node that created the data, not by any other node.

## CHAPTER 13

Data Bags

As Figure 13-1 shows, Chef Server provides a way to store shared, global data between nodes using *data bags*.

A data bag is a container for items that represent information about your infrastructure that is not tied to a single node. Data bags contain information that needs to be shared among more than one node. For example:

- Shared passwords
- License keys for software installs
- Shared lists of users and groups

Chef provides no mechanism to share data between nodes, as shown in Figure 13-2.

And even though `chef-client` does send a copy of the node attribute data to Chef Server after a successful Chef run, Figure 13-3 shows there is no way for other nodes to access this information directly.

Data bags are the only built-in mechanism Chef provides to store and access shared data between nodes.

Figure 13-4 shows what a data bag looks like. Each data bag contains a list of items. Each item is a JSON-formatted name-value pair collection expected to have exactly the same schema for every item in the data bag. However, the schema between two different data bags can differ. String values are quoted; integer values are not. Values can also contain lists of strings or integers as well.

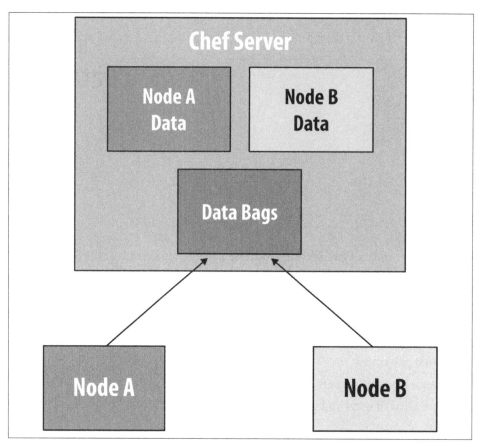

Figure 13-1. Data bags contain shared, global data

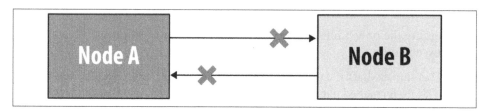

Figure 13-2. Nodes cannot share data directly

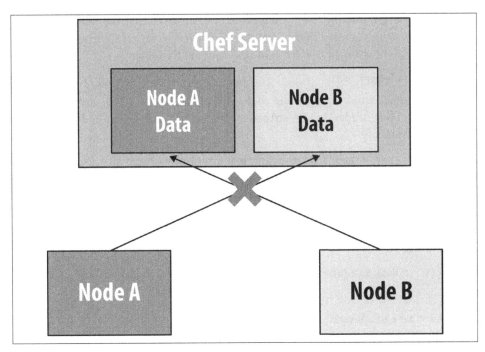

Figure 13-3. Chef Server does not a provide a way for nodes to share data directly

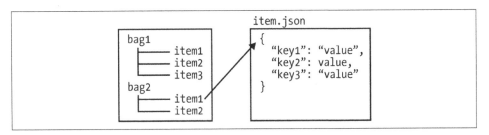

Figure 13-4. Data bag contents

Basic Command Line Data Bag Usage with Knife

Let's start by performing a search query with knife on the command line. Let's say we want to make sure that our employees alice and bob have local user accounts created on all nodes. We want to store this user list in a data bag, as we want to be able to add new employees to this list and have accounts created for them automatically. Data bags are the perfect solution for this problem because the list of users is global data that we want to share between nodes.

Use the *chef-playground* directory you created in Chapter 11. Use the same dual command prompt setup you used there. Start the `chef-zero` server on an open port in one window. We will be using port 9501 in the examples in this chapter:

```
$ chef-zero --port 9501
```

Then, in the other window, make the *chef-playground* directory the current working directory. You don't need to `knife upload nodes` for this chapter, but it doesn't hurt if you've done it already.

Make sure the `chef-playground` directory is the current working directory:

```
$ cd chef-playground
```

Create a *data_bags* directory in *chef-playground*. Also, create a new data bag called `users`. It's simply a matter of creating a new directory underneath *data_bags*.

Linux/Mac OS X:

```
$ mkdir -p data_bags/users
```

Windows:

```
> mkdir data_bags\users
```

Similar to what we did in Chapter 11 to create `node` data, create some items in your data bag by creating a *.json* file for each item. In this case, we want to create data bags for a user named `alice` and a user named `bob`. Create the files *alice.json* and *bob.json* as shown in Example 13-1 and Example 13-2. The data bag item contains key-value pairs with data relevant to a Unix user. String values are quoted; integer values are not. We'll feed this data into some Chef recipe code next, so we can show you how to make a data-driven cookbook.

Example 13-1. chefdk/chef-playground/data_bags/users/alice.json

```
{
  "id": "alice",
  "comment": "Alice Jones",
  "uid": 2000,
  "gid": 0,
  "home": "/home/alice",
  "shell": "/bin/bash"
}
```

Example 13-2. chefdk/chef-playground/data_bags/users/bob.json

```
{
  "id": "bob",
  "comment": "Bob Smith",
  "uid": 2001,
  "gid": 0,
  "home": "/home/bob",
```

```
  "shell": "/bin/bash"
}
```

To create a data bag named users on the Chef server, run the command knife data_bag create as follows:

```
$ knife data_bag create users
Created data_bag[users]
```

To create data bag items, use the knife data_bag from file command. knife da ta_bag from file assumes that the *.json* files are in a subdirectory with the specified data bag name under the directory *data_bags*:

```
$ knife data_bag from file users alice.json
Updated data_bag_item[users::alice]
$ knife data_bag from file users bob.json
Updated data_bag_item[users::bob]
```

To search data bags, use the name of the data bag in the index parameter to knife search. In this case, our data bag name is users ":". The following command will search for the list of users we created in a data bag:

```
$ knife search users "*:*"
2 items found

chef_type: data_bag_item
comment:   Alice Jones
data_bag:  users
gid:       0
home:      /home/alice
id:        alice
shell:     /bin/bash
uid:       2000

chef_type: data_bag_item
comment:   Bob Smith
data_bag:  users
gid:       0
home:      /home/bob
id:        bob
shell:     /bin/bash
uid:       2001
```

You can add specific key-value pairs in the query part of the knife search command line. The following query will return the item where id == alice:

```
$ knife search users "id:alice"
1 items found

chef_type: data_bag_item
comment:   Alice Jones
data_bag:  users
```

```
gid:      0
home:     /home/alice
id:       alice
shell:    /bin/bash
uid:      2000
```

The same search query variants we used in Chapter 12 for nodes also apply to data bags. The query fields are just slightly different as they are no longer node attributes. For example, the following query would return the items where the id is alice OR bob:

```
$ knife search users "id:alice OR id:bob"
2 items found

chef_type: data_bag_item
comment:   Alice Jones
data_bag:  users
gid:       0
home:      /home/alice
id:        alice
shell:     /bin/bash
uid:       2000

chef_type: data_bag_item
comment:   Bob Smith
data_bag:  users
gid:       0
home:      /home/bob
id:        bob
shell:     /bin/bash
uid:       2001
```

Just as we covered in Chapter 12, search results can be filtered with the -a parameter. For example, -a shell returns the value only for the users shell:

```
$ knife search users "*:*" -a shell
2 items found

data_bag_item_users_alice:
  shell: /bin/bash

data_bag_item_users_bob:
  shell: /bin/bash
```

 If the search text is a string, you'll need to put it in double quotes (""):

```
knife search users "comment:\"Alice Jones\"" -a shell
```

We have to escape the " here within the search string. On a Mac/Linux machine you could do this:

```
knife search users 'comment:"Alice Jones"' -a shell
```

But the single quote (') doesn't work in a Windows PowerShell terminal.

Creating Local Users Based on Data Bag Items in a Recipe

So far, we've created a list of users as data bag items, but we also want local accounts created for them. Let's write a Chef cookbook that creates the user accounts. We'll be using Test Kitchen and `chef_zero` to write our code, just like we did in Chapter 12.

Make sure *chef-playground/cookbooks* is the current working directory.

Linux/Mac OS X:

```
$ cd chef-playground/cookbooks
```

Windows:

```
> cd chef-playground\cookbooks
```

Then generate a `users` cookbook in the `chef-playground/cookbooks` directory.

Chef Development Kit:

```
$ chef generate cookbook users
$ cd users
```

Chef Client:

```
$ knife cookbook create users --cookbook-path .
$ cd users
$ kitchen init --create-gemfile
$ bundle install
```

Edit the *.kitchen.yml* and make sure you are using the `chef_zero` provisioner and our favorite basebox image as shown in Example 13-3. Notice there is a new addition to the `provisioner:` stanza, the `data_bags_path:`

```
provisioner:
  name: chef_zero
  data_bags_path: ../../data_bags
```

`data_bags_path` is a relative path pointing to the *chef-playground/data_bags* directory we created with our test data in the last section, similar to what we did with the `node` test data in Chapter 12.

All files in the `data_bags_path:` directory tree get uploaded to the `chef-zero` server as data bags. In production, data bags are populated with data that is not packaged with the cookbook itself. In other words, any data used for cookbook testing is normally located outside the main cookbook directory structure. In Example 13-3, we store our test data in *chef-playground/data_bags*, not under the subtree for the `users` cookbook within *cookbooks/users*.

Example 13-3. chefdk/users/.kitchen.yml

```
---
driver:
```

```
    name: vagrant

provisioner:
  name: chef_zero
  data_bags_path: ../../data_bags

platforms:
  - name: centos65
    driver:
      box: learningchef/centos65
      box_url: learningchef/centos65

suites:
  - name: default
    run_list:
      - recipe[users::default]
    attributes:
```

Let's write a recipe that queries the list of users in our users data bag and creates a local user for each item. You can use the search() method to perform the data bag query, just like you did for nodes in Chapter 12. Plus, you can make use of the Chef user resource to create a user based on the information contained in the data bag.

Enter in the code for *recipes/default.rb* that matches Example 13-4.

Example 13-4. chefdk/chef-playground/cookbooks/users/recipes/default.rb

```
#
# Cookbook Name:: users
# Recipe:: default
#
# Copyright (C) 2014
#
#
#
search("users", "*:*").each do |user_data|
  user user_data["id"] do
    comment user_data["comment"]
    uid user_data["uid"]
    gid user_data["gid"]
    home user_data["home"]
    shell user_data["shell"]
  end
end
```

We're using the each do construct similar to the code we wrote in Chapter 12, this time iterating through each item of the data bag and returning the data bag contents in user_data. user_data is a hash containing the key-value pairs in the data bag item.

The user statement within the search() block is a Chef resource. The user resource creates a local user on the node. It takes the following attributes:

comment
> One (or more) comments about the user

uid
> The numeric user identifier

gid
> The identifier for the group

home
> The location of the home directory

shell
> The login shell

The code reads these values from the user_data map and passes them to the Chef user resource.

Run kitchen converge. If all goes well, Test Kitchen should upload the cookbook code to the sandbox environment and create the data bag entries in a chef-zero instance. It should then run the cookbook code that performs a query for our user data bag items and creates corresponding users with the user resource:

```
$ kitchen converge
-----> Starting Kitchen (v1.2.2.dev)
-----> Converging <default-centos65>...
       Preparing files for transfer
...
       Preparing data bags
...
       [2014-07-23T22:18:29-07:00] INFO: Starting chef-zero on port 8889 with
       repository at repository at /tmp/kitchen
         One version per cookbook
...
       Starting Chef Client, version 11.12.8
...
       resolving cookbooks for run list: ["users::default"]
       [2014-07-23T22:18:31-07:00] INFO: Loading cookbooks [users@0.1.0]
       Synchronizing Cookbooks:
         - users
       Compiling Cookbooks...
       Converging 2 resources
       Recipe: users::default
         * user[alice] action create[2014-07-23T22:18:31-07:00] INFO:
         Processing user[alice] action create (users::default line 11)
       [2014-07-23T22:18:31-07:00] INFO: user[alice] created

           - create user user[alice]

         * user[bob] action create[2014-07-23T22:18:31-07:00] INFO:
         Processing user[bob] action create (users::default line 11)
```

```
[2014-07-23T22:18:31-07:00] INFO: user[bob] created

    - create user user[bob]

[2014-07-23T22:18:31-07:00] INFO: Chef Run complete in 0.122617779
seconds

Running handlers:
[2014-07-23T22:18:31-07:00] INFO: Running report handlers
Running handlers complete

[2014-07-23T22:18:31-07:00] INFO: Report handlers complete
Chef Client finished, 2/2 resources updated in 2.425061171 seconds
Finished converging <default-centos65> (0m5.37s).
-----> Kitchen is finished. (0m5.82s)
```

Verify Users

Let's verify that the users actually got created in our sandbox environment. Log in to the sandbox environment, and run getent password to verify that our users exist. Then make sure you exit back out to the host command prompt:

```
$ kitchen login
Last login: Sun Jul 27 14:24:53 2014 from 10.0.2.2
Welcome to your Packer-built virtual machine.
[vagrant@default-centos65 ~]$ getent passwd alice
alice:x:2000:0:Alice Jones:/home/alice:/bin/bash
[vagrant@default-centos65 ~]$ getent passwd bob
bob:x:2001:0:Bob Smith:/home/bob:/bin/bash
[vagrant@default-centos65 ~]$ exit
logout
Connection to 127.0.0.1 closed.
```

Local users alice and bob should now be created with the appropriate user data.

You can also add a new item to the users data bag collection. Let's add a new user called eve. Go back to the root *chef-playground* directory and create a new file called *chef-playground/data_bags/users/eve.json* as shown in Example 13-5.

Example 13-5. chefdk/chef-playground/data_bags/users/eve.json

```
{
  "id": "eve",
  "comment": "Eavesdrop",
  "uid": 2002,
  "gid": 0,
  "home": "/home/eve",
  "shell": "/bin/bash"
}
```

Make sure the root *chef-playground* directory is your current working directory, and run `knife data_bag from file` to add eve to the global list of users:

```
$ knife data_bag from file users eve.json
Updated data_bag_item[users::eve]
```

Make your *users* recipe the current working directory.

Linux/Mac OS X:

```
$ cd chef-playground/cookbooks/users
```

Windows:

```
> cd chef-playground\cookbooks\users
```

Run `kitchen converge` and then `kitchen login` to check to see if the new user account got created. Make sure you `exit` back out to the host prompt when you are done.

```
$ kitchen converge
$ kitchen login
Last login: Sun Jul 27 14:38:04 2014 from 10.0.2.2
Welcome to your Packer-built virtual machine.
[vagrant@default-centos65 ~]$ getent passwd eve
eve:x:2002:0:Eavesdrop:/home/eve:/bin/bash
[vagrant@default-centos65 ~]$ exit
logout
Connection to 127.0.0.1 closed.
```

You should notice that an account for eve got created. Your recipe is data driven, based on the list of users maintained in the users databag. Whenever that list changes, a node will pick up the change on its next scheduled Chef run. You didn't have to change the recipe to get a new user account created.

Encrypted Data Bags

Data bag items can be encrypted with a shared key in order to store private information on Chef Server in a secure fashion. Examples of secrets that you might want to store in an encrypted databag include:

- SSL certificates
- SSH keys
- Passwords
- License keys

Because node attributes are in plain text and can be searched—even though other nodes can't change another node's attributes—node attributes are not secure. Encrypted data bags are a great option, even when you want to secure an attribute for just one node, though secrets aren't usually node specific.

Figure 13-5 shows more detail about how encrypted data bags work. When a data bag item is created with `knife data bag create`, a file containing a shared key is passed on the command line. The shared key is used as the password to encrypt the data bag item contents. When a node wants to decrypt the data bag item and access the secret in plain text, it must also pass the same shared key on its `knife data bag` operations.

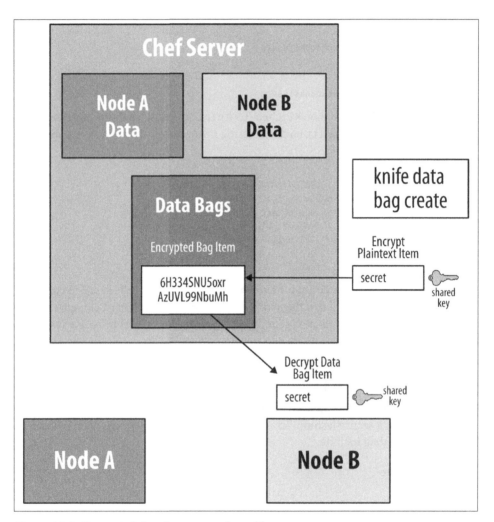

Figure 13-5. Encrypted data bags use a shared key

Let's try working with an encrypted data bag item. Make sure the root *chef-playground* directory is your current working directory.

First, generate a password to be used as a shared key. Enter in the following command line, which generates a 512-byte random key and saves it to the file encrypted_da ta_bag_secret:

```
$ openssl rand -base64 512 | tr -d '\r\n' > encrypted_data_bag_secret
```

When symmetric key encryption is used, the password is typically a random key generated by a machine instead of a human. So we used openssl tool to generate a 512-byte random key. In order to represent the binary data contained in the key, we tell openssl to use base64 encoding to represent the binary data as an ASCII string. Further, since by default the output of openssl contains linefeeds, which are different depending on the platform, we use the translate (tr) command to remove any linefeed characters from the secret key. Removing linefeed characters ensures that the bytes in the random key will be the same even if the platform is different.

For some test data, let's create a *.json* file that contains the api key to access our credit card payment system. This is definitely something we want to keep from prying eyes. In addition to the required id: field, we'll add an api_key field to store api_key.

First, create a new directory to hold the data bag under *chef-playground/data_bags* to hold our api_keys.

Linux/Mac OS X:

```
$ mkdir -p data_bags/api_keys
```

Windows:

```
> mkdir data_bags\api_keys
```

Now create the file *chef-playground/data_bags/api_keys/payment_system.json* by using the code provided in Example 13-6.

Example 13-6. chefdk/chef-playground/data_bags/api_keys/payment.json

```
{
  "id": "payment",
  "api_key": "592c879e-f37d-43e6-8b54-8c2d97cf04d4"
}
```

Create the data bag using the following command line:

```
$ knife data bag create api_keys
```

When data bag items are encrypted, use the --secret-file command line option to pass in the shared key. Create the encrypted data bag item api_keys by using the *payment.json* file that we just created, with the following:

```
$ knife data bag from file api_keys payment.json \
--secret-file encrypted_data_bag_secretUpdated data_bag_item[api_keys::payment]
```

So is the data item encrypted on Chef Server? Let's see. Try using the `knife data bag show` command, but don't pass the shared key:

```
$ knife data bag show api_keys payment
api_key:
  cipher:         aes-256-cbc
  encrypted_data: 25wUoOzKMqRAlMm3bGVch+0VAyL/IQj6/oi/K2CyYWWemP5akQo4pldal9SP
TjkFNmLH5mO8uWi9jn61UrvQdA==

  iv:             jU1uFntBuH8b1pwms09nkA==

  version:        1
id:      payment
```

Looks encrypted, doesn't it? You don't see our plain-text `api_key` anywhere in the output. The only thing that is plain text is the `id:`. The `id:` field cannot be encrypted, because the server uses this field to index and search for the associated encrypted data.

 It's worth pointing out that you lose the ability to search for data within encrypted data bags. A data bag can be searchable or secure, but not both at the same time.

If you want to decrypt the item data, just use the `--secret-file` parameter as follows. Now the data bag item is shown in plain text:

```
$ knife data bag show api_keys payment \
--secret-file encrypted_data_bag_secret
api_key: 592c879e-f37d-43e6-8b54-8c2d97cf04d4
id:      payment_system
```

There is one problem with using encrypted data bags for which Chef Software does not provide a built-in solution. How does a node get the secret key? In order for the node to decrypt the secret, it must have a copy of the shared key. Unfortunately, there is no central place to access encrypted keys, as storing encryption keys on the same system where the data resides violates all the core principles of computer security. So when you use encrypted data bags, you must find a solution to the key distribution problem.

Luckily there is a solution to this key distribution issue, which we'll cover in the next section. It's called `chef-vault`, and it is included with the Chef Development Kit.

chef-vault

Kevin Moser came up with idea for `chef-vault` in 2013 while working at Nordstrom. Kevin devised a clever solution to the key distribution issue for encrypted data bags by reusing the public/private key pairs Chef already uses for nodes to implement a key encapsulation scheme. When the data bag item is created, a shared key is generated on the node. Then, for each node that needs access to it, the shared key is encrypted with the node's public key, creating an encrypted version of the shared key in an encapsulated payload. This encrypted version of the key is stored on Chef Server.

> For those using Chef Client, you will need to install an additional gem to use `chef-vault`. Run the following to install the `chef-vault` gem:
>
> ```
> $ sudo gem install chef-vault --no-ri --no-rdoc
> ```
>
> If you're using the Chef Development Kit, you're fine, this Ruby gem has already been installed for you.

Before we can play with `chef-vault` in our `chef-playground` setup, we need to register a legitimate client key for our `devhost` node with the `chef-zero` server.

Right now, if you run `knife client list`, note that `devhost` isn't in our list of clients. Chef Server doesn't know it has a client key that allows it to store data on the server from its `chef-client` runs nor does it know that `devhost` is a node. Both of these conditions are required for a node to access encrypted data with `chef-vault`:

```
$ knife client list
chef-validator
chef-webui
$ knife node list
```

The node list must be blank for this exercise to work, as the fake nodes we created in Chapter 11 do not have accompanying client keys. If you see nodes listed, start and stop the `chef-zero` server to clear them out.

Generate a new private/public client key pair for your Development Workstation, which we call `devhost` in *chef-playground/.chef/knife.rb*. Since `chef-zero` doesn't check the contents of the *chef-playground/.chef/devhost.pem* file, it doesn't matter if we regenerate it. However, when we regenerate the client key, it ensures that a matching public key is stored on Chef Server, which does matter. Run the following command to regenerate the client key.

```
$ knife client create devhost --admin --disable-editing --file .chef/devhost.pem
Created client[devhost]
```

The `--admin` option lets the client run the APIs behind the `knife client show` and `knife node commands` on other nodes besides its own node. By default, `knife client create` displays the client info in an editor to allow tweaking before a *client.pem* is generated. In our case, however, the defaults are fine, so we just pass in `--disable-editing`. The `--file` option writes the *client.pem* out to the specified filename:

Now if you run `knife client list`, the devhost machine shows up:

```
$ knife client list
chef-validator
chef-webui
devhost
```

We also need to associate a node with our client key, so run the following:

```
$ knife node create devhost --disable-editing
```

Now devhost shows up as a node as well. This is what happens when a node is bootstrapped—a client key is generated and the node is registered with Chef Server. We are just simulating this process in `chef-zero` by hand:

```
$ knife node list
devhost
```

We're going to create a new encrypted data bag for storing root passwords, which will be managed by `chef-vault`. Create the directory *chef-playground/data_bags/passwords* to store the *.json* file we will be creating next.

Linux/Mac OS X:

```
$ mkdir -p data_bags/passwords
```

Windows:

```
> mkdir data_bags\passwords
```

Create the file shown in Example 13-7 in *chef-playground/data_bags/api_keys/mysql.json*. It stores the MySQL database root user password.

Example 13-7. chefdk/chef-playground/data_bags/passwords/mysql_root.json

```
{
  "id": "mysql_root",
  "password": "This is a very secure password"
}
```

`chef-vault` installs a knife plugin to manage encrypted data bags. It exposes `chef-vault` commands via `knife vault`. Enter in the following command to create an encrypted data bag item with a secret managed by `chef-vault`:

```
$ knife vault create passwords mysql_root \
--json data_bags/passwords/mysql_root.json --search "*:*" \
--admins "admin" --mode client
```

You must specify users or nodes that have valid `client` keys using the `--search` and `--admins` parameters. We have to use both in this example because we didn't set up the admin user to have a valid client key. If you run `knife client list`, the `admin` user isn't present.

When you are using Chef Server, you must use the option `--mode client`.

The command line options for `knife vault` are a little different than the options for `chef data_bags`. See the comprehensive documentation (*https://github.com/Nord strom/chef-vault/blob/master/KNIFE_EXAMPLES.md*) on `knife vault` command line options.

The most important takeaway you should get from this example is that `chef-vault` can encrypt data only if Chef Server has valid *client* keys. This can be hard to configure in a `chef-zero` setup. What we've done so far in this section is just enough to get `chef-vault` working with `chef-zero` in order to demo.

So is our data bag encrypted? Let's perform a check using `knife data bag show`, similar to what we did in the previous section on encrypted data bags:

```
$ knife data bag show passwords mysql_root
id:        mysql_root
password:
  cipher:        aes-256-cbc
  encrypted_data: K+PZ4zemMt2Hp7FTgTTHxGa1bWez1RqJbYGUNSJIgLDLu8cBlr9Uuu+gL9hT
  AH9jtIRms9BEjHXVn63SEzHMZQ==

  iv:            //KVXQRwdu81zOUXaSAC0Q==

  version:       1
```

Looks encrypted to us!

Run `knife vault show` as follows to display the decrypted data bag content:

```
$ knife vault show passwords mysql_root --mode client
id:        mysql_root
password: This is a very secure password
```

Summary

We covered data bags in this chapter. Data bags are a powerful feature of Chef Server that let you store global information that can be shared among nodes. We also presented an overview of how data bag contents can be secured with encrypted data bags. Unfortunately, because encrypted data bags use symmetric key encryption, there is no way to distribute the shared keys to nodes that need to encrypt the data. We showed how `chef-vault` helps address this key distribution issue.

In the next chapter we'll cover roles. Roles are a great way to capture patterns that exist across nodes belonging to a single job function.

## CHAPTER 14

Roles

Roles are a way of classifying the different types of services in your infrastructure, as shown in Figure 14-1.

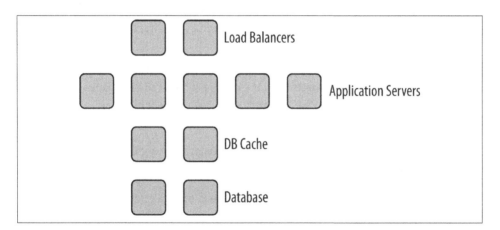

Figure 14-1. Roles overview

Roles can be used to represent the types of servers in your infrastructure:

- Load balancer
- Application server
- Database cache
- Database
- Monitoring

Although you can add recipes directly to a node's run list, that's not how your infrastructure works. Think about how you normally refer to servers:

- "It's a *web server*."
- "It's a *database server*."
- "It's a *monitoring server*."

Roles allow you to conveniently encapsulate the run lists and attributes required for a server to be what you already think it is. Roles make it easy to configure many nodes identically without repeating yourself each time.

In addition to obvious roles, such as a "web server," it is common practice to group any functionality that goes together into a role. The most common example is a *base role*, where you include all the recipes that should be run on every node.

Create a Web Server Role

Roles can be created and managed in the same fashion as data bags—there is a directory under *chef-playground* in which they are organized. The directory name is *roles* by default.

Use the *chef-playground* directory you created in Chapter 11. Use the same dual command prompt setup you used there. Start the `chef-zero` server on an open port in one window. We will be using port 9501 in the examples in this chapter:

```
$ chef-zero --port 9501
```

Make sure the *chef-playground* directory is the current working directory:

```
$ cd chef-playground
```

Now run `knife upload nodes` to load up `chef-zero` with fake node data:

```
$ knife upload nodes
Created nodes/snowman.json
Created nodes/atwood.json
Created nodes/susu.json
```

Create a *roles* directory in *chef-playground*:

```
$ mkdir roles
```

We're going to create a *.json* file representing the role data. A basic role has a `name:`, `description:`, and `run_list`. The role can be used to encapsulate a long list of recipes into just one alias. Create file *chef-playground/roles/webserver.json* with the code in Example 14-1.

Example 14-1. chef-playground/roles/webserver.json

```
{
  "name": "webserver",
  "description": "Web Server",
  "json_class": "Chef::Role",
  "chef_type": "role",
  "run_list": [
    "recipe[motd]",
    "recipe[users]",
    "recipe[apache]"
  ]
}
```

Then run `knife role from file` passing in the *webserver.json* file. Similar to data bags, `knife role from file` assumes *webserver.json* is located in a subdirectory named *roles*, and not in the current directory.

```
$ knife role from file webserver.json
Updated Role webserver!
```

Run `knife show role` as follows to display the details about the `webserver` role:

```
$ knife role show webserver
chef_type:           role
default_attributes:
description:         Web Server
env_run_lists:
json_class:          Chef::Role
name:                webserver
override_attributes:
run_list:
  recipe[motd]
  recipe[users]
  recipe[apache]
```

You can reset a node's run list with the `knife node set` command. Change the run list of the `snowman` node to use the `webserver` role you just created, using the following command on Linux/Mac OS X:

```
$ knife node run_list set snowman "role[webserver]"
snowman:
  run_list: role[webserver]
```

or, on Windows:

```
$ knife node run_list set snowman "'role[webserver]'"
snowman:
  run_list: role[webserver]
```

During the Chef run, the reference to the web server role will be expanded to the entries in the role's run list:

- recipe[motd]
- recipe[users]
- recipe[apache]

Roles are a powerful abstraction that let you think of your infrastructure as arrays of functionality. It is quite common for a role to contain dozens of recipes. Imagine needing to assign dozens of recipes to the run list of, say, hundreds of nodes. Roles make this process much easier.

Attributes and Roles

Roles can contain attributes as well.

Create a *.json* file to represent a base role. This role will include references to the chef-client::delete_validation and chef-client::default recipes, both of which we recommended running on every node in Chapter 10. In this case, we'll also set an attribute to tell the chef-client::default recipe to set the init_style to use runit instead of the default. Create the file *chef-playground/roles/base.json* with the code provided in Example 14-2.

Example 14-2. chef-playground/roles/base.json

```
{
  "name": "base",
  "description": "Common recipes for all nodes",
  "json_class": "Chef::Role",
  "chef_type": "role",
  "run_list": [
    "recipe[chef-client::delete_validation]",
    "recipe[chef-client]"
  ],
  "default_attributes": {
    "chef_client": {
      "init_style": "runit"
    }
  }
}
```

Then run knife role from file passing in the *webserver.json* file. Similar to data bags, knife role from file assumes *webserver.json* is located in a subdirectory named *roles*, and not in the current directory:

```
$ knife role from file base.json
Updated Role base!
```

When you run knife role show base as follows, notice that the role has attributes set as well as items in a run list:

```
$ knife role show base
chef_type:          role
default_attributes:
  chef_client:
    init_style: runit
description:         Common recipes for all nodes
env_run_lists:
json_class:         Chef::Role
name:               base
override_attributes:
run_list:
  recipe[chef-client::delete_validation]
  recipe[chef-client]
```

As we discussed in Chapter 8, it is recommended that you restrict your use of attributes in roles to those of default priority, to make it easier to follow the composition of attributes when they come from multiple sources.

Because roles can have attributes, they have a place in the attribute hierarchy of precedence. Figure 14-2 is a modified version of the attribute precedence diagram we showed you in Figure 8-3 that includes roles. Roles can override attributes defined in recipes or attribute files, but they have a lower priority than the automatic attributes defined by ohai. Attribute settings in roles are intended to be global settings that override attributes set within cookbooks.

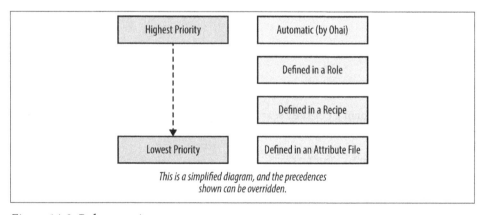

Figure 14-2. Roles overview

Roles and Search

Roles can be search items as well. The following example shows how you can search for a recipe in the run list of a role. Note that you must use the \ character to escape the [and] characters in the query string:

```
$ knife search role "run_list:recipe\[apache\]"
1 items found

chef_type:           role
default_attributes:
description:         Web Server
env_run_lists:
json_class:          Chef::Role
name:                webserver
override_attributes:
run_list:
  recipe[motd]
  recipe[users]
  recipe[apache]
```

Because roles introduce the idea that a list of recipes in a run list can be expanded, there are two ways to search for recipes in a node's run list:

knife search node "recipe:<recipe_name>"
> When you *do not* want the search to include the expanded set of recipes within roles

knife search node "recipes:<recipe name>"
> When you *do* want the search to expand role references

Recall that earlier in the chapter we assigned the snowman node to have the webserver role in its run list. Implicitly, when the role reference is expanded during a Chef run, the node will run the following recipes in the webserver role's run_list:

- recipe[motd]
- recipe[users]
- recipe[apache]

However, if you perform a recipe: search for, say, the recipe[apache::config], you might not get the results you intended:

```
$ knife search node "recipe:apache"
2 items found

Node Name:    atwood
...
Node Name:    susu
...
```

Notice when the reference to "role[webserver]" is expanded, snowman does have "recipe[apache]" in its run list. But it doesn't have "recipe[apache]" directly in its run list if it is not expanded. So, snowman does not show up in the search results because the recipe search does not expand the node's run list.

Similar to the square bracket characters ([]), the colon (::) characters in a cookbook recipe reference must be individually escaped on
a command line with the backslash (\) character: `chef-client\:`
`\:config`. This is treated as if it were `chef-client::config`.

If you want to fully expand all the recipe references in a run list, perform a `recipes:`
search instead. Then `snowman` shows up in the search results:

```
$ knife search node "recipes:apache"
3 items found

Node Name:  atwood
...
Node Name:  snowman
...
Node Name:  susu
...
```

There are similar search commands with expansion for roles as there are for recipes:

`knife search node role:<role_name>`
When you *do not* want the search to include the expanded set of role references

`knife search node "roles:<role_name>"`
When you *do* want the search to expand role references

Role Cookbook

Another issue related to the expansion of roles is that when a change gets made to a
role, it gets reflected immediately across your entire infrastructure. Roles are not versioned in any way.

This usually has the most impact with run lists. Say, for example, one of your Chef
infrastructure developers decided to remove the `recipe[apache]` role from the `web`
`server` role we have been using in this chapter. We'll say this developer made the change
because she didn't want web servers to default to using the Apache web server, but
instead wanted to offer cookbook developers the choice of using the Apache or Nginx
web servers for their apps:

```
{
  "name": "webserver",
  "description": "Web Server",
  "json_class": "Chef::Role",
  "chef_type": "role",
  "run_list": [
    "recipe[motd]",
    "recipe[users]"
```

```
    ]
  }
```

If the webserver role were used widely across your infrastructure, this could have un-intended consequences for cookbooks that assumed the old behavior where the recipe[apache] was included in the role. Or conversely, if developers are careful not to make changes to the run lists of existing roles, it can result in a proliferation of differently named roles with similar functions. For example, that Chef developer might have instead chosen to create two new roles—webserver-apache and webserver-nginx —to make her intention to complement the existing webserver role more clear.

Because cookbooks are versioned, a pattern of using a *role cookbook* in lieu of using the run list feature of roles is one technique many Chef developers use. They still use roles for common attributes, but the role run list is moved to a cookbook. A recipe can emulate a role run list easily through the use of the include_recipe command we introduced in "Include_Recipe" on page 137.

For example, in this case, we could create a webserver cookbook where the default recipe includes the apache cookbook:

```
#
# Cookbook Name:: webserver
# Recipe:: default
#
# Copyright (C) 2014
#
#
#

include_recipe "motd"
include_recipe "user"
include_recipe "apache"
```

Nodes could still include the webserver role as a classification mechanism and for any shared attributes. It can still be handy to run this command to find all the web servers on your network:

```
knife search node role:webserver
```

 chef-zero currently does not seem to index roles for searching, so the preceding command will not work with the test setup in this chapter. Instead, you'll need to use a full Chef Server setup.

In this scenario, the run list of the webserver role would be blank, and instead nodes would add the cookbook recipe[webserver] to their run list. Cookbooks are versioned, and with environments, which we'll introduce in the next chapter, you can ensure that a subset of nodes in your infrastructure is fixed to use specific versions of a cookbook. This is referred to as *version pinning* a node (or *pinning* a node).

Summary

We covered roles in this chapter. Roles provide a way to classify patterns of use in your infrastructure. Roles can contain attributes and a list of recipes and other roles as a run list. This allows you to package all the settings for a node configuration into a single role reference.

In the next and final chapter of this book, we'll cover environments, which provide a different code of abstraction—a way to map your organization's app deployment workflow to a set of server configurations and cookbook versions.

## CHAPTER 15

Environments

Environments are a feature of Chef Server used to model the server configurations required during each phase of your software development lifecycle, as shown in Figure 15-1.

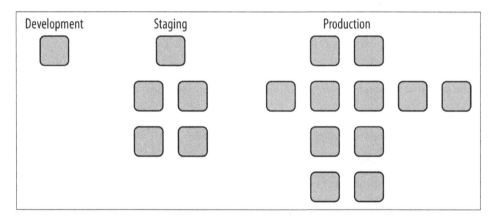

Figure 15-1. Environments overview

Environments reflect your patterns and workflow, and can be used to model the life stages of your application, such as:

- Development
- Testing
- Staging
- Production

Every Chef Server starts out with a single environment, the `_default` environment.

Environments might include attributes necessary for configuring your infrastructure, such as:

- The URL of a payment service API
- The location of a package repository
- The version of Chef configuration files that should be used

Environments allow for isolating resources on a Chef Server because environments can contain version constraints, unlike with roles. Environments still have a use even when you have Test Kitchen at your disposal, because you'll probably want to do some testing against servers in your production environment.

Create a Dev Environment

Environments can be created and managed in the same fashion as data bags and roles, organized in a directory under *chef-playground*. The directory name is *environments* by default.

Use the *chef-playground* directory you created in Chapter 11. Use the same dual command prompt setup you used there. Start the `chef-zero` server on an open port in one window. We will be using port 9501 in the examples in this chapter:

```
$ chef-zero --port 9501
```

Make sure that the *chef-playground* directory is the current working directory:

```
$ cd chef-playground
```

Create an `environments` directory in *chef-playground*:

```
$ mkdir environments
```

We're going to create a *.json* file representing the new environment. A basic environment has a `name:` and `description:`. Environments can have one or more cookbook constraints as well. The ability to "pin" cookbooks to particular versions is the most useful feature of environments. Create the file *chef-playground/roles/dev.json* containing the code provided in Example 15-1.

Example 15-1. chef-playground/environments/dev.json

```
{
  "name": "dev",
  "description": "For developers!",
  "cookbook_versions": {
    "apache": "= 0.2.0"
  },
  "json_class": "Chef::Environment",
  "chef_type": "environment"
}
```

There are other options for a version constraint besides "equal to" (=). Equality is the recommended practice. To learn more about the other options, refer to *http://bit.ly/abt_cookbook_versions*.

Run `knife environment from file` passing in the *dev.json* file. `knife environment from file` assumes *dev.json* is located in a subdirectory called *environments*, and not in the current directory:

```
$ knife environment from file dev.json
Updated Environment dev
```

Run `knife environment show dev` as follows to display the details about the dev environment:

```
$ knife environment show dev
chef_type:          environment
cookbook_versions:
  apache: = 0.2.0
default_attributes:
description:         For developers!
json_class:         Chef::Environment
name:               dev
override_attributes:
```

Attributes and Environments

Environments can contain attributes. Let's experiment with this by creating a *.json* file to represent a `production` environment. This environment will pin production to the older version of the `apache` cookbook, the `0.1.0` that is not currently under development. We'll also make sure that in the production environment, the message of the day is set to a suitable message of the day for production. Create the file *chef-playground/environments/production.json* with the code provided in Example 15-2.

Example 15-2. chef-playground/environments/production.json

```
{
  "name": "production",
  "description": "For prods!",
  "cookbook_versions": {
    "apache": "= 0.1.0"
  },
  "json_class": "Chef::Environment",
  "chef_type": "environment",
  "override_attributes": {
    "motd": {
      "message": "A production-worthy message of the day"
    }
```

```
    }
}
```

Then run `knife environment from file` passing in the *production.json* file, as follows:

```
$ knife environment from file production.json
Updated Environment production
```

`knife show environment` displays more detailed information about an environment:

```
$ knife environment show production
chef_type:           environment
cookbook_versions:
  apache: = 0.1.0
default_attributes:
description:          For prods!
json_class:          Chef::Environment
name:                production
override_attributes:
  motd:
    message: A production-worthy message of the day
```

Things get a little more complicated with attribute precedence when environments come into the picture. Figure 15-2 shows that an environment has a priority less than a role, but greater than a cookbook recipe or attribute file.

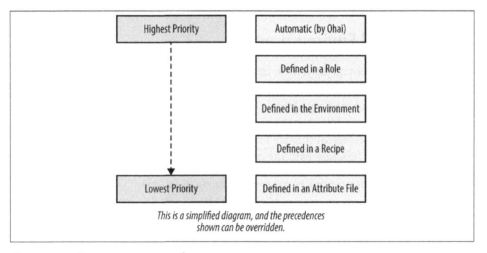

Figure 15-2. Environment precedence

Because an environment can override and pin specific cookbook versions, it seems more reasonable that environments should have a higher priority than the default. So in this particular instance with environments, it does make sense to use `override_at tributes` instead of `default_attributes` for any environment attributes.

Putting All the Pieces Together

Let's go through a complete example using the `apache` cookbook from Chapter 7, making use of environments and roles as you would in a production Chef setup.

Simulate a Production Environment

Create a directory called *chef-zero*. This will be structured similar to *chef-repo* in Chapter 9 and *chef-playground*, with *cookbooks*, *environments*, and *roles* as subdirectories. Once you create the directory, make it the current working directory as follows:

```
$ mkdir chef-zero
$ cd chef-zero
```

Create a *chef-zero/environments* subdirectory to contain our environment definitions in the JSON file format, and make it the current working directory:

```
$ mkdir environments
$ cd environments
```

Let's say our `apache` cookbook is ready to go and we are making use of attributes, environments, and roles in our production environment. First, let's simulate the production environment with Test Kitchen.

Create an environment definition in *chef-zero/environments* as shown in Example 15-3. This will represent a `production` environment, like we covered earlier in this chapter. There is also an attribute set for node[`'motd'`][`'message'`] as an attribute with override precedence.

Example 15-3. chefdk/chef-zero/environments/production.json

```
{
  "name": "production",
  "description": "For prods!",
  "cookbook_versions": {
    "apache": "= 0.1.0"
  },
  "json_class": "Chef::Environment",
  "chef_type": "environment",
  "override_attributes": {
    "motd": {
      "message": "A production-worthy message of the day"
    }
  }
}
```

Our production environment uses roles. Create a directory parallel to `environments` called `roles`, and make it the current working directory, as follows:

```
$ cd ..
$ mkdir roles
$ cd roles
```

In our production environment, we use a `webserver` role just like we covered in Chapter 14 to denote nodes that are web servers. Create the file *chef-zero/roles/webserver.json* as shown in Example 15-4. It contains the *apache* directory in its run list and the attribute `node['apache']['port']` set at the default attribute precedence. We'll be using this attribute to show how we can change the behavior of the cookbook depending on whether the node is in production.

Example 15-4. chefdk/chef-zero/roles/webserver.json

```
{
  "name": "webserver",
  "description": "Web Server",
  "json_class": "Chef::Role",
  "chef_type": "role",
  "default_attributes": {
    "apache": {
      "port": 80
    }
  },
  "run_list": [
    "recipe[apache]"
  ]
}
```

Create a directory called *cookbooks*, parallel to the others you have created so far in this chapter, and make it the current working directory:

```
$ cd ..
$ mkdir cookbooks
$ cd cookbooks
```

So far, your *chef-zero* directory should resemble the following structure:

```
chef-zero
    ├── cookbooks
    ├── environments
    │   └── production.json
    └── roles
        └── webserver.json
```

We'll be recreating a version of the `apache` cookbook for this chapter, with a few additions. Create an apache cookbook in the cookbooks subdirectory by using `chef gener ate cookbook` or `knife cookbook create`, as per your Chef development tool setup.

Chef Development Kit:

```
$ chef generate cookbook apache
$ cd apache
```

Chef Client:

```
$ knife cookbook create apache --cookbook-path .
$ cd apache
$ kitchen init --create-gemfile
$ bundle install
```

Create a *.kitchen.yml* file as shown in Example 15-5. There's a lot more going on in this version than we have seen in previous chapters.

For this example, we must use the chef_zero provisioner because we are making use of Chef Server features, so make sure that is being set in the provisioner: stanza of the *.kitchen.yml*. We need Test Kitchen to spin up a Chef Zero instance for us.

Also in the provisioner: stanza, we tell Test Kitchen where the *roles* and *environments* directories are relative to the location of the *.kitchen.yml*:

```
provisioner:
  name: chef_zero
  environments_path: ../../environments
  roles_path: ../../.roles
```

Don't miss that we are setting the Test Kitchen suite name to be prod in the suites: stanza. We're using a special suite name in this chapter because eventually there are going to be two suites, one for each environment, and we need a way of telling them apart. The suite for production will have the suite name prod.

We're also introducing some new syntax in the suites: stanza. We set the environment for our sandbox node in its */etc/chef/client.rb*, like so:

```
suites:
  - name: prod
    provisioner:
      client_rb:
        environment: production
  ...
```

Nodes can be a member of only one environment at a time. The environment is a setting in the */etc/chef/client.rb* file. If this is not set, a node uses the default environment named _default.

Outside of this simulated setup, you would use the chef-client::config recipe to change the value of the environment setting in */etc/chef/client.rb*, using the following node attribute, similar to how we set ssl_verify_mode in Chapter 10:

```
node.default['chef_client']['config']['environment'] = 'production'
```

We also show how a private_network IP address can be set in the suites: stanza instead of the provisioner: stanza:

```
suites:
  - name: prod
```

```
...
driver:
  network:
  - ["private_network", {ip: "192.168.33.15"}]
```

When a value is set in the provisioner: stanza in Test Kitchen, the values are inherited by all the items in the suites: stanza. In this case, we're going to want our production and dev sandbox environments to have different IP addresses, so we move the private_network setting to be under suites.

Example 15-5. chefdk/chef-zero/cookbooks/apache/.kitchen.yml

```
---
driver:
  name: vagrant

provisioner:
  name: chef_zero
  environments_path: ../../environments
  roles_path: ../../.roles

platforms:
  - name: centos65
    driver:
      box: learningchef/centos65
      box_url: learningchef/centos65

suites:
  - name: prod
    provisioner:
      client_rb:
        environment: production
    driver:
      network:
      - ["private_network", {ip: "192.168.33.15"}]
    run_list:
      - recipe[apache::default]
    attributes:
```

Check the syntax of your *.kitchen.yml* with kitchen list. The output should resemble the following:

```
$ kitchen list
Instance        Driver   Provisioner  Last Action
prod-centos65  Vagrant  ChefZero      <Not Created>
```

Edit *apache/metadata.rb*, filling in the maintainer, maintainer_email, and license. We filled in ours like in Example 15-6.

Example 15-6. chefdk/chef-zero/cookbooks/apache/metadata.rb

```
name              'apache'
maintainer        'Mischa Taylor'
```

```
maintainer_email 'mischa@misheska.com'
license          'MIT'
description      'Installs/Configures apache'
long_description 'Installs/Configures apache'
version          '0.1.0'
```

Because we will be using attributes in this version of the apache cookbook, create a *default.rb* attributes file.

Chef Development Kit:

```
$ chef generate attribute default
```

Chef Client:

```
$ touch attributes/default.rb
```

Provide default settings for all the attributes we're going to be using in our cookbook by creating *attributes/default.rb* as shown in Example 15-7. In order to test attribute precedence, we're going to set the default values for node['apache']['port'] and node['motd']['message'] to something different than what is being set in the role and in the environment we are using. We also moved the root location for our *index.html* file to an attribute.

Example 15-7. chefdk/chef-zero/apache/attributes/default.rb

```
default['apache']['document_root'] = '/var/www/html'
default['apache']['port'] = 3333
default['motd']['message'] = 'Default message'
```

Create the recipe file *recipes/default.rb* as shown in Example 15-8. Most of this recipe code should look familiar.

We are adding a new template resource to create a *custom.conf* file on the sandbox node, along with an accompanying directory resource to create the required directory on the node. *custom.conf* is an optional file used to configure apache web server settings. In this file we're going to set the default listening port and the document root.

We are introducing an alternative template resource syntax:

```
template '/etc/httpd/conf.d/custom.conf' do
  ...
  variables(
    :document_root => node['apache']['document_root'],
    :port => node['apache']['port']
  )
  ...
end
```

We covered the use of notifies in Chapter 9.

You can pass a hash of variables to be used when the template file is evaluated using the
variables() attribute. This is a way to pass local instance variables in a recipe to a
template, or to use shorter, more memorable variable names in the template file.

Example 15-8. chefdk/chef-zero/apache/recipes/default.rb

```
#
# Cookbook Name:: apache
# Recipe:: default
#
# Copyright (C) 2014
#
#
#

package 'httpd'

service 'httpd' do
  action [ :enable, :start ]
end

# Add a template for Apache virtual host configuration
template '/etc/httpd/conf.d/custom.conf' do
  source 'custom.erb'
  mode '0644'
  variables(
    :document_root => node['apache']['document_root'],
    :port => node['apache']['port']
  )
  notifies :restart, 'service[httpd]'
end

document_root = node['apache']['document_root']

# Add a directory resource to create the document_root
directory document_root do
  mode '0755'
  recursive true
end

template "#{document_root}/index.html" do
  source 'index.html.erb'
  mode '0644'
  variables(
    :message => node['motd']['message'],
    :port => node['apache']['port']
  )
end
```

Generate the template file *templates/default/index.html.erb*, using the appropriate command line for your Chef development setup.

Chef Development Kit:

```
$ chef generate template index.html
```

Chef Client - Linux/Mac OS X:

```
$ touch templates/default/index.html.erb
```

Chef Client - Windows:

```
$ touch templates\default\index.html.erb
```

Create the file *templates/default/index.html.erb* as shown in Example 15-9. We are using the short variable instance forms we defined in the `variables()` attribute of the template resource. Also, for some variety, we left one of them as the standard form: `node["ipad dress"]`. You can mix and match these forms as you like.

Example 15-9. chefdk/chef-zero/apache/templates/default/index.hmtl.erb

```
<html>
  <body>
    <h1><%= @message %></h1>
    <%= node["ipaddress"] %>:<%= @port %>
  </body>
</html>
```

Generate one more template file, *templates/default/custom.erb*, which will be used as an apache configuration file.

Chef Development Kit:

```
$ chef generate template custom
```

Chef Client - Linux/Mac OS X:

```
$ touch templates/default/custom.erb
```

Chef Client - Windows:

```
$ touch templates\default\custom.erb
```

Create *templates/default/custom.erb* as shown in Example 15-10. We're using this optional apache configuration file to set the port the server is listening on via the `Listen` setting and the `DocumentRoot`.

We will explain the `if` syntax in the template in more detail in Chapter 16. In short for now, you can place conditional logic in templates when it is enclosed by `<% %>` (vs. `<%= %>` when you want to evaluate a string). Also, if the closing tag has a minus sign in it, such as `-%>`, the line is removed from the resultant template output when it is evaluated. Therefore, in Example 15-10, these three lines are processed when the template file is evaluated: `<% if @port != 80 -%>`, `Listen <%= @port %>`, and `<% end -%>`. When the evaluated output is written to the resultant template file, it becomes just one line, because there are `-%>` symbols on the first and the third lines: `Listen <%= @port %>`.

Further, the single line with `Listen <%= @port %>` is only written to the resultant template file if the conditional logic evaluates to a port number besides 80.

We need this conditional logic in the template because the `Listen` line is required in the *.conf* file when any port besides 80 is used. If we left out the conditional, we'd get an error configuring the website if it evaluates to port 80.

Example 15-10. chefdk/chef-zero/apache/templates/default/custom.erb

```
<% if @port != 80 -%> ❶
  Listen <%= @port %> ❷
<% end -%> ❸

<VirtualHost *:<%= @port %>>
  ServerAdmin webmaster@localhost

  DocumentRoot <%= @document_root %>
  <Directory />
    Options FollowSymLinks
    AllowOverride None
  </Directory>
  <Directory <%= @document_root %>>
    Options Indexes FollowSymLinks MultiViews
    AllowOverride None
    Order allow,deny
    allow from all
  </Directory>
</VirtualHost>
```

❶   This line is omitted from the resultant template file.

❷   Only this line is written to the resultant template file.

❸   This line is omitted from the resultant template file.

Run `kitchen converge` to deploy your cookbook to the sandbox node using the pro duction environment:

```
$ kitchen converge prod-centos65
```

If all goes well, you should be able to view the production website on the sandbox node at *http://192.168.33.15* on the default web port 80—it should resemble Figure 15-3. The port 80 setting in the role overrides the default attribute set in the apache cookbook. Also, the message attribute set in the environment takes precedence.

Figure 15-3. Production web server

Simulate a Development Environment

Let's say we want to start a new development cycle for our apache cookbook, adding some new requested functionality. For the purposes of this chapter, we don't care what the enhancements are, we just want our new cookbook development not to interfere with the stable 0.1.0 version we already have in production. We will perform our development on a node allocated to an environment called dev.

First, before doing anything else, increment the current cookbook version 0.1.0 to the next minor version number 0.2.0. We recommend that you follow semantic versioning (*http://semver.org*) guidelines when you version your cookbooks, incrementing the second digit when there are new changes that won't break existing functionality. This is the intent with these hypothetical changes we might make to the apache cookbook.

Example 15-11. chefdk/chef-zero/cookbooks/apache/metadata.rb

```
name              'apache'
maintainer        'Mischa Taylor'
maintainer_email  'mischa@misheska.com'
license           'MIT'
description       'Installs/Configures apache'
long_description  'Installs/Configures apache'
version           '0.2.0'
```

If you try to deploy this new cookbook to the production node, you should get an error saying *could not satisfy version constraints*. Now we know that our production environment is enforcing the policy we set to pin the apache cookbook to version 0.1.0. When we tried to deploy version 0.2.0, we got an error:

```
$ kitchen converge prod-centos65
...
        Missing Cookbooks:
        ------------------
```

```
        Could not satisfy version constraints for: apache
    ...
    Chef Client failed. 0 resources updated in 1.626076356 seconds
        [2014-08-22T17:59:26-07:00] ERROR: 412 "Precondition Failed "
        [2014-08-22T17:59:26-07:00] FATAL: Chef::Exceptions::ChildConvergeError:
        Chef run process exited unsuccessfully (exit code 1)
    >>>>>> Converge failed on instance <prod-centos65>.
    >>>>>> Please see .kitchen/logs/prod-centos65.log for more
    details
    >>>>>> ------Exception-------
    >>>>>> Class: Kitchen::ActionFailed
    >>>>>> Message: SSH exited (1) for command: [sudo -E
    chef-client -z --config /tmp/kitchen/client.rb --log_level info
    --chef-zero-port 8889 --json-attributes /tmp/kitchen/dna.json]
    >>>>>> --------------------
```

Add a new environment definition to `chef-zero/environments` as shown in Example 15-12. We'll pin the environment to use the latest cookbook version `0.2.0`. Also, set the `node['apache']['port']` and `node['motd']['message']` to use developer-specific overrides.

Example 15-12. chefdk/chef-zero/environments/dev.json

```
{
  "name": "dev",
  "description": "For developers!",
  "cookbook_versions": {
    "apache": "= 0.2.0"
  },
  "json_class": "Chef::Environment",
  "chef_type": "environment",
  "override_attributes": {
    "apache": {
      "port": 8080
    },
    "motd": {
      "message": "Developers, developers, developers!"
    }
  }
}
```

Add a new `dev` suite to *chef-zero/cookbooks/apache/.kitchen.yml* as shown in Example 15-13. It's in the same format as our `prod` instance—it just uses the `dev` environment and the IP address `192.168.33.16`.

Example 15-13. chefdk/chef-zero/cookbooks/apache/.kitchen.yml

```
---
driver:
  name: vagrant

provisioner:
```

```
  name: chef_zero
  environments_path: ../../environments
  roles_path: ../../.roles

platforms:
  - name: centos65
    driver:
      box: learningchef/centos65
      box_url: learningchef/centos65

suites:
  - name: prod
    provisioner:
      client_rb:
        environment: production
    driver:
      network:
      - ["private_network", {ip: "192.168.33.15"}]
    run_list:
      - recipe[apache::default]
    attributes:

  - name: dev
    provisioner:
      client_rb:
        environment: dev
    driver:
      network:
      - ["private_network", {ip: "192.168.33.16"}]
    run_list:
      - recipe[apache::default]
    attributes:
```

Run kitchen list to check your *.kitchen.yml* syntax. Now you should see two instances, like so:

```
$ kitchen list
Instance        Driver   Provisioner  Last Action
prod-centos65   Vagrant  ChefZero     Converged
dev-centos65    Vagrant  ChefZero     <Not Created>
```

Run kitchen converge against the dev-centos65 instance, as follows:

```
$ kitchen converge dev-centos65
```

If all goes well, you should be able to view the development website on the sandbox node at *http://192.168.33.16:8080*—it should resemble Figure 15-4. The port 8080 setting in the environment overrides the default attribute set in the apache cookbook and in the role. Also, the message attribute set in the environment takes precedence.

Figure 15-4. Development web server

Run kitchen destroy with no parameters to destroy the virtual machines associated with both of the sandbox instances and to release all resources used:

```
$ kitchen converge dev-centos65
-----> Starting Kitchen (v1.2.2.dev)
-----> Destroying <prod-centos65>...
       ==> default: Forcing shutdown of VM...
       ==> default: Destroying VM and associated drives...
       Vagrant instance <prod-centos65> destroyed.
       Finished destroying <prod-centos65> (0m3.00s).
-----> Destroying <dev-centos65>...
       ==> default: Forcing shutdown of VM...
       ==> default: Destroying VM and associated drives...
       Vagrant instance <dev-centos65> destroyed.
       Finished destroying <dev-centos65> (0m3.00s).
-----> Kitchen is finished. (0m6.49s)
```

Summary

In this chapter we have covered environments and how they provide the ability to fix settings to match the different stages of your deployment workflow. We also walked you through a realistic example that made use of both environments and roles to change cookbook behavior. You can use environments to match the promotion model you use as your Chef code travels from development to production.

In the next, and final, chapter of this book, we're going to show you how to test your automation code.

## CHAPTER 16

Testing

In this final chapter of the book, we will cover how to test your Chef automation code. It is important to perform testing and verification steps before deploying your Chef code to production to ensure it works as intended.

In nearly all the exercises in this book, we've taken care to add sections highlighting how to manually verify that your Chef code is working properly. In this chapter, we'll show you how to automate this process.

Testing Rationale

Using a configuration management tool like Chef gets you 50% of the way there in automating testing and verification. Because Chef automates infrastructure in a repeatable manner, it inherently makes apps running in these environments more testable. This is why we introduced Test Kitchen so early in the book, in Chapter 5, so that you could see this in action. Throughout the book, you've deployed your Chef code to a local development sandbox environment. Using Test Kitchen should give you confidence that if you deployed the same code to a production Chef environment, it will behave in the same manner.

The other 50% of the testing rationale, besides using Chef in the first place, is to be strategic when testing and deploying automation code. Just as it is best to introduce change to application code in small batches, it is also best to introduce change to your infrastructure in small batches. As Figure 16-1 shows, you should work in short bursts, performing a short build-test-deploy cycle. This approach can help ensure that enough testing gets done to result in an infrastructure and application of high quality.

Figure 16-1. Using short build→test→deploy cycles

It's harder to estimate when long, drawn-out development cycles will complete than shorter "baby step" development increments as advocated in Figure 16-1. As Figure 16-2 shows, what almost inevitably happens with long, drawn-out development cycles is that testing is done at the last minute and it ultimately takes longer to deliver a large feature than intended. At the same time, the shorter testing period sacrifices quality, and this can lead to the "throw it over the wall to operations" scenario where applications work fine in development but don't work in production. Configuration management tools like Chef try to address this problem.

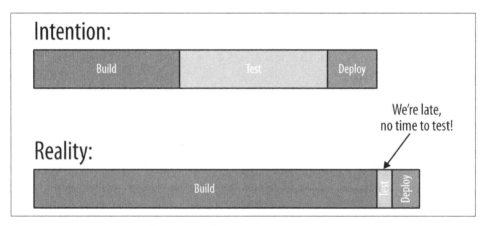

Figure 16-2. Testing crunches in lengthy development projects

Further, there is a monetary cost associated with finding and fixing bugs in your software and infrastructure code, and that cost goes up the further out in the development cycle you discover issues. Figure 16-3 shows the relative cost of fixing a software bug as development progresses. Your infrastructure code is no different than application code in this respect:

- Requirements
- Design
- Coding

- Development testing
- Acceptance testing
- Operations/production

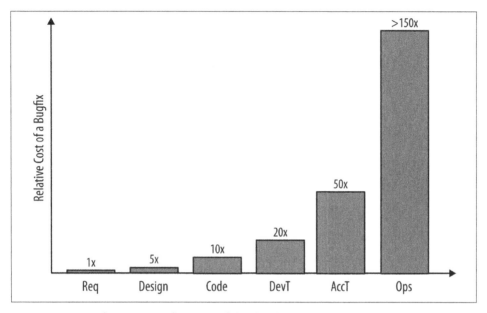

Figure 16-3. Bugfix costs as a function of the development stage

Finding and fixing issues during the requirements and design phase is not very expensive. However, the cost goes up the further out in the development lifecycle you go. When you wait to find bugs after they have been coded, the costs are 20 times to 50 times greater than if you had caught them earlier. During the production phase, the cost is 150 times greater.

This graphic serves as a good reminder of how you should always approach a Chef coding project:

1. Code right the first time, because it costs a lot more to fix things later.
2. Find bugs and issues as early as possible, ideally before they ever get in, or at least as close to the time of coding as possible.
3. Make changes in small batches—the smaller the change, the less likely you are to introduce a lot of new defects. It's also easier to test in small batches.

Chef includes testing tools that support this approach. As Figure 16-4 shows, Chef provides multiple testing tools specialized to give you feedback on issues with your code at the earliest possible time during the cookbook authoring process.

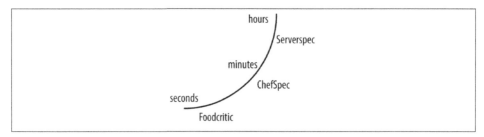

Figure 16-4. Chef's testing tools for every phase of development

There are multiple tools because each is tailored to run in a particular cookbook authoring phase. Following is a brief overview of each tool and when you use it:

- In your text editor when you type:
  - — Foodcritic analyzes your Chef coding style.
- Before you deploy to a test node:
  - — ChefSpec helps you document and organize your code.
- After you deploy to a test node:
  - — Serverspec verifies that a cookbook behaves as intended.

 In this chapter, we use the terms *test* and *example* interchangeably.

For those using Chef Client, you will need to install some additional gems to support testing. Run the following to install the required tools for this chapter:

```
$ sudo gem install foodcritic --no-ri --no-rdoc
$ sudo gem install chefspec --no-ri --no-rdoc
```

If you're using the Chef Development Kit, you're fine, these Ruby gems have already been installed for you.

Revisiting the Apache Cookbook

For people new to automated testing, Serverspec is the most easily understood tool, so we'll start with it first. We will test it by revisiting a cookbook we created in Chapter 7. We'll be adding tests to this cookbook in this chapter.

 We are covering Serverspec v2 syntax.

Generate a cookbook called `apache-test`.

Chef Development Kit:

```
$ chef generate cookbook apache-test
$ cd apache-test
```

Chef Client:

```
$ knife cookbook create apache-test --cookbook-path .
$ cd apache-test
$ kitchen init --create-gemfile
$ bundle install
```

Edit the *.kitchen.yml* as shown in Example 16-1. Use the `chef_zero` provisioner and our favorite basebox image. Additionally, configure a `private_network` with an IP address of `192.168.33.38` so you can access the website from your host development workstation like you did in Chapter 7.

Example 16-1. chefdk/apache-test/.kitchen.yml

```
---
driver:
  name: vagrant

provisioner:
  name: chef_zero

platforms:
  - name: centos65
    driver:
      box: learningchef/centos65
      box_url: learningchef/centos65
      network:
      - ["private_network", {ip: "192.168.33.38"}]

suites:
  - name: default
    run_list:
```

```
    - recipe[apache-test::default]
  attributes:
```

Make sure there are no syntax errors in your *.kitchen.yml* by running `kitchen converge`:

```
$ kitchen converge
```

Create a `default` recipe with the same code we used in Chapter 7.

Example 16-2. chefdk/apache-test/recipes/default.rb

```
#
# Cookbook Name:: apache-test
# Recipe:: default
#
# Copyright (C) 2014
#
#
#

package "httpd"

service "httpd" do
  action [ :enable, :start ]
end

template "/var/www/html/index.html" do
  source 'index.html.erb'
  mode '0644'
end
```

Create an ERB template for the *index.html* file.

Chef Development Kit:

```
$ chef generate template index.html
```

Chef Client:

```
$ touch templates/default/index.html.erb
```

Let's do a little something new with the *index.html.erb* template. In "Introducing the Template Resource" on page 124 we learned that the ERB template processor looks for tags such as <%= %> in *.erb* files, evaluates the expression within the tag, and returns a string as output:

```
This site was set up by <%= node['hostname'] %>
```

If the tag does not have an equal sign, it is evaluated as a *scriptlet* instead of a string. Within Chef templates, this mechanism is used to add conditional logic. For example, take a close look at this ERB template:

```
<% for @interface in node['network']['interfaces'].keys %>
  * <%= @interface %>
<% end %>
```

 Pay close attention to where <% %> is used and where <%= %> is used.

On my test node, which has three network interfaces—lo, eth0, and eth1 —the scriptlet will render the following output:

```
* lo
* eth0
* eth1
```

The lines in the ERB template *without* an equal sign <% %> are evaluated as *scriptlets*; the expression is evaluated but not rendered in the output file as a string. Then we use the ERB tag *with* an equals sign <%= %> to print out a line in the resulting output each time we run through the conditional logic.

 In order to determine that node['network']['interfaces'] was the correct variable syntax, we inspected the output of ohai, looking for the values that we wanted to display.

In your cookbook, edit *index.html.erb* as shown in Example 16-3. We'll use a variant of the preceding logic that prints out each interface name on the node and its IP address, using more idiomatic Ruby and some bare-bones HTML.

Example 16-3. chefdk/apache-test/templates/default/index.hmtl.erb

```
<html>
<body>
<pre><code>
This site was set up by <%= node['hostname'] %>
My network addresses are:
<% node['network']['interfaces'].keys.each do |iface_name| %>
  * <%= iface_name %>:
      <%= node['network']['interfaces'][iface_name]['addresses'].keys[1] %>
<% end %>
</code></pre>
</body>
</html>
```

This is admittedly horrible HTML! But it will render readable output, which is our only goal. Thankfully, this is a book on Chef, not HTML.

Perform a final `kitchen converge` to ensure there are no syntax errors in your code:

```
$ kitchen converge
```

Verify that the website functions as intended by visiting it at `192.168.33.38`. It should render as shown in Figure 16-5.

Figure 16-5. Your apache site on 192.168.33.38

Test Automation with Serverspec

In the last section, we verified that our cookbook worked by running `kitchen converge` and verifying that the website worked by checking it manually. Let's automate our website verification process by writing some tests in Serverspec and running the tests with Test Kitchen.

Write Your First Serverspec Test

By default, Test kitchen will look in the *test/integration* subdirectory for test-related files. Serverspec looks for its own files a few more directory levels below *test/integration*. First there needs to be a directory name underneath *test/integration* that matches the *suite name*:

```
<cookbook_root>
└── test
    └── integration
        └── <suite_name>
```

As Figure 16-6 shows, the name of the suite can be found in the `suites:` stanza of the *.kitchen.yml*. `default` is the suite name that is initially generated. Although not covered in this book, you can use the suite capability of Test Kitchen to run sets of tests with different run lists and attributes, perhaps exercising conditional functionality in your cookbook.

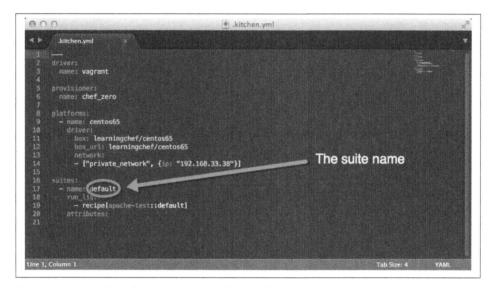

Figure 16-6. Finding the suite name in the .kitchen.yml

In our case, the suite name is `default`, so create a directory for that now under the apache-test cookbook root.

Linux/Mac OS X:

```
$ mkdir -p test/integration/default
```

Windows:

```
> mkdir test\integration\default
```

Further, we need to create a directory underneath *test/integration/default* to tell test kitchen that we want to use the `serverspec` test plugin. Rather than specifying this in the *.kitchen.yml* file, Test Kitchen infers this from the directory structure underneath *test/integration*. Create the *test/integration/default/serverspec* directory now.

Linux/Mac OS X:

```
$ mkdir -p test/integration/default/serverspec
```

Windows:

```
$ mkdir test\integration\default\serverspec
```

By convention, Serverspec expects files containing test code to end in the suffix *spec.rb*. Create the file *default_spec.rb* in the *test/integration/default/serverspec* subdirectory of your cookbook, as shown in Example 16-4.

Example 16-4. chefdk/apache-test/test/integration/default/serverspec/default_spec.rb

```
require 'serverspec'

set :backend, :exec

describe 'web site' do
  it 'responds on port 80' do
    expect(port 80).to be_listening 'tcp'
  end
end
```

There are three major components to the *spec.rb* file, which we've labeled 1, 2, and 3:

```
require 'serverspec' ❶

set :backend, :exec ❷

describe 'web site' do ❸
  it 'responds on port 80' do
    expect(port 80).to be_listening 'tcp'
  end
end
```

❶ The `require` statement is used to load the gem library for `serverspec`, so we can reference Serverspec classes and methods, such as the `set` method.

❷ The `set` statement lets us configure how `serverspec` runs. In this case, we set the `:backend` property to `:exec` to tell `serverspec` that the test code will be running on the same machine as where it is being evaluated.

❸ Tests are written using the RSpec DSL using `describe` and `it` statements. In this case, we're using the RSpec DSL to write a test that checks to see if our website is listening on port 80 using the TCP protocol (the standard port/protocol for an HTTP website).

We'll go over the RSpec DSL and test syntax in more detail in "RSpec DSL Syntax" on page 279. For now, just accept that this is the syntax to specify a test that checks to see if something is listening on port 80.

In order to run this test code, you first need to make sure all the necessary gem files are loaded on the test node. We do that with the `kitchen setup` command. Go ahead and run `kitchen setup` now:

```
$ kitchen setup
-----> Starting Kitchen (v1.2.1)
-----> Setting up <default-centos65>...
```

```
Fetching: thor-0.19.0.gem (100%)
Fetching: busser-0.6.2.gem (100%)
        Successfully installed thor-0.19.0
        Successfully installed busser-0.6.2
        2 gems installed
-----> Setting up Busser
        Creating BUSSER_ROOT in /tmp/busser
        Creating busser binstub
        Plugin serverspec installed (version 0.4.0)
-----> Running postinstall for serverspec plugin
        Finished setting up <default-centos65> (0m14.02s).
-----> Kitchen is finished. (0m14.64s)
```

When the `kitchen setup` command runs, it inspects the directory structure in the *test/ integration/<suite>/<plugin>* subfolder on your development host. Test Kitchen will then load any plugins required for testing *in your sandbox instance* as indicated by the *<plugin>* directory name. Because we created the directory subfolder *test/integration/ default/serverspec*, Test Kitchen makes sure that the test node has all the necessary libraries and gems for running `serverspec` tests.

Once the test node has all the appropriate test libraries, you can run your tests using the `kitchen verify` command. Do that now. Barring any errors in your code syntax, the output should successfully indicate that the website is running and responding on port 80:

```
$ kitchen verify
-----> Starting Kitchen (v1.2.1)
-----> Verifying <default-centos65>...
        Suite path directory /tmp/busser/suites does not exist, skipping.
        Uploading /tmp/busser/suites/serverspec/default_spec.rb (mode=0644)
-----> Running serverspec test suite
        /opt/chef/embedded/bin/ruby -I/tmp/busser/suites/serverspec
        -I/tmp/busser/gems/gems/rspec-support-3.1.2/lib:/tmp/busser/gems/gems/
        rspec-core-3.1.7/lib /opt/chef/embedded/bin/rspec --pattern /tmp/busser
        /suites/serverspec/\*\*/\*_spec.rb --color --format documentation
        --default-path /tmp/busser/suites/serverspec

        web site
          responds on port 80

        Finished in 0.04131 seconds (files took 0.20083 seconds to load)
        1 example, 0 failures
        Finished verifying <default-centos65> (0m0.90s).
-----> Kitchen is finished. (0m1.36s)
```

You can use these RSpec DSL test statements to express checks in code that you would do manually to verify that your cookbook is working.

However, did this test really do anything? Let's verify this by temporarily disabling the website on the test node and running the test code again.

Log in to the test node with `kitchen login`, stop the web server with `service httpd stop`, and `exit` back out to your host development workstation command prompt, as shown in the following code block:

```
$ kitchen login
Last login: Mon Aug 11 21:01:36 2014 from 10.0.2.2
Welcome to your Packer-built virtual machine.
[vagrant@default-centos65 ~]$ sudo service httpd stop
Stopping httpd:                                        [  OK  ]
[vagrant@default-centos65 ~]$ exit
logout
Connection to 127.0.0.1 closed.
```

Run your test again using `kitchen verify` (you only need to run `kitchen setup` once to initialize the configuration on the test node). This time, it should report that the test failed, which is exactly what should happen:

```
$ kitchen verify
-----> Starting Kitchen (v1.2.1)
-----> Verifying <default-centos65>...
       Removing /tmp/busser/suites/serverspec
       Uploading /tmp/busser/suites/serverspec/default_spec.rb (mode=0644)
-----> Running serverspec test suite
       /opt/chef/embedded/bin/ruby -I/tmp/busser/suites/serverspec
       -I/tmp/busser/gems/gems/rspec-support-3.1.2/lib:/tmp/busser/gems/gems
       /rspec-core-3.1.7/lib /opt/chef/embedded/bin/rspec --pattern /tmp/busser
       /suites/serverspec/\*\*/\*_spec.rb --color --format documentation
       --default-path /tmp/busser/suites/serverspec

       web site
         responds on port 80 (FAILED - 1)

       Failures:

         1) web site responds on port 80
            Failure/Error: expect(port 80).to be_listening 'tcp'
              expected Port "80" to be listening "tcp"
              /bin/sh -c netstat\ -tunl\ \|\ grep\ --\ :80

            # /tmp/busser/suites/serverspec/default_spec.rb:7:in `block (2
            levels) in <top (required)>'

       Finished in 0.03284 seconds (files took 0.2051 seconds to load)
       1 example, 1 failure
    ...
```

So yes, our test is actually performing checks against the live configuration on the test node.

Before we finish this section, go ahead and run `kitchen converge` again to restore the configuration back to what it should be. During the Chef run, the Chef engine will detect that the `httpd` service is not running and start it up again:

```
$ kitchen converge
```

Once the web server is restored, run `kitchen verify` one final time. The test should pass once again:

```
$ kitchen verify
-----> Starting Kitchen (v1.2.1)
-----> Setting up <default-centos65>...
-----> Setting up Busser
       Creating BUSSER_ROOT in /tmp/busser
       Creating busser binstub
       Plugin serverspec already installed
       Finished setting up <default-centos65> (0m1.06s).
-----> Verifying <default-centos65>...
       Removing /tmp/busser/suites/serverspec
       Uploading /tmp/busser/suites/serverspec/default_spec.rb (mode=0644)
-----> Running serverspec test suite
       /opt/chef/embedded/bin/ruby -I/tmp/busser/suites/serverspec
       -I/tmp/busser/gems/gems/rspec-support-3.1.2/lib:/tmp/busser/gems/gems
       /rspec-core-3.1.7/lib /opt/chef/embedded/bin/rspec --pattern /tmp/busser
       /suites/serverspec/\*\*/\*_spec.rb --color --format documentation
       --default-path /tmp/busser/suites/serverspec

       web site
         responds on port 80

       Finished in 0.03131 seconds (files took 0.19949 seconds to load)
       1 example, 0 failures
       Finished verifying <default-centos65> (0m0.90s).
-----> Kitchen is finished. (0m2.66s)
```

RSpec DSL Syntax

Before we continue learning more about how to use Serverspec, let's go over some of the fundamentals of the RSpec DSL syntax, so you know the basics of the Serverspec test syntax.

The RSpec DSL uses a `describe` block to contain a group of tests. A `describe` block has the following form:

```
describe '<entity>' do
  <tests here>
end
```

The purpose of the `describe` block is to group tests in a meaningful manner and describe the entity or thing being tested. The description is just a string passed as a parameter to `describe`. This string serves as documentation for human beings to read in the test output. In Example 16-4, we used the following `describe` form to note that we are testing our website:

```
describe 'web site' do
  <tests here>
end
```

 Under the hood, the RSpec DSL creates a Ruby class in which to group tests.

The actual tests are contained within an `it` block inside a `describe`, which needs to be in the following form:

```
describe '<entity>' do
  it '<description>'
    <examples here>
  end
end
```

The `it` block also accepts a string for documentation on the specific check that will be performed. For example, in Example 16-4 we supplied the string *responds on port 80* to indicate that our test will be checking to see if the website responds on port 80, the standard HTTP port:

```
describe 'web site' do
  it 'responds on port 80' do
    ...
  end
end
```

As of RSpec 3.0, the version of RSpec that ships with current versions of the Chef Development Kit and Chef Client, the tests themselves should be written in *expect form*. Here's what *expect form* looks like:

```
describe '<entity>' do
  it '<description>'
    expect(resource).to matcher matcher_parameter
  end
end
```

A *resource* (also known as a *subject* or *command*) is the first argument for an `expect` block, and it expresses the "thing" to be tested. Testing frameworks such as Serverspec and ChefSpec supply custom resource class implementations that perform a wide variety of checks.

A *matcher* is used to define positive or negative expectations on a resource, via the expect(…).to and expect(…).not_to forms, respectively. These are also supplied as custom class implementations in testing frameworks.

In Example 16-4, we used the port resource and the be_listening matcher with the parameter tcp to check to see if the website is listening on port 80 over TCP:

```
describe 'web site' do
  it 'responsponds on port 80' do
    expect(port 80).to be_listening 'tcp'
  end
end
```

How did we know about this port resource and the be_listening matcher? We referred to the Serverspec test framework documentation listing the resource and matcher classes it provides. See the Serverspec documentation (*http://serverspec.org*). As of this writing, click on the *Resource Types* link at the top of the page, and you will see links to all the Serverspec custom resources, as shown in Figure 16-7.

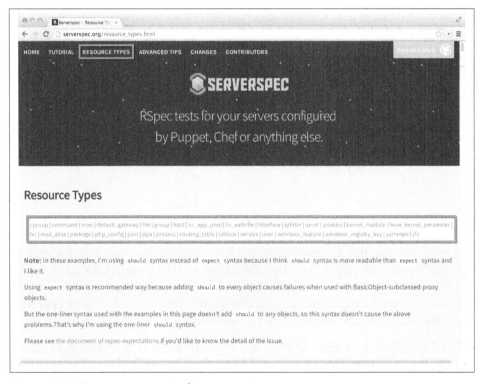

Figure 16-7. Serverspec resource documentation

When you click on a resource, you'll see more detail on all the matchers available, as shown in Figure 16-8.

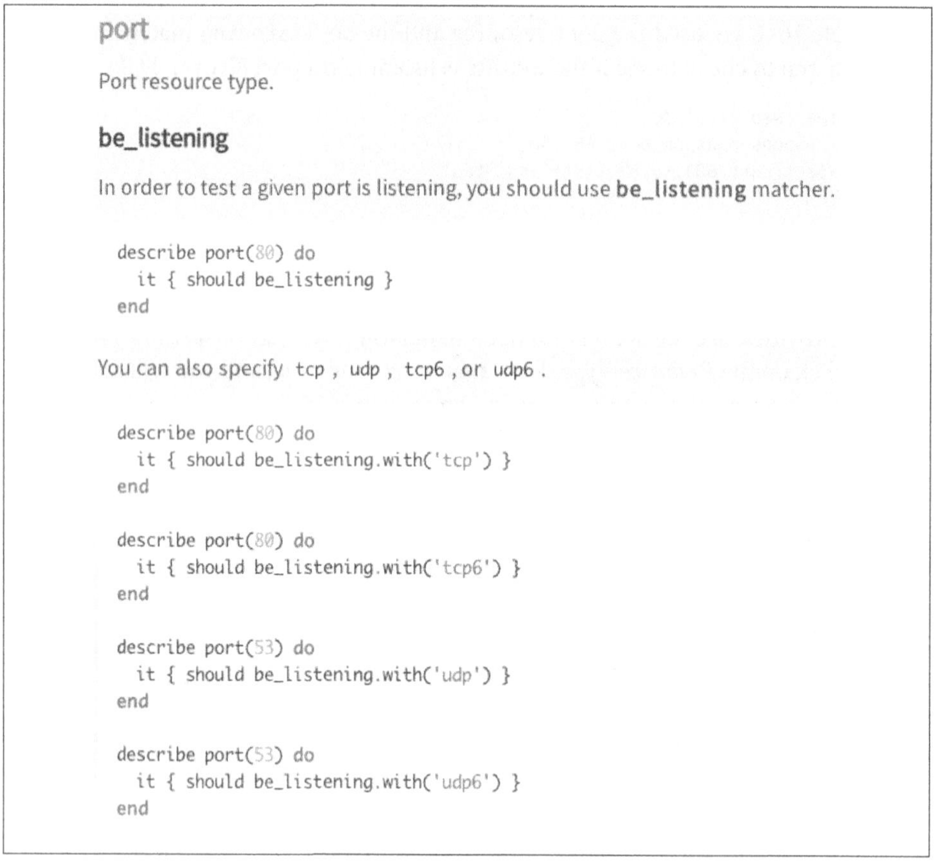

port

Port resource type.

be_listening

In order to test a given port is listening, you should use **be_listening** matcher.

```
describe port(80) do
  it { should be_listening }
end
```

You can also specify `tcp` , `udp` , `tcp6` , or `udp6` .

```
describe port(80) do
  it { should be_listening.with('tcp') }
end

describe port(80) do
  it { should be_listening.with('tcp6') }
end

describe port(53) do
  it { should be_listening.with('udp') }
end

describe port(53) do
  it { should be_listening.with('udp6') }
end
```

Figure 16-8. Serverspec port resource be_listening matcher documentation

As you can see from this documentation, you'll also encounter a legacy RSpec form that was used prior to RSpec 3.0: the *should form* (*https://github.com/rspec/rspec-expectations/blob/master/Should.md*). The *should form* was deprecated with RSpec 3.0, because it can produce unexpected results for some testing code edge cases. However, some sites, such as the Serverspec documentation site, haven't been updated.

Figure 16-9 shows how you can map old documentation in *should form* to *expect form*. With *should form*, the `resource` is in a describe block around the `it` clause. With *expect form*, this is a parameter passed to *expect*. You can also see how the matcher form differs. With *should*, expectations are expressed as *should* or *should not*, for positive and negative expectations, respectively. With *expect*, expectations are expressed as the chained methods `.to` or `.not_to`. Finally, in *should form*, matcher parameters are expessed using a chained `.with()` syntax, whereas in *expect* form, it is just a parameter to the matcher.

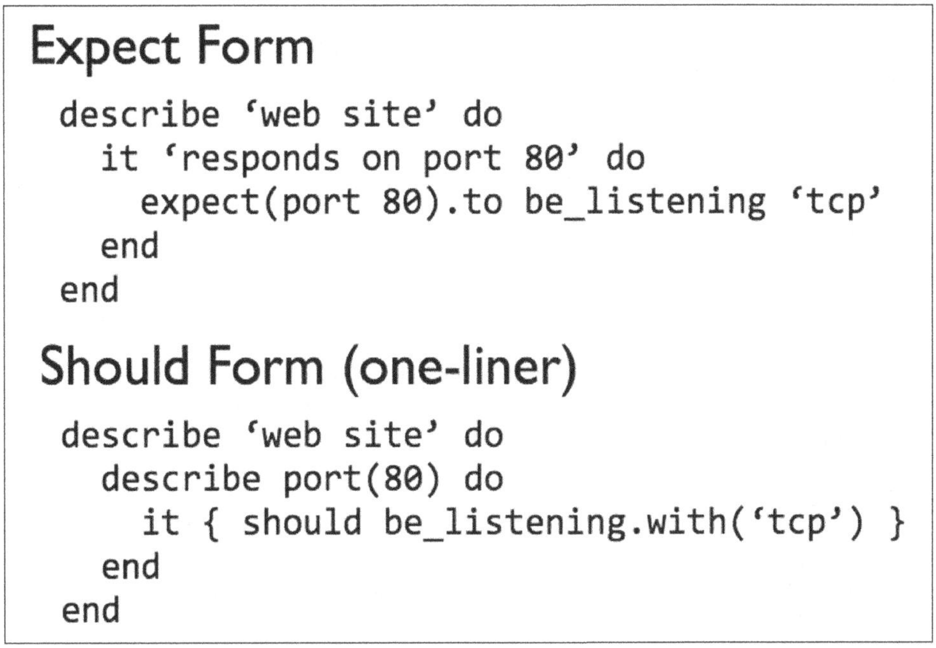

Expect Form

```
describe 'web site' do
  it 'responds on port 80' do
    expect(port 80).to be_listening 'tcp'
  end
end
```

Should Form (one-liner)

```
describe 'web site' do
  describe port(80) do
    it { should be_listening.with('tcp') }
  end
end
```

Figure 16-9. Expect versus should form

More Serverspec Resources

Common code can be moved to a file called *spec_helper.rb*. We only have one file with tests in our example, but imagine there are multiple files. Create a *spec_helper.rb* as shown in Example 16-5. Notice that the file contains the first two lines from *default_spec.rb*. Those lines would need to be repeated in every file that contains tests.

Example 16-5. chefdk/apache-test/test/integration/default/serverspec/spec_helper.rb

```
require 'serverspec'

set :backend, :exec
```

Now that you have a *spec_helper.rb* file, modify *default_spec.rb* to use the `spec_help er`. Change the `require` statement and remove the `set` line, as shown in Example 16-6.

Example 16-6. chefdk/apache-test/test/integration/default/serverspec/default_spec.rb

```
require 'spec_helper'

describe 'web site' do
```

```
  it 'responds on port 80' do
    expect(port 80).to be_listening 'tcp'
  end
end
```

Rerun `kitchen verify`. You should notice no net change in the tests. It should still report that one example succeeded.

```
$ kitchen verify
```

Although it is a little silly to use a *spec_helper.rb* file in this contrived example, we hope you see how this file could be used to contain any duplicate code between multiple files with tests.

You can add more than one example with tests in a `describe` block. Normally, there will a handful to perhaps a dozen. Let's add one more example to *default_spec.rb*.

Although we've written one example that checks to see that our website is responding on port 80, we don't really know if it is serving up the correct content. Let's write an example that inspects the website output to see if it seems OK.

If you look at the Serverspec documentation, you'll find that there isn't an obvious resource that seems to do what we want. In cases like this, Serverspec lets you run arbitrary command lines via the `command` resource as shown in Figure 16-10. We'll use the `command` resource to run a `curl` command to inspect the website output, just as we did in Chapter 7.

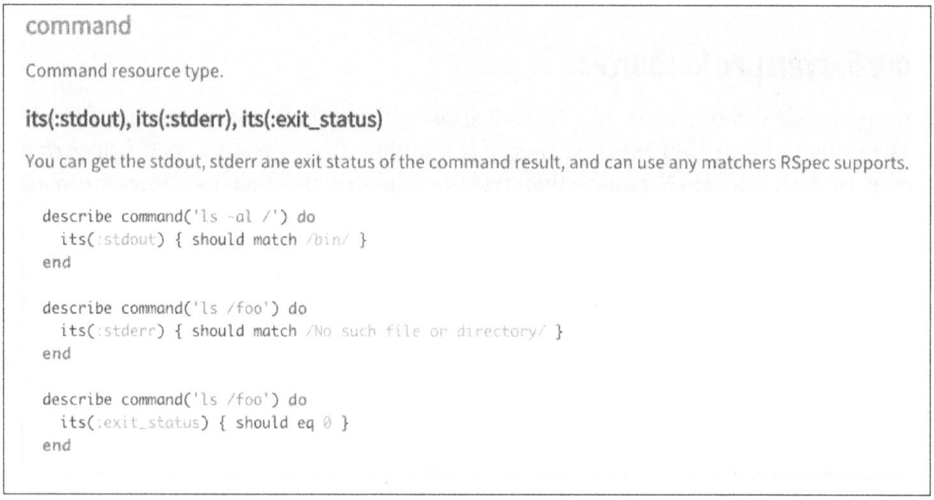

---

command

Command resource type.

its(:stdout), its(:stderr), its(:exit_status)

You can get the stdout, stderr ane exit status of the command result, and can use any matchers RSpec supports.

```
describe command('ls -al /') do
  its(:stdout) { should match /bin/ }
end

describe command('ls /foo') do
  its(:stderr) { should match /No such file or directory/ }
end

describe command('ls /foo') do
  its(:exit_status) { should eq 0 }
end
```

Figure 16-10. Command resource

The `its` method is a way to access attributes of a resource in *should* form. To access resource attributes in *expect* form, use a chained method with the attribute name, using statements like:

```
expect(command(...).attribute)
```

Add a new example to *default_spec.rb* as shown in Example 16-7. By running the `curl localhost` command, you can inspect the HTML output of the website to ensure that it is working correctly.

Using the `stdout` attribute of the `command` resource, we can take a look at the output of the `curl` command returned on *standard output*. It is a convention that programs generate their output to two different standard file handles: `stdout` and `stderr`, for regular program output and errors, respectively. This way, other computer programs can open these file handles and inspect the contents in an automated fashion. Our example does not care about any errors happening on `stderr` because getting notified that an error happened through Ruby exceptions is enough for test code. This error exception generation process happens automatically in Serverspec. We only care about the program output being generated on `stdout`.

The results of running `curl localhost:80` are returned to our example code as a string. We use a feature of Ruby called a *regular expression* and the `match` RSpec matcher to search for content in the output generated by `curl`. In Ruby, strings containing regular expressions are enclosed by forward slash characters (`//`) instead of the usual single quotes (`"`) or double quotes (`""`).

A regular expression is a special string format that is used to specify a search string. In this case, we use a regular expression to search for the string `eth1` in the program output. This seems like a reasonable and simple way to check that our website is working. It isn't likely that the string `eth1` would appear in the output otherwise. Using the string `eth1` also implicitly checks to make sure that the vagrant box had its `eth1` adapter enabled, which is another assumption we'd like to check as well. When there are opportunities to implicitly check more than one condition in your tests, take the opportunity to do so.

Example 16-7. chefdk/apache-test/test/integration/default/serverspec/default_spec.rb

```
require 'spec_helper'

describe 'web site' do
  it 'responds on port 80' do
    expect(port 80).to be_listening 'tcp'
  end

  it 'returns eth1 in the HTML body' do
    expect(command('curl localhost:80').stdout).to match /eth1/
```

```
        end
end
```

There's a great website (*http://rubular.com*) for learning more about regular expressions in Ruby. You can use this website to check regular expressions against test strings. Let's use it to check our regular expression.

First, log in to the node with `kitchen login` and run the same `curl localhost:80` command that we will run in our test. The output is shown in the following example. Copy and paste the program output to your clipboard from your terminal window. Then `exit` back out to your host prompt:

```
$ kitchen login
Last login: Sun Aug 17 10:39:34 2014 from 10.0.2.2
Welcome to your Packer-built virtual machine.
[vagrant@default-centos65 ~]$ curl localhost:80
<html>
<body>
<pre><code>
This site was set up by default-centos65
My network addresses are:
  * lo: ::1
  * eth0: 10.0.2.15
  * eth1: 192.168.33.38
</code></pre>
</body>
</html>
[vagrant@default-centos65 ~]$ exit
logout
Connection to 127.0.0.1 closed.
```

Once you have the program output in your host clipboard, paste it into the *test string* field as shown in Figure 16-11.

Once you have a test string, you can enter in any regular expression between the forward slash characters in the *Your regular expression* field. Once you enter a regular expression, the Rubular site will show you if it would match any results in the test string.

Regular expressions containing strings without any special symbols will match the string itself. For more information about the special characters that can be used, refer to the *Regex quick reference* section of the Rubular website, below the editing pane. As Figure 16-12 shows, if we use the `eth1` regular expression and the program output contains `eth1`, we'll get a match. And conversely, if the program output does not contain `eth1`, we won't get a match. Thus, we make a match if the regular expression `eth1` against the program output of `curl localhost:80` on `stdout` is a success condition for our example.

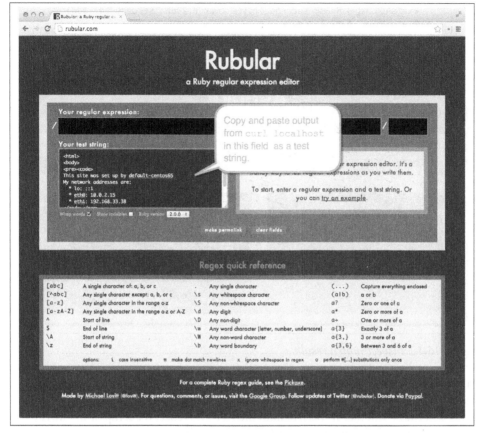

Figure 16-11. Copy and paste a test string on Rubular

Run `kitchen verify`. Notice from the Serverspec report that the second example succeeds. Serverspec ran `curl localhost:80` on the node and got the expected regular expression match in the program output:

```
$ kitchen verify
-----> Starting Kitchen (v1.2.1)
...
-----> Running serverspec test suite
       /opt/chef/embedded/bin/ruby -I/tmp/busser/suites/serverspec
       -I/tmp/busser/gems/gems/rspec-support-3.1.2/lib:/tmp/busser/gems/gems
       /rspec-core-3.1.7/lib /opt/chef/embedded/bin/rspec --pattern /tmp/busser
       /suites/serverspec/\*\*/\*_spec.rb --color --format documentation
       --default-path /tmp/busser/suites/serverspec

       web site
         responds on port 80
         returns eth1 in the HTML body
```

```
        Finished in 0.03838 seconds (files took 0.20863 seconds to load)
        2 examples, 0 failures
        Finished verifying <default-centos65> (0m1.25s).
-----> Kitchen is finished. (0m1.71s)
```

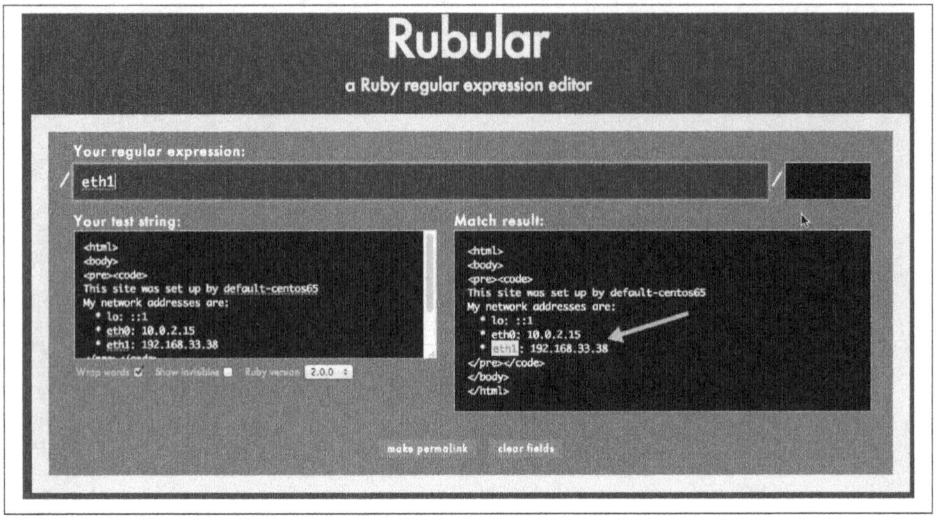

Figure 16-12. Inspect match results

Just from these two simple examples, we can be fairly certain about whether the website our Chef code produces actually works. Further, when an error occurs, we can more easily determine whether it was a fault in the Apache webserver setup or in our HTML code because we check these two conditions separately.

There's one more thing we need to cover before you can go about using all of the Serverspec resources in your own test code. Many Serverspec resources require Serverspec to detect information about the test node operating system so it can run the correct commands for the platform. We've taken care so far not to use any commands that need this extra support.

The `package` resource is a command that requires Serverspec to detect OS information. Figure 16-13 shows the documentation from the Serverspec site on the `service` resource. It can be used to detect whether a package is installed. Behind the scenes, it needs to know what OS is being used so it can use the `rpm -q` command on RedHat and variants or `dpkg-query` on Ubuntu/Debian to perform this query, for example.

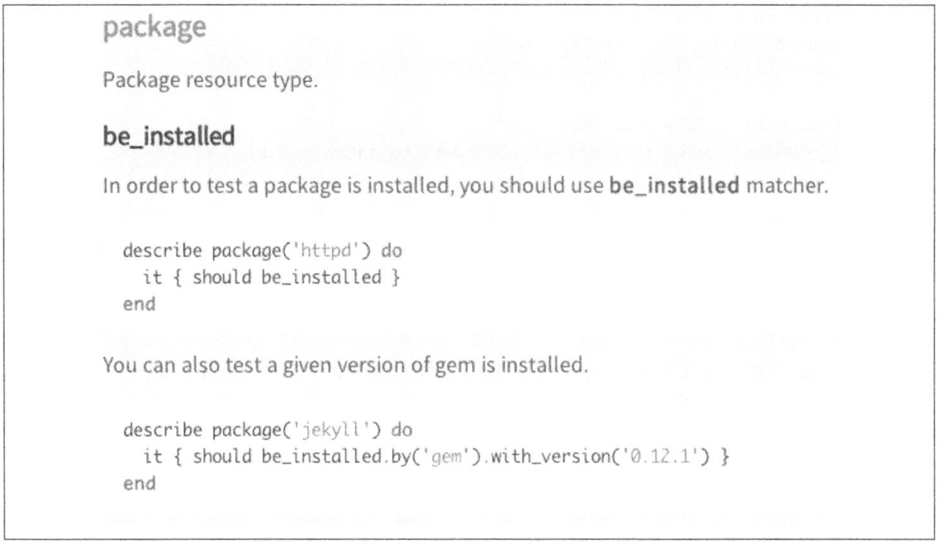

package

Package resource type.

be_installed

In order to test a package is installed, you should use **be_installed** matcher.

```
describe package('httpd') do
  it { should be_installed }
end
```

You can also test a given version of gem is installed.

```
describe package('jekyll') do
  it { should be_installed.by('gem').with_version('0.12.1') }
end
```

Figure 16-13. Serverspec package resource

By default, Serverspec tries to automatically detect the OS, which works for most Linux/Unix variants. However, on some platforms you'll need to override the default OS setting, using the `set` method.

In particular, you'll need to add the following line to all your *_spec.rb* files for test code that you plan to run on Windows guests, as Serverspec is unable to automatically detect the Windows OS, as of this writing. The exact `set` commands needed vary by platform. Refer to the Serverspec documentation for more information.

Here's what a *_spec.rb* file might look like for Windows, which uses the `set` command to give Serverspec a cue on what OS is running:

```
require 'spec_helper'
set :backend, :cmd
set :os, :family => 'windows'
```

In this book, we're using a Linux variant as our guest OS, so the Serverspec autodetect logic should work just fine. Make sure you check this out on your test platform by using a resource that requires OS platform detection, like the `package` command.

Let's add an example to *default_spec.rb* using the `package` command. As shown in Example 16-8, let's check to see if the `httpd` package is installed.

Example 16-8. chefdk/apache-test/test/integration/default/serverspec/default_spec.rb

```
require 'spec_helper'

describe 'web site' do
```

```
it 'responds on port 80' do
  expect(port 80).to be_listening 'tcp'
end

it 'returns eth1 in the HTML body' do
  expect(command('curl localhost:80').stdout).to match /eth1/
end

it 'has the apache web server installed' do
  expect(package 'httpd').to be_installed
end
end
```

Run `kitchen verify` for Serverspec. The command works fine because Serverspec automatically detected the OS:

```
$ kitchen verify
-----> Starting Kitchen (v1.2.1)
...
-----> Running serverspec test suite
       /opt/chef/embedded/bin/ruby -I/tmp/busser/suites/serverspec
       -I/tmp/busser/gems/gems/rspec-support-3.1.2/lib:/tmp/busser/gems/gems
       /rspec-core-3.1.7/lib /opt/chef/embedded/bin/rspec --pattern /tmp/busser
       /suites/serverspec/\*\*/\*_spec.rb --color --format documentation
       --default-path /tmp/busser/suites/serverspec

       web site
         responds on port 80
         returns eth1 in the HTML body
         has apache installed

       Finished in 0.03944 seconds
       3 examples, 0 failures
       Finished verifying <default-centos65> (0m1.25s).
-----> Kitchen is finished. (0m1.74s)
```

If for some reason we need to tell Serverspec that we are specifically running CentOS 6 because of issues with a command, we can add the following `set` line as shown in Example 16-9:

```
set :os, :family => 'redhat', :release => 6
```

CentOS is in the RedHat family of operating systems. Specifying a `:release` attribute is optional.

Example 16-9. chefdk/apache-test/test/integration/default/serverspec/default_spec.rb

```
require 'spec_helper'

set :os, :family => 'redhat', :release => 6

describe 'web site' do
  it 'responds on port 80' do
```

```
    expect(port 80).to be_listening 'tcp'
  end

  it 'returns eth1 in the HTML body' do
    expect(command('curl localhost:80').stdout).to match /eth1/
  end

  it 'has the apache web server installed' do
    expect(package 'httpd').to be_installed
  end
end
```

When you are not interactively coding tests, you probably want to run kitchen converge, kitchen setup, and so on all in one fell swoop instead of needing to remember all the individual Test Kitchen actions to run tests.

The kitchen test command will run the following commands in sequence:

1. kitchen destroy (if necessary)
2. kitchen create
3. kitchen converge
4. kitchen setup
5. kitchen verify
6. kitchen destroy

You wouldn't want to use this command locally when you are writing tests, as for some cookbooks the process of creating a virtual machine and performing an initial converge can be quite time consuming, and you wouldn't want the environment automatically destroyed in the end. But Test Kitchen is a perfect command for a continual integration environment such as Jenkins. It's also a good idea to do a final kitchen test run against a clean setup before committing your Chef code to source control.

Go ahead and run kitchen test now, so you can see it in action. Plus, it will destroy our test environment. Note that kitchen test runs all five phases automatically for you:

```
$ kitchen test
-----> Starting Kitchen (v1.2.1)
-----> Cleaning up any prior instances of <default-centos65>
-----> Destroying <default-centos65>...
...
-----> Testing <default-centos65>
-----> Creating <default-centos65>...
       Bringing machine 'default' up with 'virtualbox' provider...
...
       Vagrant instance <default-centos65> created.
```

```
        Finished creating <default-centos65> (0m35.57s).
-----> Converging <default-centos65>...
        Preparing files for transfer
        Resolving cookbook dependencies with Berkshelf 3.1.5...
        Removing non-cookbook files before transfer
-----> Installing Chef Omnibus (true)
...

        Thank you for installing Chef!
        Transferring files to <default-centos65>
        [2014-08-11T18:33:39-07:00] INFO: Starting chef-zero on host localhost,
        port 8889 with repository at repository at /tmp/kitchen
            One version per cookbook


        [2014-08-11T18:33:39-07:00] INFO: Forking chef instance to converge...
        Starting Chef Client, version 11.14.2
        [2014-08-11T18:33:39-07:00] INFO: *** Chef 11.14.2 ***
...

        [2014-08-11T18:33:42-07:00] INFO: Starting Chef Run for default-centos65
...

        Converging 3 resources
...

        [2014-08-11T18:33:56-07:00] INFO: Report handlers complete
        Chef Client finished, 4/4 resources updated in 17.027821539 seconds
        Finished converging <default-centos65> (1m11.46s).
-----> Setting up <default-centos65>...
Fetching: thor-0.19.0.gem (100%)
Fetching: busser-0.6.2.gem (100%)
        Successfully installed thor-0.19.0
        Successfully installed busser-0.6.2
        2 gems installed
-----> Setting up Busser
        Creating BUSSER_ROOT in /tmp/busser
        Creating busser binstub
        Plugin serverspec installed (version 0.2.6)
-----> Running postinstall for serverspec plugin
        Finished setting up <default-centos65> (0m24.61s).
-----> Verifying <default-centos65>...
        Suite path directory /tmp/busser/suites does not exist, skipping.
        Uploading /tmp/busser/suites/serverspec/default_spec.rb (mode=0644)
        Uploading /tmp/busser/suites/serverspec/spec_helper.rb (mode=0644)
-----> Running serverspec test suite
        /opt/chef/embedded/bin/ruby -I/tmp/busser/suites/serverspec
        -I/tmp/busser/gems/gems/rspec-support-3.1.2/lib:/tmp/busser/gems/gems
        /rspec-core-3.1.7/lib /opt/chef/embedded/bin/rspec --pattern /tmp/
        busser/suites/serverspec/\*\*/\*_spec.rb --color
        --format documentation --default-path /tmp/busser/suites/serverspec

        web site
          responds on port 80
          returns eth1 in the HTML body
          has the apache web server installed
```

```
                  Finished in 0.03922 seconds
                  3 examples, 0 failures
                  Finished verifying <default-centos65> (0m1.14s).
          -----> Destroying <default-centos65>...
                  ==> default: Forcing shutdown of VM...
                  ==> default: Destroying VM and associated drives...
                  Vagrant instance <default-centos65> destroyed.
                  Finished destroying <default-centos65> (0m2.89s).
                  Finished testing <default-centos65> (2m19.03s).
          -----> Kitchen is finished. (2m19.48s)
```

For more on Serverspec, the Jenkins community cookbook (*https://github.com/opscode-coobkooks/jenkins*) is chock-full of advanced Serverspec techniques. It is a great starting point to learn more about how to perform end-to-end testing of cookbooks.

Test Automation with Foodcritic

Severspec is an invaluable tool for performing end-to-end testing of cookbook functionality. However, spinning up a sandbox instance and performing a full Chef converge can take a long time.

Use the power of Test Kitchen and Serverspec judiciously. Other tools can provide more limited forms of feedback faster. One example of a tool that can provide limited feedback quickly is Foodcritic.

Foodcritic is designed to be used as you are writing Chef code, and it can even be integrated into your editor. Foodcritic provides feedback on your Chef coding style. It does this by performing checks against your code called *rules*.

You can find all the default rules used by Foodcritic in its documentation (*http://acrmp.github.io/foodcritic/#*), as shown in Figure 16-14. You'll need to scroll down a bit on the web page to see them.

You run `foodcritic` on your development host instead of in a sandbox environment, so it is fast. Give it a try now. Make sure the root `apache-test` root cookbook is your current working directory, and run the following. The results you see might differ depending on whether you are using the Chef Development Kit or Chef Client.

Chef Development Kit:

```
$ foodcritic .
```

Chef Client:

```
$ foodcritic .
FC008: Generated cookbook metadata needs updating: ./metadata.rb:2
FC008: Generated cookbook metadata needs updating: ./metadata.rb:3
```

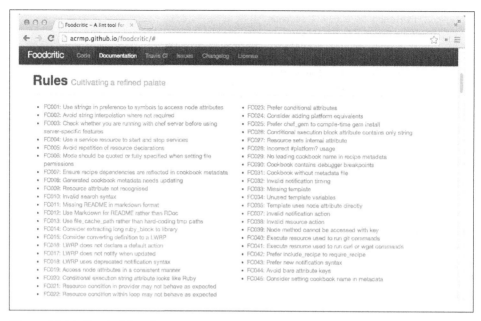

Figure 16-14. Foodcritic rules

As of this writing, there is a bug in the version of Foodcritic shipping with Chef Development Kit 0.2.0-2. It should check to see whether the *metadata.rb* file needs updating, as shown in Figure 16-15, but it doesn't currently work with the cookbook output generated by chef cookbook generate.

We're not sure if this rule will be fixed in future versions, if a new rule will be added to check for the Chef Development Kit version, or something else. So for now, if you are using the Chef Development Kit, change your *metadata.rb* file to match the Chef Client-generated version, as shown in Example 16-10.

Example 16-10. chefdk/apache-test/metadata.rb

```
name             'apache-test'
maintainer       'YOUR_COMPANY_NAME'
maintainer_email 'YOUR_EMAIL'
license          ''
description      'Installs/Configures apache-test'
long_description 'Installs/Configures apache-test'
version          '0.1.0'
```

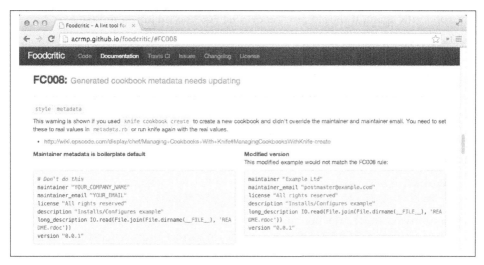

Figure 16-15. Foodcritic in action, telling us that some cookbook metadata needs updating

After this change, the Chef Development Kit result should match the Chef Client version.

Chef Development Kit:

```
$ foodcritic .
FC008: Generated cookbook metadata needs updating: ./metadata.rb:2
FC008: Generated cookbook metadata needs updating: ./metadata.rb:3
```

As shown in Figure 16-15, when Foodcritic detects an issue in your Chef code, you can look up more detail on the issue and how it can be fixed. In this case, FC008 indicates that you should modify the *metadata.rb* file `maintainer` and `maintainer_email` fields to be something besides the default boilerplate text.

Let's modify the *metadata.rb* file appropriately. Example 16-11 shows how we changed our file.

Example 16-11. chefdk/apache-test/metadata.rb

```
name             'apache-test'
maintainer       'Mischa Taylor'
maintainer_email 'mischa@misheska.com'
license          'MIT'
description      'Installs/Configures apache-test'
long_description 'Installs/Configures apache-test'
version          '0.1.0'
```

Run Foodcritic again. It should now report that FC008 is no longer an issue:

```
$ foodcritic .
```

Let's create one more issue with our code. We'll say that a Chef developer forgot to commit a *README.md* file into source control. Simulate this state by renaming the *README.md* file. Run the following move command:

```
$ mv README.md README.md.old
```

Run Foodcritic as follows and you should see a new issue:

```
$ foodcritic .
FC011: Missing README in markdown format: ./README.md:1
```

As you can see from the documentation on FC11, as shown in Figure 16-16, it is important to provide a *README* file in markdown format because Chef Supermarket expects your cookbooks to have documentation in a *README.md* file.

Figure 16-16. FC011: Missing README in markdown

Ideally, you would fix this issue by writing some great documentation, but for now, just move the *README.md* boilerplate back to its original name:

```
$ mv README.md.old README.md
```

Run Foodcritic again, and it should report that FC011 is no longer an issue:

```
$ foodcritic .
```

Performing these Foodcritic checks should be a regular part of your Chef cookbook development cycle. The Foodcritic documentation (*http://acrmp.github.io/foodcritic*) has more information on how to integrate Foodcritic with various build tools.

You can even use Foodcritic with many popular text editors, so it can perform Foodcritic runs while you type or when you save your Chef code.

You can create your own custom rules to extend the checks performed by Foodcritic. Etsy has published its set of custom Foodcritic rules (*https://github.com/etsy/foodcritic-rules*) online. You can use its custom rules as an example of how you can write rules more relevant to your environment.

Not all Foodcritic rules are trivial checks to see if you filled in the *metadata.rb* file or provided documentation. The Etsy custom Foodcritic rules, for example, check for issues that have caused outages in their production environment, such as ETSY001, as shown in Figure 16-17.

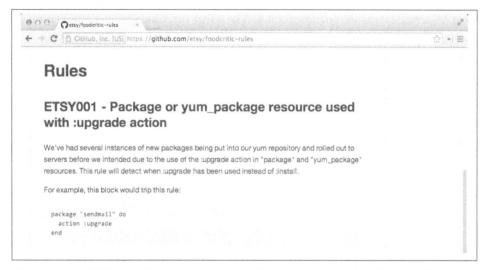

Figure 16-17. ETSY001 - Package or yum_package resource used with :upgrade action

Foodcritic can be used to perform vital checks similar to ETSY001, to catch bugs in your code even before it gets deployed to a testing sandbox environment. A way to start might be to look through recent help desk incidents where you have identified the root cause being related to server configuration issues, and encode them as Foodcritic rules. This is the process Etsy used to develop its custom Foodcritic rule set.

We hope this section on Foodcritic shows you how you can catch bugs earlier in your Chef development process, closer to the time of coding. Catching issues early saves time and money.

Although limited in the feedback it can provide, Foodcritic is a great tool for catching many bugs early. You still need to do some form of end-to-end testing using a tool like Serverspec, but you shouldn't have to rely on end-to-end testing exclusively to find issues.

Test Automation with ChefSpec

Another great tool that can help you run tests early in your development cycle is Chef Spec. You can even use it to catch errors *before* you code. ChefSpec can be used to produce *runnable documentation*. Its primary purpose is to help document and organize your code.

As a side benefit, ChefSpec tests and checks can uncover bugs when you make changes. Plus, your Chef code will be improved when it is guided by tests.

Similar to Serverspec, ChefSpec builds on RSpec. ChefSpec uses the RSpec description form to create runnable documentation. The form for ChefSpec documentation is slightly different from Serverspec's, resembling the following:

```
describe '<recipe_name>' do
  <perform in-memory Chef run>
  <examples here>
end
```

For example, you would use the following describe block to contain examples performing tests against the apache-test::default cookbook:

```
describe 'apache-test::default' do
  ...
end
```

To perform an in-memory Chef run, you would add the following statements to the basic describe form, using classes and methods from the chefspec gem. In this example, to test the apache-test::default cookbook, you would use the following code:

```
require 'chefspec'

describe 'apache::default' do
  chef_run = ChefSpec::Runner.new.converge('apache-test::default')
  <descriptions here>
end
```

ChefSpec uses an expect form similar to Serverspec's. There are just different commands and matchers for ChefSpec. Following is a ChefSpec example that checks to make sure there is a reference in your Chef code to install the httpd package:

```
require 'chefspec'

describe 'apache::default' do
  chef_run = ChefSpec::Runner.new.converge('apache-test::default')

  it 'installs apache2' do
    expect(chef_run).to install_package('httpd')
  end
end
```

Keep in mind that the preceding code is just runnable documentation. The `expect` statement *does not* perform an `httpd` package installation during the in-memory Chef run. Instead, ChefSpec merely performs the in-memory Chef run to verify the cookbook syntax; in this case, to ensure that your code instructed Chef to install the package. This form of documentation-based testing is good enough for well-tested Chef primitives, such as the `package` resource.

Commands in ChefSpec are usually the results of an in-memory Chef run. ChefSpec matchers are documented[ChefSpec matchers] are documented as shown in Figure 16-18.

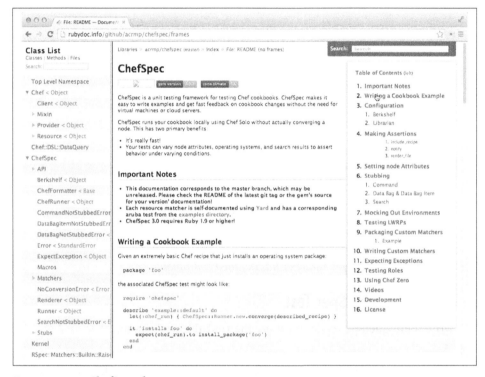

Figure 16-18. ChefSpec documentation

If you expand the ChefSpec tree in the index on the left, you'll see all the ChefSpec matchers listed, plus detailed examples, as shown in Figure 16-19.

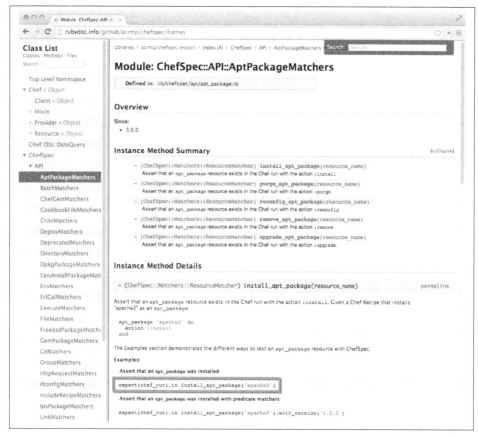

Figure 16-19. Each ChefSpec matcher has detailed examples

Write Your First ChefSpec Test

Let's write some ChefSpec code. We'll use the `install_package` matcher, as shown in Figure 16-20.

The default location for ChefSpec tests are in a `spec` folder underneath your cookbook root. Make sure that the *apache-test* root cookbook directory is the current working directory, and create a *spec* directory as follows:

```
$ mkdir spec
```

Figure 16-20. install_package matcher

Create a file called *default_spec.rb* with the content shown in Example 16-12. Files con‐
taining ChefSpec code by convention are expected to end in the suffix *_spec.rb*.

Example 16-12. chefdk/apache-test/spec/default_spec.rb

```
require 'chefspec'

describe 'apache-test::default' do
  chef_run = ChefSpec::Runner.new.converge('apache-test::default')

  it 'installs apache2' do
    expect(chef_run).to install_package('httpd')
  end
end
```

ChefSpec does not require any special `chefspec` command to run as it just extends RSpec. In the *apache-test* cookbook root, run `rspec --color` as shown in the following example to perform a ChefSpec run:

```
$ rspec --color
.

Finished in 0.00042 seconds (files took 1.12 seconds to load)
1 example, 0 failures
```

When `rspec` runs, ChefSpec will inspect your Chef code and make sure it uses the `package` resource to install the `httpd` package. If ChefSpec verifies that your code does this, the test passes, as in the `rspec` command you just ran.

Lazy Evaluation with Let

We need to introduce one more bit of RSpec syntax: lazy evaluation using the `let` helper method, which is part of the RSpec core. Figure 16-21 shows how ChefSpec commonly uses `let` helper method to cache the results of the `ChefSpec::Runner` object.

```
                   require 'chefspec'

                   describ 'apache::default' do
                     let (:chef_run) \
                   { ChefSpec::Runner.new.converge(described_recipe) }

     Lazy            it 'installs apache2' do
  evaluation           expect(chef_run).to install_package('httpd')
                     end
                   end
```

Figure 16-21. Using ChefSpec with the let helper method

A call to the `ChefSpec::Runner` is fairly heavyweight. A call to `let()` delays the evaluation of the `ChefSpec::Runner` until when it is first used instead of when it is referenced in the source—thus the evaluation is "lazy." Using `let()` allows RSpec to cache the results of `ChefSpec::Runner` when it is used multiple times in the same example.

Further, the `let()` call permits you to specify the recipe under test only once in your `describe` block as documentation. Compare the following *Without let* and *With let* code examples, and notice that the call to `ChefSpec::Runner` uses a `described_recipe` macro to evaluate the recipe name instead of repeating the recipe string. A small optimization, but a useful one.

Without let:

```
require 'chefspec'

describe 'apache::default' do
  chef_run = ChefSpec::Runner.new.converge('apache-test::default')

  it 'installs apache2' do
    expect(chef_run).to install_package('httpd')
  end
end
```

With let:

```
require 'chefspec'

describe 'apache::default' do
  let (:chef_run) { ChefSpec::Runner.new.converge(described_recipe) }

  it 'installs apache2' do
    expect(chef_run).to install_package('httpd')
  end
end
```

Change the source in *default_spec.rb* to use the let() helper method as shown in Example 16-13.

Example 16-13. chefdk/apache-test/spec/default_spec.rb

```
require 'chefspec'

describe 'apache-test::default' do
  let (:chef_run) { ChefSpec::Runner.new.converge(described_recipe) }

  it 'installs apache2' do
    expect(chef_run).to install_package('httpd')
  end
end
```

When you rerun rspec, you should notice no net change in the test results:

```
$ rspec --color
.

Finished in 0.00042 seconds (files took 1.12 seconds to load)
1 example, 0 failures
```

Generate a Coverage Report

Another ChefSpec helper method is ChefSpec::Coverage.report!. It will generate a list of resources that have corresponding examples as documentation. You can let this report guide your testing.

Edit *default_spec.rb* as shown in Example 16-14. The `at_exit` method is a part of core Ruby that permits you to register a block to execute when the program exits. In this case, we want to run the `ChefSpec::Coverage.report!` method. The exclamation point (!) in the `report!` method name is a Ruby convention that indicates a method is *dangerous*. In this case, the cautions are that `ChefSpec::Coverage.report!` must be run after all tests are complete and not run more than once in a program. We use `at_exit` to ensure that `report!` is run once after the tests have finished.

Example 16-14. chefdk/apache-test/spec/default_spec.rb

```
require 'chefspec'

at_exit { ChefSpec::Coverage.report! }

describe 'apache-test::default' do
  let (:chef_run) { ChefSpec::Runner.new.converge(described_recipe) }

  it 'installs apache2' do
    expect(chef_run).to install_package('httpd')
  end
end
```

Run `rspec --color` with the new `at_exit` code, and notice that now a helpful report is generated, telling you the total number of resources in your code and how many have been tested in your specs:

```
$ rspec --color
.

Finished in 0.00337 seconds (files took 1.11 seconds to load)
1 example, 0 failures

ChefSpec Coverage report generated...

  Total Resources:    3
  Touched Resources:  1
  Touch Coverage:     33.33%

Untouched Resources:

  service[httpd]                         /recipes/default.rb:12
  template[/var/www/html/index.html]     /recipes/default.rb:16
```

Let this report guide you in choosing other tests to write for your code.

Share Test Code with spec_helper.rb

ChefSpec supports moving common code used in your tests to a *spec_helper.rb* file, similar to Serverspec.

As with Serverspec, you'll have to imagine there are many test files in this example, and we'll move the shared code to *spec_helper.rb*.

Create the file *spec/spec_helper.rb* with the content shown in Example 16-15. We are moving the `require` and `at_exit` calls to this shared file.

Example 16-15. chefdk/apache-test/spec/spec_helper.rb

```
require 'chefspec'

at_exit { ChefSpec::Coverage.report! }
```

Now edit *spec/default_spec.rb* as shown in Example 16-16 so it references `spec_helper`.

Example 16-16. chefdk/apache-test/spec/default_spec.rb

```
require 'spec_helper'

describe 'apache-test::default' do
  let (:chef_run) { ChefSpec::Runner.new.converge(described_recipe) }

  it 'installs apache2' do
    expect(chef_run).to install_package('httpd')
  end
end
```

When you run `rspec`, you should notice no net change in the program output from when you ran `rspec` in the last section, as all we did was move around some code:

```
$ rspec --color
.

Finished in 0.00337 seconds (files took 1.11 seconds to load)
1 example, 0 failures

ChefSpec Coverage report generated...

  Total Resources:   3
  Touched Resources: 1
  Touch Coverage:    33.33%

Untouched Resources:

  service[httpd]                        /recipes/default.rb:12
  template[/var/www/html/index.html]    /recipes/default.rb:16
```

Summary

In this chapter we discussed how to test your Chef automation using Serverspec, Food-critic, and ChefSpec. You need multiple tools because each is tailored to give you fast feedback at every stage of the Chef development lifecycle.

To learn more about test automation with Chef, check out the slides for the one-day course (*http://bit.ly/testing_automation_code*) written by one of the authors of this book. This chapter was based on these slides.

## CHAPTER 17

Conclusion

We have reached the end of this book. We hope you have enjoyed learning the basics of Chef and that our book encourages you to pursue more knowledge of the language.

Here are some Chef resources you might want to check out after reading this book:

- Learn Chef (*http://learnchef.com*)
- GetChef YouTube Channel (*https://www.youtube.com/user/GetChef*)
- The Chef Mailing List (*http://lists.opscode.com*)
- Food Fight Podcast (*http://foodfightshow.org/*)
- The Ship Show (*http://theshipshow.com/*)
- Code School—Ruby Bits Part 2 (*http://bit.ly/adv_ruby_tutorial*)—Teaches you how DSLs are implemented, like the Chef DSL
- Code School—Git Real 1 and Git Real 2 (*http://bit.ly/cs_git_tutorial*)—Teaches you how to use the Git source control system
- *Customizing Chef*, by Jon Cowie (O'Reilly)
- *Test-Driven Infrastructure with Chef, 2nd Edition*, by Stephen Nelson-Smith (O'Reilly)

Open Source Chef Server

This appendix is a variant of the instructions provided in Chapter 9 for Open Source Chef Server.

How to Install Open Source Chef Server Manually

First, download the Chef Server install package from *http://www.getchef.com/chef/ install*. We'll be installing Open Source Chef server on CentOS 6.5, so choose "Enterprise Linux > 6 > x86_64", as shown in Figure A-1. Choose to Download version 11.1.4 to get a download link to the package.

 The download page might not match the images in this book exactly. However, the download and installation procedure should be the same.

The remaining steps necessary to install Chef Server are displayed below the download link:

1. Install the chef-server package.
2. Run `sudo chef-server-ctl reconfigure`.

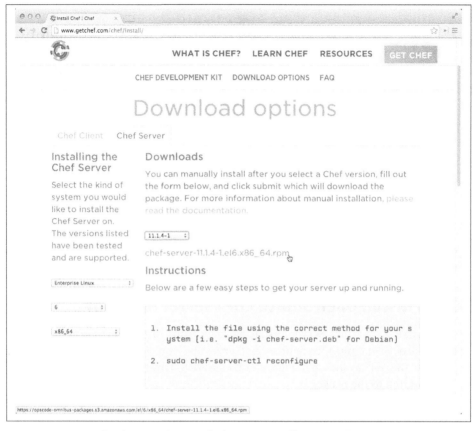

Figure A-1. Download Open Source Chef Server installation package

Install Open Source Chef Server

Assuming you have sufficient resources to install Chef Server locally along with a test node, let's create a chef-server cookbook, which we'll use to install Open Source Chef Server. To maintain consistency with Hosted Enterprise Chef, create the directory *chef-repo/cookbooks* and create the chef-server cookbook in that directory.

Create the *chef-repo/cookbooks* directory, and make it the current working directory.

Linux/Mac OS X:

```
$ mkdir -p chef-repo/cookbooks
$ cd chef-repo/cookbooks
```

Windows:

```
$ mkdir chef-repo\cookbooks
$ cd chef-repo\cookbooks
```

Now generate the `chef-server` cookbook with `chef generate cookbook` or `knife cookbook create`, depending on whether you are using the Chef Development Kit or the Chef Client, respectively. Also, enable the cookbook to use Test Kitchen. We're going to go through the cookbook creation steps quickly in this chapter. If you need a refresher on what each of these commands mean and the expected output, refer back to Chapter 7.

Chef Development Kit:

```
$ chef generate cookbook chef-server
$ cd chef-server
```

Chef Client:

```
$ knife cookbook create chef-server --cookbook-path .
$ cd chef-server
$ kitchen init --create-gemfile
$ bundle install
```

Edit the *.kitchen.yml* file to use the CentOS 6.5 basebox we prepared specifically for this book. Also, assign a private network address like we did in Chapter 7. This time, we're going to use the IP address 192.168.33.36. If this conflicts with an address already being used on your local network, change it to be a nonconflicting one. We also need more memory than the default 512 MB Test Kitchen allocates, so add a `customize:` block with a `memory:` statement to increase the memory to 1.5 GB (memory is specified in megabytes only).

 Make sure you use the `chef_solo` provisioner for this cookbook, as the in-memory Chef Server that the `chef_zero` provisioner spawns will cause a conflict with the hands-on exercises coming up in Chapter 10. As of this writing, if you want to automate the installation of a Chef Server with Chef cookbooks, the use of Chef Solo is recommended so that the deployment code doesn't get confused by the presence of the in-memory Chef Server used in Chef Zero.

Example A-1. /chefdk/chef-repo/cookbooks/chef-server/.kitchen.yml

```
---
driver:
  name: vagrant

provisioner:
  name: chef_solo

platforms:
  - name: centos65
    driver:
      box: learningchef/centos65
      box_url: learningchef/centos65
      network:
```

```
    - ["private_network", {ip: "192.168.33.36"}]
suites:
  - name: default
    run_list:
      - recipe[chef-server::default]
    attributes:
```

Generate a default attributes file in *attributes/default.rb*.

Chef Development Kit:

```
$ chef generate attribute default
```

Chef Client:

```
$ touch attributes/default.rb
```

Add an attribute specifying the download URL for the Chef Server package that you obtained from *http://www.getchef.com/chef/install*. We recommend using the 11.1.4 version URL shown in Example A-2, as we wrote the examples for this chapter using this version.

Example A-2. /chefdk/chef-repo/cookbooks/chef-server/attributes/default.rb

```
default['chef-server']['url'] = \
'https://opscode-omnibus-packages.s3.amazonaws.com/el/6/x86_64'\
'/chef-server-11.1.4-1.el6.x86_64.rpm'
```

Let's take an initial stab at coding a recipe to replicate the manual steps required to install Chef Server outlined in "How to Install Open Source Chef Server Manually" on page 309. Enter in the first version of the code as shown in Example A-3. Let's go over some of the highlights of the code in the following paragraphs.

Rather than typing in long variable names such as node['chef-server']['url'], feel free to use temporary local variables in a recipe with shorter names, such as:

```
package_url = node['chef-server']['url']
```

Remember that you have the full power of Ruby classes and methods available to you in your Chef recipes, so don't be afraid to use it. For example, you can use the ::File.basename() method to extract the package name from the URL. The package name is the last component of the URL after the forward slash ("/"): chef-server-11.1.4-1.el6.x86_64.rpm. Refer to the Ruby core API documentation (*http://ruby-doc.org/core-1.9.3/File.html*) for more information on the ::File class:

```
package_name = ::File.basename(package_url)
```

Unfortunately, the package resource does not work with URLs, so we're introducing a new resource, the remote_file resource. The remote_file resource will download files from a remote location. Rather than hardcoding a path like "/tmp" for the package

---

download, Chef provides a variable you should use instead: `Chef::Config[:file_cache_path]`. Let Chef choose the best place to store temporary files for you. Pass the local path where you want to store the file as a string parameter to `remote_file` or as a `name` attribute; in this case, we use the `package_local_path` variable. The download URL should be passed to `remote_file` as the `source` attribute.

The `package` resource should be familiar to you by now—we used it in Chapter 7.

In order to execute the `chef-server-ctl reconfigure`, we need to introduce another resource, the `execute` resource. When you fail to find a resource that meets your needs, you can use the `execute` resource to run arbitrary shell commands. Pass the shell command you want to execute as a string parameter to the `execute` resource.

The full code is in Example A-3.

Example A-3. /chefdk/chef-repo/cookbooks/chef-server/recipes/default.rb

```
#
# Cookbook Name:: chef-server
# Recipe:: default
#
# Copyright (C) 2014
#
#
#

package_url = node['chef-server']['url']
package_name = ::File.basename(package_url)
package_local_path = "#{Chef::Config[:file_cache_path]}/#{package_name}"

# omnibus_package is remote (i.e., a URL) let's download it
remote_file package_local_path do
  source package_url
end

package package_local_path

# reconfigure the installation
execute 'chef-server-ctl reconfigure'
```

Run `kitchen converge` to install Chef Server, and use `kitchen login` to verify that the `chef-server` package was installed:

```
$ kitchen converge default-centos65
$ kitchen login default-centos65
[vagrant@default-centos65 ~]$ rpm -q chef-server
chef-server-11.1.4-1.el6.x86_64
[vagrant@default-centos65 ~]$ exit
logout
Connection to 127.0.0.1 closed.
```

Introducing Idempotence

Although the recipe we created in Example A-3 is a good first attempt, it is not *idempotent*. When Chef code is idempotent, it can be run multiple times on the same system and the results will always be identical, without producing unintended side effects. All Chef default resources are guaranteed to be *idempotent* with the exception of the exe cute resource.

execute resources generally are not idempotent, because most command-line utilities can be run only once. They assume that a human being is interacting with the system and understands the state of the system. For example, assuming the file */learningchef/file1.txt* exists, the following mv command will work the first time it is run, but it will fail the second time:

```
$ mv /learningchef/file1.txt /file1.txt
```

A great way to test to see if your recipe is idempotent is to run kitchen converge *twice*. When a recipe has no unintended side effects, there should be 0 resources updated on the second run.

Does our recipe pass the idempotency test? Sadly, no. Here's a sampling of the output from an initial kitchen converge:

```
$ kitchen converge default-centos65
-----> Starting Kitchen (v1.2.2.dev)
-----> Creating <default-centos65>...
...
       Starting Chef Client, version 11.14.2
       [2014-08-17T23:06:15-07:00] INFO: *** Chef 11.14.2 ***
       [2014-08-17T23:06:15-07:00] INFO: Chef-client pid: 2386
       [2014-08-17T23:06:16-07:00] INFO: Setting the run_list to ["recipe[chef
       -server::default]"] from CLI options
       [2014-08-17T23:06:16-07:00] INFO: Run List is [recipe[chef-server
       ::default]]
       [2014-08-17T23:06:16-07:00] INFO: Run List expands to [chef-server
       ::default]
       [2014-08-17T23:06:16-07:00] INFO: Starting Chef Run for default-centos65
       [2014-08-17T23:06:16-07:00] INFO: Running start handlers
       [2014-08-17T23:06:16-07:00] INFO: Start handlers complete.
       Compiling Cookbooks...
       Converging 3 resources
...
       [2014-08-17T23:10:39-07:00] INFO: Chef Run complete in 262.973873452
       seconds

       Running handlers:
       [2014-08-17T23:10:39-07:00] INFO: Running report handlers
       Running handlers complete
       [2014-08-17T23:10:39-07:00] INFO: Report handlers complete
       Chef Client finished, 3/3 resources updated in 264.583736069 seconds
```

```
        Finished converging <default-centos65> (4m48.72s).
-----> Kitchen is finished. (5m27.52s)
```

Here's the output from the second run. Chef thinks there's still stuff it needs to do—2/3 resources updated in this second run, when we expected it to be 0/3:

```
$ kitchen converge
-----> Starting Kitchen (v1.2.2.dev)
-----> Converging <default-centos65>...
...
        Converging 3 resources
        Recipe: chef-server::default
    * remote_file[/tmp/kitchen/cache/chef-server-11.1.4-1.el6.x86_64.rpm] action
    create      [2014-08-17T23:13:55-07:00] INFO: Processing remote_file[/tmp
    /kitchen/cache/chef-server-11.1.4-1.el6.x86_64.rpm] action create (chef-server
    ::default line 15)
            (up to date)
          * package[/tmp/kitchen/cache/chef-server-11.1.4-1.el6.x86_64.rpm]
          action install
    [2014-08-17T23:13:58-07:00] INFO: Processing package[/tmp/kitchen/cache
    /chef-server-11.1.4-1.el6.x86_64.rpm] action install (chef-server
    ::default line 19)

            - install version 11.1.4-1.el6 of package /tmp/kitchen/cache/chef
            -server-11.1.4-1.el6.x86_64.rpm
          * execute[chef-server-ctl reconfigure] action run[2014-08-17T23:14:08
          -07:00] INFO: Processing execute[chef-server-ctl reconfigure] action
          run (chef-server::default line 22)
    [2014-08-17T23:14:20-07:00] INFO: execute[chef-server-ctl reconfigure]
    ran successfully

            - execute chef-server-ctl reconfigure
    [2014-08-17T23:14:20-07:00] INFO: Chef Run complete in 24.635708065
    seconds

        Running handlers:
    [2014-08-17T23:14:20-07:00] INFO: Running report handlers
        Running handlers complete
    [2014-08-17T23:14:20-07:00] INFO: Report handlers complete
        Chef Client finished, 2/3 resources updated in 26.532340506 seconds
        Finished converging <default-centos65> (0m28.53s).
-----> Kitchen is finished. (0m29.20s)
```

We've shown that the package resource is *idempotent*. As we mentioned earlier, most default Chef resources are. Notice that the *remote_file* resource is idempotent. It is reporting (up to date).

There are some issues with the package and execute resources, however, as on the second kitchen converge run Chef:

1. Reinstalled the rpm package, unnecessarily

2. Executed `chef-server-ctl reconfigure` a second time

Let's fix these idempotency issues in our code now. Example A-4 has the final idempotent version of the code.

The first issue is a common one that Chef developers encounter with the package resource when they try to install from a downloaded `rpm` instead of using a package repository. Instead of using a `package` one-liner for a downloaded `rpm`, you need to tell the `package` resource to explicitly use the RPM provider via the `provider` attribute, and you need to tell it where the source RPM is located using the `source` attribute, like so:

```
package package_name do
  source package_local_path
  provider Chef::Provider::Package::Rpm
end
```

 You can use the `rpm_package` short name to specify the RPM provider to the `package` resource, if you prefer. The following code is equivalent to the preceding code:

```
rpm_package package_name do
  source package_local_path
end
```

Fixing the second issue with the `execute` resource is a little more involved. That's why you should prefer built-in Chef resources over using the `execute` resource, because it's up to you to make the `execute` resources idempotent.

One way to fix this issue is with a `not_if` *guard* to the `execute` resource. Guards are used to make a resource idempotent by allowing the resource to test for a desired state, and if the desired state is present, the resource should do nothing. In this case, we'll test to see if the chef-server package is already installed, by adding a `not_if` clause to the `execute` resource as follows. `not_if` will test to see if the exit code of the command is 0, and if so the resource does nothing. (If you need to test the reverse of this logic, which is more typical on Windows, there is also an `only_if` guard—take a look at *http://bit.ly/common_functionality* for more information:

```
execute "chef-server-ctl reconfigure" do
  not_if "rpm -q chef-server"
end
```

While this is a reasonable way to address the issue, it's a little clunky. You have to figure out a way to detect whether Chef Server is installed, and the method used in the previous example is not very reliable. A better approach is to trigger the execute when the package resource installs the package. You can trigger events in other resources with a *notifies* statement.

In order to use `notifies`, we'll need to change the `execute` resource statement a bit. First, you'll want to change the resource so it does nothing by default when `execute` is evaluated during the Chef run by adding an `action :nothing` attribute. Also, you'll want to move the actual command line explicitly to the `command` attribute, so that you can use a short name to trigger the execute block. By default, the `name` passed to the `execute` resource as a string parameter is used as the `command` attribute, which is great for a self-documenting one-liner, but not so great when you want to trigger the command by name. So let's transform the `execute` resource like so:

```
# reconfigure the installation
execute 'reconfigure-chef-server' do
  command 'chef-server-ctl reconfigure'
  action :nothing
end
```

Now add the `notifies` attribute as follows. The `notifies` attribute takes three parameters: an action, the name of the resource to notify, and a timer indicating when the action should be performed. As shown in the following example, we want to perform the `:run` action on the `execute[reconfigure-chef-server]` resource, and we want the action performed `:immediately`. For more information on `notifies` parameters, refer to the Chef documentation (*http://docs.opscode.com/resource_common.html*):

```
package package_name do
  source package_local_path
  provider Chef::Provider::Package::Rpm
  notifies :run, 'execute[reconfigure-chef-server]', :immediately
end
```

Example A-4 shows what the final version of our idempotent code looks like.

Example A-4. chef-server/chefdk/chef-repo/cookbooks/chef-server/recipes/default.rb

```
# Cookbook Name:: chef-server
# Recipe:: default
#
# Copyright (C) 2014
#
#
#

package_url = node['chef-server']['url']
package_name = ::File.basename(package_url)
package_local_path = "#{Chef::Config[:file_cache_path]}/#{package_name}"

# omnibus_package is remote (i.e., a URL) let's download it
remote_file package_local_path do
  source package_url
end

package package_name do
```

```
  source package_local_path
  provider Chef::Provider::Package::Rpm
  notifies :run, 'execute[reconfigure-chef-server]'
end

# reconfigure the installation
execute 'reconfigure-chef-server' do
  command 'chef-server-ctl reconfigure'
  action :nothing
end
```

Try running `kitchen converge` against this revised recipe, and note that it reports 0/2 resources updated, which is the result we are looking for: 0 resources updated after running `kitchen converge` for the second time without any other changes to the cookbook:

```
$ kitchen converge
-----> Starting Kitchen (v1.2.2.dev)
-----> Converging <default-centos65>...
       ...
       Converging 3 resources
       Recipe: chef-server::default
         * remote_file[/tmp/kitchen/cache/chef-server-11.1.4-1.el6.x86_64.rpm]
         action create[2014-08-17T23:18:31-07:00] INFO: Processing remote_file[
         /tmp/kitchen/cache/chef-server-11.1.4-1.el6.x86_64.rpm] action create
         (chef-server::default line 15)
         (up to date)
         * package[chef-server-11.1.4-1.el6.x86_64.rpm] action install[2014-08
         -17T23:18:34-07:00] INFO: Processing package[chef-server-11.1.4-1.el6
         .x86_64.rpm] action install (chef-server::default line 19)
         (up to date)
         * execute[reconfigure-chef-server] action nothing[2014-08-17T23:18:34
         -07:00] INFO: Processing execute[reconfigure-chef-server] action
         nothing (chef-server::default line 26)
         (skipped due to action :nothing)
       [2014-08-17T23:18:34-07:00] INFO: Chef Run complete in 2.725841396
       seconds

       Running handlers:
       [2014-08-17T23:18:34-07:00] INFO: Running report handlers
       Running handlers complete
       [2014-08-17T23:18:34-07:00] INFO: Report handlers complete
       Chef Client finished, 0/2 resources updated in 4.347711133 seconds
       Finished converging <default-centos65> (0m5.81s).
-----> Kitchen is finished. (0m6.28s)
```

Always check your recipes to see if they are idempotent before deploying them to production. If we had deployed the first version of this recipe in production, given that the chef-client usually runs on a periodic timer performing Chef runs, all our nodes would have been reinstalling the Chef Server package and reconfiguring the server every 15 minutes!

Configure Open Source Chef Server

If your Open Source Chef Server installed properly, you should be able to access the web admin console using the `private_network` IP address you configured in your *.kitchen.yml*. In our case, we used the address 192.168.33.36. After you dismiss a warning about the use of a self-signed SSL certificate, log in with the default admin username and password, as shown in Figure A-2.

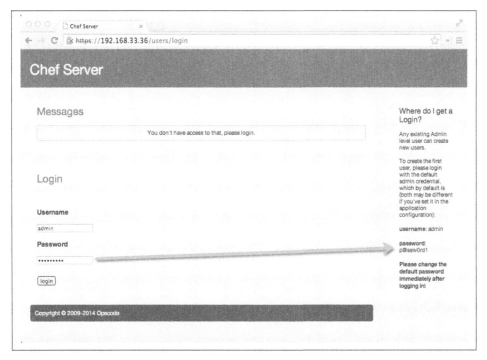

Figure A-2. Log in as admin

You will be immediately prompted to reset the `admin` user's password as shown in Figure A-3. Enter in a new password for the `admin` user and then:

1. Click on the *Save User* button.

2. Click on the *Create* tab when the *admin* user's public key is shown to create a user account for yourself.

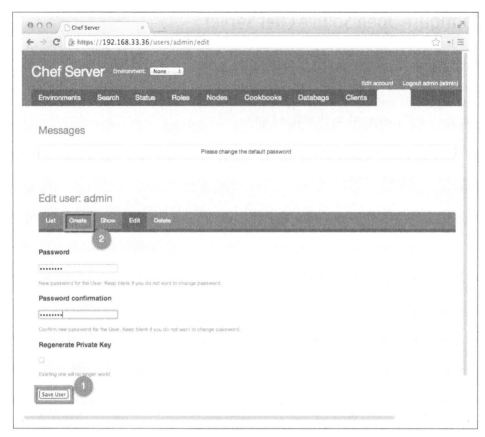

Figure A-3. Reset admin password

When you click on the Create tab, you will be prompted to enter in a username and password for your user account. Enter in your username and password of choice. Make sure the *Admin* checkbox is selected, then click on the *Create User* button (see Figure A-4.

Finally, as shown in Figure A-5, you must download a copy of your user key, as this is used as your password for Chef Server and will be displayed only once. Copy the contents of the *Private Key* to the clipboard, and save it as *<your_username>.pem*. For example, our username is *misheska*, so we saved the file as *misheska.pem*.

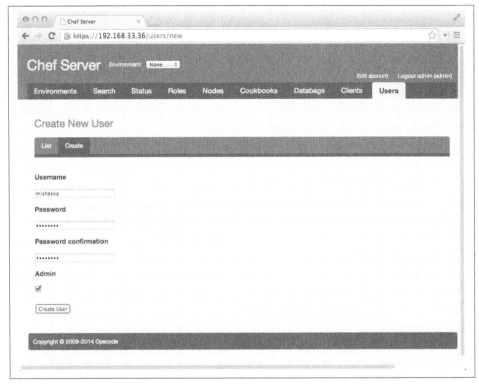

Figure A-4. Create a user

In the *chef-repo* directory you created in "Install Open Source Chef Server" on page 310, create a subdirectory called *.chef*. Our *chef-repo* is in our home directory; change the following command if your *chef-repo* is located elsewhere:

```
$ cd $HOME/chef-repo
$ mkdir .chef
```

After creating the *chef-repo/.chef* directory, copy the *<username>.pem* file you just created.

You also need to get a copy of the */etc/chef-server/chef-validator.pem* key from Chef Server. Run the following scp command to download the key as root. The password is vagrant:

```
$ scp root@192.168.33.36:/etc/chef-server/chef-validator.pem .
root@192.168.33.36's password: vagrant
chef-validator.pem                          100% 1675     1.6KB/s   00:00
```

Figure A-5. Copy user key

Finally, create a file in *chef-repo/.chef* called *knife.rb*. Example A-5 shows what our *knife.rb* file looks like; change the `node_name` and `client_key` fields in your version of the file to match your username for *<username>.pem*. Also, if you used a different IP address for your Chef Server, change the `chef_server_url` field accordingly.

Example A-5. chefdk/chef-repo/.chef/knife.rb

```
current_dir = File.dirname(__FILE__)
log_level                :info
log_location             STDOUT
node_name                "misheska"
client_key               "#{current_dir}/misheska.pem"
validation_client_name   "chef-validator"
validation_key           "#{current_dir}/chef-validator.pem"
chef_server_url          "https://default-centos65.vagrantup.com:443"
cache_type               "BasicFile"
cache_options( :path => "#{ENV['HOME']}/.chef/checksums" )
cookbook_path            ["#{current_dir}/../cookbooks"]
```

Once you have finished creating the *<user>.pem*, *chef-validator.pem*, and *knife.rb* files, your *chef-repo/.chef* directory should resemble the following:

```
chef-repo/.chef
├── chef-validator.pem
├── knife.rb
└── misheska.pem
```

The *.chef* directory now contains three important files:

- *<username>.pem*
- *chef-validator.pem*
- *knife.rb*

<username> is the username you created in the Chef Server web admin tool. The *<username>.pem* file is a unique identifier used to authenticate *you* against Chef Server. This should be treated like a password; do not share it with anyone, and do not alter the contents of the file.

The *chef-validator.pem* file is a unique identifier used to authenticate *your organization* against Chef Server. This should be treated like a password, but it must also be shared among all your Chef developers. Anyone needing access to your Chef organization will also need a copy of this file. Do not alter the contents of this file, either.

RSA Key-Pairs

The *.pem* files are actually RSA private keys generated during the signup process. Chef generates an RSA key-pair for your username and your organization. Those private keys are packaged into your ZIP download. The associated public keys are stored on the Hosted Enterprise Chef Server and used to authenticate you and your organization when making requests to Chef Server.

Unlike the *.pem* files, the *knife.rb* file is meant to be edited, altered, and customized. The *knife.rb* file is recognized as Ruby and read by Chef when it issues commands:

```
current_dir = File.dirname(__FILE__)
log_level                 :info
log_location              STDOUT
node_name                 "<username>"
client_key                "#{current_dir}/<username>.pem"
validation_client_name    "chef-validator"
validation_key            "#{current_dir}/chef-validator.pem"
chef_server_url           "https://default-centos65.vagrantup.com:443"
cache_type                "BasicFile"
cache_options( :path =>   "#{ENV['HOME']}/.chef/checksums" )
cookbook_path             ["#{current_dir}/../cookbooks"]
```

As you can see, the *knife.rb* file sets some default configuration values, such as the log level, caching options, and cookbook paths. Additionally, the *knife.rb* configures the file `client_key`, `validation_client_name`, and `validation_key`. The URL points to your Chef Server installation.

Note that the `chef_server_url_` field uses a fake DNS hostname of `default-centos65.vagrantup.com` because that's the hostname vagrant set up. If you try to visit the URL *https://default-centos65.vagrantup.com:443*, you will discover that it is not valid.

Chef Server requires that hosts have valid fully qualified domain names set up in your local domain name service (DNS). In production, you would have your Chef Server hostname configured in your Domain Name System (DNS) server before installing. Let's add a temporary host entry for `default-centos65.vagrantup.com` in your local host database in lieu of making a DNS change, as we are just doing a book exercise.

Run one of the following commands to add a host entry. Following are the commands we ran on our machine. If you used an IP address other than 192.168.33.36, make sure it matches when you run the command.

Linux/Mac OS X:

```
$ sudo sh -c "echo '192.168.33.36 default-centos65.vagrantup.com' >> /etc/hosts"
```

Windows Command Prompt:

```
> echo 192.168.33.36 default-centos65.vagrantup.com >> \
%WINDIR%\System32\Drivers\Etc\Hosts
```

Windows PowerShell:

```
PS> ac -Encoding UTF8 $env:windir\system32\drivers\etc\hosts \
"192.168.33.36 default-centos65.vagrantup.com"
```

Now if you try to visit *https://default-centos65.vagrantup.com* in your web browser, your local host should think this is a valid hostname.

You can add additional values to the *knife.rb*, such as EC2 credentials, proxy information, and encrypted data bag settings. Although certain pieces of the *knife.rb* will be common among your team members, the contents of the file generally should be unique to you and your machine. However, unless you have access keys and passwords in your *knife.rb*, you do not need to treat it like a password.

Testing the Connection

You should run the following commands from inside the Chef repo. Open your terminal or command prompt and make *chef-repo* the current working directory. If you placed your Chef repo in a different location, use that instead:

```
$ cd ~/chef-repo
```

Now you can use `knife`, the command-line tool for Chef Server, to test your connection and authentication against Chef Server. At the time of this writing, Chef does not provide a "connection test" command. However, asking Chef Server to list the clients will verify:

- Your network can connect to Chef Server.
- The authentication files are in the correct location.
- The authentication files can be read by Chef.
- The response from Chef Server is received by your workstation.

Issue the `knife client list` command on your terminal. You should see the following:

```
$ knife client list
chef-validator
chef-webui
```

If you get an error, check the following:

1. You can access `https://192.168.33.36:443` from a web browser.
2. You are running commands from inside the *chef-repo*.
3. The *.chef* directory contains two *.pem* files and a *knife.rb*.
4. Your authentication files have the correct file permissions (they should be only user readable).

If you have confirmed the preceding steps and are still unable to connect to Chef Server, please consult the Chef online documentation (*http://docs.opscode.com*).

Now that you have verified that your host can connect to Chef Server, let's create another cookbook for a node instance and register it to be managed by Chef Server. If you created Chef Server locally in a sandbox environment in this chapter, leave it running—we'll be using it in the next chapter.

Bootstrapping a Node

In Chef, the term "bootstrapping" refers to the process by which a remote system is prepared to be managed by Chef. This process includes installing Chef Client and registering the target node with Chef Server.

Create a Node

Let's use Test Kitchen to define a project that spins up a node in a sandbox environment, similar to what we did back in Chapter 5 before we learned how to create cookbooks.

Create a node directory alongside the chef-server cookbook you created in Chapter 9. This technically isn't a cookbook—it's just a Test Kitchen project—but putting it beside the chef-server cookbook directory makes it convenient to go back and forth between the two.

Create the directory ~/chef-repo/cookbooks/node, and make it the current working directory:

```
$ cd ~/chef-repo/cookbooks
$ mkdir node
$ cd node
```

Assuming that you set up knife to communicate with your Chef Server following either the instructions in Chapter 9 or Appendix B, the knife client list command should work even in this subdirectory. Verify this now:

```
$ knife client list
chef-validator
chef-webui
```

This node directory will just be a test kitchen project, not a cookbook, so run the following commands to create a .kitchen.yml file for Test Kitchen:

```
$ kitchen init --create-gemfile
$ bundle install
```

Edit the .kitchen.yml file to use the CentOS 6.5 basebox we prepared specifically for this book. Also assign a private network address like we did in Chapter 7. This time, we're going to use the IP address 192.168.33.37. Make sure this address does not conflict with the IP address of your Chef Server. It should be 192.168.33.36.

Note that we also changed the suite name to be node, as this sandbox environment will be running our node, and have the other sandbox environment running our Chef Server. Having different names will disambiguate the two environments.

Example A-6. chefdk/chef-repo/cookbooks/node/.kitchen.yml

```
---
driver:
```

```
  name: vagrant

provisioner:
  name: shell

platforms:
  - name: centos65
    driver:
      box: learningchef/centos65
      box_url: learningchef/centos65
      network:
      - ["private_network", {ip: "192.168.33.37"}]

suites:
  - name: node
    run_list:
    attributes:
```

Spin up the node environment with `kitchen create`:

```
$ kitchen create node-centos65
```

Bootstrap the Node with Knife

Figure A-6 presents an overview of the current setup we've configured so far. We've configured a Chef Server (or used Hosted Enterprise Chef), and we configured a *knife.rb* with the appropriate keys, so that we can communicate with the Chef server from our host, the administrator's workstation. We've established that this communication channel works by verifying that `knife client list` produces the expected output.

Now let's set up our node like we would in production by "bootstrapping" the node with `knife bootstrap`. (We won't be able to use Test Kitchen in production!) When we run `knife bootstrap` on the our host, it will install Chef Client on the node and register it to be managed by Chef Server.

Nodes must have valid, fully qualified domain names set up in your local domain name service (DNS) as well. Let's add an entry to our local host database for the node just like we did for Chef Server.

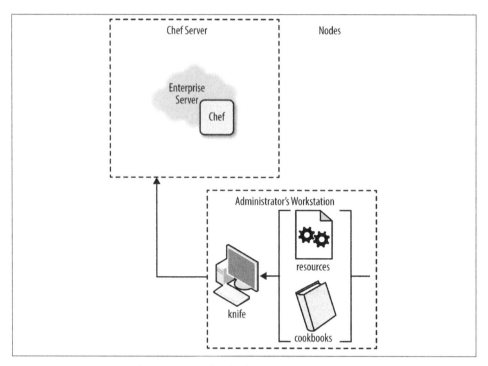

Figure A-6. Overview of our setup so far, before nodes

Run one of the following commands to add a node entry. Following are the commands we ran on our machine. If you used an IP address other than 192.168.33.35, make sure it matches when you run the command.

Linux/Mac OS X:

```
$ sudo sh -c "echo '192.168.33.37 node-centos65.vagrantup.com' >> /etc/hosts"
```

Windows Command Prompt:

```
> echo 192.168.33.37 node-centos65.vagrantup.com >> \
%WINDIR%\System32\Drivers\Etc\Hosts
```

Windows PowerShell:

```
PS> ac -Encoding UTF8 $env:windir\system32\drivers\etc\hosts \
"192.168.33.37 node-centos65.vagrantup.com"
```

You also need to kitchen login to the node and configure the local host database on the node to provide it the name of the server where you will run chef-client. Once this is complete, exit back out to your host prompt. As mentioned before, in production, you'd just make sure the DNS was configured with these hostnames before installing Chef Server and any nodes:

```
$ kitchen login node-centos65
Last login: Fri Jul  4 14:48:27 2014 from 10.0.2.2
Welcome to your Packer-built virtual machine.
[vagrant@node-centos65 ~]$ sudo sh -c "echo \
'192.168.33.36 default-centos65.vagrantup.com' >> /etc/hosts"
[vagrant@node-centos65 ~]$ exit
logout
Connection to 127.0.0.1 closed.
```

Run the following command to bootstrap your node:

```
$ knife bootstrap --sudo --ssh-user vagrant --ssh-password \
vagrant --no-host-key-verify node-centos65.vagrantup.com
Connecting to node-centos65.vagrantup.com
node-centos65.vagrantup.com Installing Chef Client...
...
node-centos65.vagrantup.com Thank you for installing Chef!
node-centos65.vagrantup.com Starting first Chef Client run...
...
node-centos65.vagrantup.com Starting Chef Client, version 11.14.2
node-centos65.vagrantup.com Creating a new client identity for
node-centos65.vagrantup.com using the validator key.
node-centos65.vagrantup.com resolving cookbooks for run list: []
node-centos65.vagrantup.com Synchronizing Cookbooks:
node-centos65.vagrantup.com Compiling Cookbooks...
node-centos65.vagrantup.com [2014-08-18T00:05:44-07:00]
WARN: Node node-centos65.vagrantup.com has an empty run list.
node-centos65.vagrantup.com Converging 0 resources
node-centos65.vagrantup.com
node-centos65.vagrantup.com Running handlers:
node-centos65.vagrantup.com Running handlers complete
node-centos65.vagrantup.com Chef Client finished, 0/0 resources updated in
2.595912205 seconds
```

You can tell from the output that it successfully installed Chef Client, and even performed a courtesy Chef Client run, but there were no cookbooks in the run list.

To verify that the node is now registered on the Chef server, log into the web interface and click on the *Nodes* tab. Now you should see that you have a node registered with your Chef Server, as shown in Figure A-7.

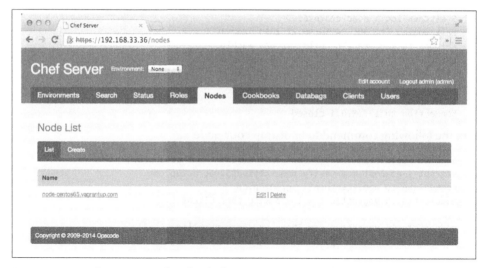

Figure A-7. Node is registered with Chef Server

If you click on the link to the node, you should see that Chef Server displays information about the node as shown in Figure A-8. The values you see under attributes should look familiar—these are the attributes generated automatically by ohai. They are stored on Chef Server for each node, and the data is searchable by all clients.

We are now done with both our Chef Server and node. Go ahead and kitchen destroy both of them:

```
$ cd ~/chef-repo/cookbooks/chef-server
$ kitchen destroy
$ cd ~/chef-repo/cookbooks/node
$ kitchen destroy
```

> Don't forget to remove the entries for *default-centos65.vagrantup.com* and *node-centos65.vagrantup.com* from */etc/hosts* on Linux/Mac OS X or *%WINDIR%\system32\drivers\etc\hosts* on Windows.

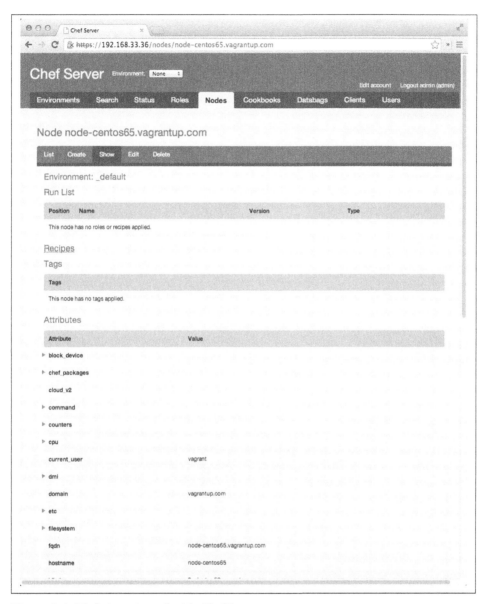

Figure A-8. Node is registered with Chef Server

Hosted Enterprise Chef

Hosted Enterprise Chef is the cloud-based version of Chef Server. You can sign up for Hosted Enterprise Chef at no cost to you to manage up to five nodes, more than enough for getting started with Chef Server.

Go to *https://manage.opscode.com/signup* to sign up for a Hosted Enterprise Chef account. Complete the required fields.

Upon submitting the form, you will be redirected to a page with helpful links and documentation. Click on the Download Starter Kit button as shown in Figure B-1. This will download a ZIP file containing all your authentication keys, as well as a pre-populated Chef repo.

Extract the archive and move the *chef-repo* folder into your home directory. The *chef-repo* directory should resemble the following:

```
chef-repo/
├── .chef
│   ├── <username>.pem
│   ├── <organization>-validator.pem
│   └── knife.rb
├── .gitignore
├── README.md
├── Vagrantfile
├── cookbooks
└── roles
```

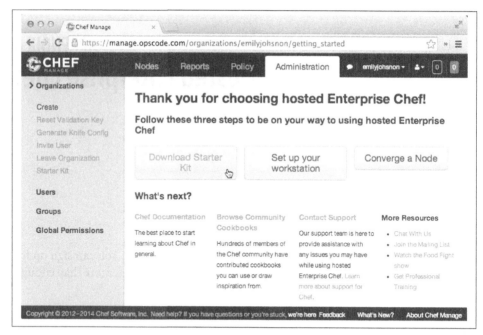

Figure B-1. Hosted Enterprise Chef post-signup page

 If you do not see a *.chef* directory, you might need to enable the display of system files in your file manager. Because the *.chef* directory starts with a dot, some operating systems will hide its presence.

The *.chef* directory contains three important files:

- *<username>.pem*
- *<organization>-validator.pem*
- *knife.rb*

<username> is the username you used when you signed up for your Hosted Chef Server account. *<organization>* is the name of the company or organization you used when signing up for Hosted Chef Server. If you registered with the username "seth" and the organization "houseofbacon", your *.chef* directory would contain:

- *seth.pem*
- *houseofbacon.pem*
- *knife.rb*

The *<username>.pem* file is a unique identifier used to authenticate *you* against Chef Server. This should be treated like a password; do not share it with anyone, and do not alter the contents of the file.

The *<organization>.pem* file is a unique identifier used to authenticate *your organization* against Chef Server. This should be treated like a password, but it must also be shared among all your Chef developers. Anyone needing access to your Chef organization will also need a copy of this file. Do not alter the contents of this file, either.

RSA Key-Pairs

The *.pem* files are RSA private keys generated during the signup process. Chef generates an RSA key-pair for your username and your organization. Those private keys are packaged into your ZIP download. The associated public keys are stored on the Hosted Enterprise Chef Server and used to authenticate you and your organization when making requests to Chef Server.

Unlike the *.pem* files, the *knife.rb* file is meant to be edited, altered, and customized. The *knife.rb* file is recognized as Ruby and read by Chef when it issues commands:

```
current_dir = File.dirname(__FILE__)
log_level                 :info
log_location              STDOUT
node_name                 "<username>"
client_key                "#{current_dir}/<username>.pem"
validation_client_name    "<organization>-validator"
validation_key            "#{current_dir}/<organization>-validator.pem"
chef_server_url           "https://api.opscode.com/organizations/<organization>"
cache_type                'BasicFile'
cache_options( :path => "#{ENV['HOME']}/.chef/checksums" )
cookbook_path             ["#{current_dir}/../cookbooks"]
```

As you can see, the *knife.rb* file sets some default configuration values, such as the log level, caching options, and cookbook paths. Additionally, the *knife.rb* configures the files *client_key*, *validation_client_name*, and *validation_key*. These values were automatically configured when you downloaded your starter kit. The `chef_server_url` configures the endpoint for Chef Server. Because we are using Hosted Enterprise Chef, this points to Opscode's Chef API. If you were using Enterprise Chef or Open Source Chef Server, the URL would point to your Chef Server installation.

You can add other values to the *knife.rb*, such as EC2 credentials, proxy information, and encrypted data bag settings. Although certain pieces of the *knife.rb* will be common across your team, the contents of the file generally should be unique to you and your machine. However, unless you have access keys and passwords in your *knife.rb*, you do not need to treat it like a password.

Testing the Connection

You should run the following commands from inside the Chef repo. Open your terminal or command prompt, and make *chef-repo* the current working directory. If you placed your Chef repo in a different location, use that instead:

```
$ cd ~/chef-repo
```

Now you can use knife, the command-line tool for Chef Server, to test your connection and authentication against Chef Server. At the time of this writing, Chef does not provide a "connection test" command. However, asking Chef Server to list the clients will verify:

- Your network can connect to Chef Server.
- The authentication files are in the correct location.
- The authentication files can be read by Chef.
- The response from Chef Server is received by your workstation.

Issue the knife client list command on your terminal:

```
$ knife client list
```

Depending on the speed of your Internet connection, it might take a few seconds to get a response, but you should see the following:

```
$ knife client list
<organization>-validator
```

For example, if I named my Chef organization houseofbacon, the output would be:

```
$ knife client list
houseofbacon-validator
```

If you get an error, check the following:

1. You can access *https://api.opscode.com* from a web browser.
2. You are running commands from inside the *chef-repo*.
3. The *.chef* directory contains two *.pem* files and a *knife.rb*.
4. Your authentication files have the correct file permissions.

If you have confirmed the preceding steps and are still unable to connect to Chef Server, please consult the Chef online documentation (*http://docs.opscode.com*).

Glossary

Argument

See *Parameter*

Chef

a broad term for Opscode products including Chef Server (Erchef), Chef Client, Chef Solo, Hosted Chef, and Private (Enterprise) Chef; however, most commonly refers to Chef Client

Chef Client

the agent or service that runs locally on a machine managed by Chef

Chef Shell

formerly `shef`, the Chef Shell (`chef-shell`) is an interactive REPL for using Chef via the command line (similar to `irb` in Ruby or `python` in Python)

Chef Server

the centralized store for configuration data in your infrastructure

Chef Solo

an open source version of Chef that does not require Chef Server, but lacks some features that might be important to power users, such as search and centralized data

Client

See *Chef Client*

Convergent

See *Convergence*

Convergence

a stronger version of idempotency that guarantees the command will not be executed if action is not required

See also *Idempotency*

Cookbook

a single unit of configuration and policy information; an encapsulation of recipes, attributes, metadata, templates, files, and more

Domain Specific Language

a language or syntax written to handle a specific problem domain or set of concerns

DSL

See *Domain Specific Language*

Data Bag

a JSON key-value file that is used to file global organizational data such as users or API keys

Embedded Ruby

a Ruby templating language that lets you run Ruby and output the results; useful for configuration templates

Encrypted Data Bag

an AES-256-CBC encrypted version of a Data Bag that requires a secret key to read and write the contents

Enterprise Chef
Chef Server inside an organization's firewall; formerly called Private Chef

Environment
logical grouping of nodes either horizontally (i.e., staging and production) or vertically (i.e., east coast and west coast)

ERB
See *Embedded Ruby*

File
a static file or binary for distribution onto a node

Hosted Chef
See *Hosted Enterprise Chef*

Hosted Enterprise Chef
the cloud-based Software-as-a-Service version of Chef; formerly called Hosted Chef

Idempotent
See *Idempotency*

Idempotency
a mathematical property of certain operations such that the operation can be applied multiple times, but the end result is always the same

Interactive Ruby
the read-eval-print-loop (REPL) for Ruby on the command line

Interactive Ruby Shell
See *Interactive Ruby*

IRB
See *Interactive Ruby*

Knife
the command-line tool for working with Chef and your infrastructure; knife supports a plugin model for easy customization

Metadata
additional information, such as the name, version, description, dependencies, and recommendations for a given cookbook

Multi-tenancy
See *Organization*

Node
any machine or device managed by Chef

Open Source Chef Server
a free and open source version of Chef Server that contains much of the same functionality of Hosted Chef, but requires additional setup, maintenance, configuration, and management

Organization
a top-level grouping of nodes, policies, and users; a feature found only in Hosted Chef and Enterprise Chef, often called "multi-tenancy"

Parameter
An object (such as a String or Array) passed as an argument to a method in Ruby or Chef

Private Chef
See *Enterprise Chef*

Provider
platform-specific implementation of a resource (such as apt or useradd); commonly referred to as the "how"

Recipe
a set of instructions written in Chef's Ruby DSL that instructs the Chef Client what commands to execute on a target node

Resource
cross-platform abstraction of an item managed by Chef (such as a package or user); commonly referred to as the "what"

Role
a logical group of recipes or other roles

Ruby
an object-oriented programming language that is the base language in which Chef Client is executed

Run List
an ordered list of recipes or roles that are applied to a Chef node *in the order specified*

Template
embedded Ruby templates that are rendered or compiled on a target node

Index

Symbols

A

We'd like to hear your suggestions for improving our indexes. Send email to index@oreilly.com.

G

gedit text editor, 11
gems
    defined, 18
    installation location for, 19
    location on Linux, 19
    location on Mac OS X, 26
    location on Windows, 31
gem_package resource, 52
Git, installing on Windows, 32
GitHub, 179
GNU Emacs text editor, 10
group resource, 52

H

Hallet, Tom, 6
Hansson, David Heinemeier, 37
hashes, 43–45
Heartbleed Virus, 213
HIPPA compliance, 147
Hosted Chef, 147
Hosted Enterprise Chef, 147, 333–336
    node limit on, 149
    setting up, 333–335
    testing connection to, 336
HTTPS, 89, 183
Hunt, Andy, 38

I

Idempotence, 155–160
IDEs, 11
if keyword, 45
IIS web services, 179
include_recipe statement, 137–140
infrastructure
    automation, ix
    self-healing, 6
instance, 74
integrated development environments (IDEs),
    11
IntelliJ IDEA IDE, 11
interpolation of strings, 41
inventory queries, 213
IP address, specifying, 126
IT, 1
    automating, 2
it block (RSpec), 280

its method (Serverspec), 285

J

Jacob, Adam, 4
Java, 37
Jenkins community cookbook, 293
JetBrains, 11
JSON format
    in YAML files, 80
    ohai tool and, 94

K

kitchen converge command, 107–109
kitchen create command, 74
kitchen setup command, 88
kitchen test command, 291–293
Knife
    bootstrapping nodes with, 171–176
    chef generate command versus, 99
    chef-zero and, 206
    configuring for SSL, 192
    cookbook site plugin, 185
    creating data bags with, 227
    deploying environments with, 253
    deploying roles with, 243
    downloading cookbooks with, 187–189
    generating cookbooks with, 103
    local mode, 209
    searching with, 186, 214–217
    Server configuration file, 163
    testing Chef Server connection with, 168
    uploading node information with, 211
knife cookbook site commands, 186
    download, 187
    managing supermarket cookbooks with,
        187–189
    search, 186
    show, 187
knife.rb file, 163, 166

L

lazy evaluation (RSpec), 302
Learning Ruby (Fitzgerald), 38
let helper method (RSpec), 302
linefeeds, removing from SSL keys, 235
link resource, 52

Winsor, Jamie, 116

Y

YAML, 79–81

YAML files, JSON format in, 80
yum_package resource, 122

About the Authors

Mischa Taylor is a consultant at Chef, a fast-growing Seattle-based startup responsible for creating the Chef platform, which makes it easy to quickly automate development processes and move business processes into the cloud. He has spent his career focusing on building high quality products and increasing engineering productivity within organizations. Mischa is an author, speaker, and mentor on software development topics and neuromorphic computing.

Seth Vargo is currently a software engineer and open source advocate at at HashiCorp. Previously, Seth worked at Chef (Opscode), CustomInk, and a few Pittsburgh-based startups. He is passionate about inequality in technology and organizational culture. When he is not writing software or working on open source, Seth enjoys speaking at local user groups and conferences. He is a coorganizer for DevOps Days Pittsburgh and loves all things bacon. You can find him on the Internet as @sethvargo or at *https://sethvargo.com*.

Colophon

The animal on the cover of *Learning Chef* is a Wahlberg's honeyguide, also known as a brown-backed honeybird (*Protodiscus regulus*).

The Wahlberg's honeyguide is a small bird native to the thornveld and other mesic habitats of southern Africa. Inconspicuous and mostly residential, the honeyguide feeds primarily on scale insects and practices *brood parasitism*, in which offspring are smuggled into the broods of other birds—in this case, into the spherical nests of cisticolas and warblers—in order to spare the brood-parasite the investment of raising young.

This bird was given its name by Johan August Wahlberg, a Swedish naturalist who, during his travels in southern Africa between 1838 and 1856, also gave his name to a species of eagle, cormorant, fruit bat, frog, and tree. Wahlberg met his end near the Thamalakane river in modern-day Botswana in 1856, trampled by a wounded elephant. Wahlberg's subsequent election to the Royal Swedish Academy of Science before news of his death could reach Sweden makes him the only member to have been elected posthumously.

Many of the animals on O'Reilly covers are endangered; all of them are important to the world. To learn more about how you can help, go to *animals.oreilly.com*.

The cover image is from Cassell's *Natural History*. The cover fonts are URW Typewriter and Guardian Sans. The text font is Adobe Minion Pro; the heading font is Adobe Myriad Condensed; and the code font is Dalton Maag's Ubuntu Mono.

Get even more for your money.

Join the O'Reilly Community, and register the O'Reilly books you own. It's free, and you'll get:

- $4.99 ebook upgrade offer
- 40% upgrade offer on O'Reilly print books
- Membership discounts on books and events
- Free lifetime updates to ebooks and videos
- Multiple ebook formats, DRM FREE
- Participation in the O'Reilly community
- Newsletters
- Account management
- 100% Satisfaction Guarantee

Signing up is easy:

1. Go to: oreilly.com/go/register
2. Create an O'Reilly login.
3. Provide your address.
4. Register your books.

Note: English-language books only

To order books online:
oreilly.com/store

For questions about products or an order:
orders@oreilly.com

To sign up to get topic-specific email announcements and/or news about upcoming books, conferences, special offers, and new technologies:
elists@oreilly.com

For technical questions about book content:
booktech@oreilly.com

To submit new book proposals to our editors:
proposals@oreilly.com

O'Reilly books are available in multiple DRM-free ebook formats. For more information:
oreilly.com/ebooks

O'REILLY®

Have it your way.

Lightning Source UK Ltd.
Milton Keynes UK
UKOW07f2255260315

248581UK00004B/10/P